The Girl with the Saddest Secret

Other books by Angela Hart

The Girl with the Saddest Secret

The True Story of a Troubled Little Girl
and the Foster Carer Who Gives her Hope

ANGELA HART

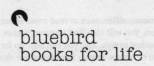

bluebird
books for life

First published 2020 by Bluebird
an imprint of Pan Macmillan
The Smithson, 6 Briset Street, London EC1M 5NR
Associated companies throughout the world
www.panmacmillan.com

ISBN 978-1-5290-2445-6

1 3 5 7 9 8 6 4 2

A CIP catalogue record for this book is available from the British Library.

Typeset by Palimpsest Book Production Ltd, Falkirk, Stirlingshire

Printed and bound by CPI Group (UK) Ltd, Croydon, CR0 4YY

This book is sold subject to the condition that it shall not, by way of
trade or otherwise, be lent, resold, hired out, or otherwise circulated without
the publisher's prior consent in any form of binding or cover other than
that in which it is published and without a similar condition including
this condition being imposed on the subsequent purchaser.

The Girl with the Saddest Secret

1

'Just a couple of nights'

'Anything interesting?'

Jonathan was clutching a pile of post he'd picked up from the doormat.

'Mostly junk and a couple of bills by the looks of it.'

Having taken Erica to school, we were having a quick cuppa before starting work in our florist next door. Jonathan opened one of the letters and winced.

'What's the matter?'

'It's our buildings and contents insurance. It's gone up again! Can you believe this quote? I think we'd better shop around.'

I took one look and immediately agreed. 'I'll do it, you get on.'

I poured a cup of tea for our assistant, Barbara, which Jonathan took through to the shop with him. After setting off the dishwasher and checking the rest of the post I called our insurance broker. The number was busy so I left a message, requesting a call back.

Minutes later, the phone rang. *That was quick,* I thought, picking up a pen as I lifted the receiver.

'Morning, Angela!'

It was our support social worker, Caitlin, sounding her usual chirpy self.

'Oh, hello! I wasn't expecting it to be you.'

'Have I called at a bad time?'

'No, not at all. I'm waiting for a call from the insurance company but I'd much prefer to talk to you.'

Caitlin explained that she had an eight-year-old girl who needed looking after and wondered if we could help.

'Her foster carer is asking for some respite cover. Just a couple of nights. I know you've got a houseful at the moment, but if you can help us out, I'd be very grateful.'

Jonathan and I had trained as specialist carers for teen-agers with complex needs some twenty years earlier, after starting our foster career in the late eighties. Alongside troubled teens we continued to take in children of all ages, whether they needed specialist care or not. There wasn't much that fazed us and we always tried to help Social Services if we could. Having said that, we did need to consider little Erica, who had been living with us for six months. She was nine years old and could be quite a shy and sensitive soul.

We also had my mum staying with us temporarily, as she was recovering from an operation on her back, plus eighteen-year-old Anthony, who was a former foster child we were helping out. We were passed to take in up to three children at any one time and had three bedrooms we normally used for the kids we took in, but with Mum and

Anthony occupying two of the rooms, this little girl would have to go in the bunk bed in Erica's room.

'What can you tell me about her?' I asked Caitlin. 'I'm just thinking about Erica, because she'd have to share a room with her.'

'I'm afraid I don't have any information on why her foster carer is asking for respite. Her name's Jasmine and like I say she's eight. She's in her first term of Year 4 and she isn't statemented.'

We knew very well that the fact a child didn't have a statement of educational needs (SEN) did not necessarily mean they didn't have special needs. They may simply not have gone through the process of being statemented yet, so this didn't really tell us a great deal.

'Can you give me a minute and I'll check with Jonathan and give you a buzz back?'

'Of course. Thanks, Angela. I'm heading out shortly, but I'll be on the mobile and if I don't pick up I'll call you back as soon as I can.'

Caitlin was an extremely efficient and hard-working support social worker, one of the best we'd had. No sooner had she arranged one placement than another child in need would come on to her books. Despite having such a heavy caseload, she didn't ever complain or get flustered; in fact, she was generally upbeat. It was always easy to get hold of her, nothing was ever too much trouble and she didn't make us feel under pressure to take a child in, even though we knew full well that it would create extra work and stress for her if we said no.

A minority of kids on Caitlin's books might be waiting for adoptive parents to be cleared to take them in, which meant they would be best matched with foster carers who preferred to do short rather than long-term or open-ended placements. The future for the rest of the children would be much more uncertain. They might have just been taken into care, either having been removed by the courts or placed voluntarily in care by their family, or they might have been in care for some time but now needed a new home, perhaps because their previous placement was breaking down or because they had been placed in a secure unit or children's home as there was nowhere else to go. Some kids simply needed a short respite stay, away from their family home or from their current placement, like Jasmine. Others might be working towards returning to their family, in which case the length of their stay could be very unpredictable. We've always made ourselves available to any children in need of foster care, no matter what their situation or how long they might stay with us, and so our lives had become very unpredictable too!

I nipped through to the shop. Though Jonathan and I had been working as a team for such a long time and trusted and supported each other's decisions completely, we still always checked with each other before agreeing to take in a new child.

'An eight-year-old girl? Two nights?'

'Yes, that's what Caitlin said. Respite from her current placement, she doesn't know why it's been requested.'

'Well, I'm sure we can manage that. She'll have to share with Erica and go in the bunk beds, won't she?'

'Yes, the girls can share, that was the first thing I thought of too and I mentioned it to Caitlin. Just as well we've got the bunk beds and the girls are close in age.'

Jonathan and I always did our level best to help and I don't think we once said no to Caitlin. In turn, I don't think Caitlin ever said no when she was asked to help her colleagues in an emergency.

'I'll phone Caitlin back.'

Jonathan grinned and gave me a thumbs-up. We always feel a mixture of nervous anticipation and excitement whenever we agree to foster another child, and that has not changed, even now, after fostering more than fifty children over three decades. Many people have told us they admire us for being foster carers for all these years. They often tell us things like, 'I couldn't do it, you are so selfless!' But the truth is, we've carried on fostering because we love doing it, and part of that enjoyment comes from the lift we all get as humans when we help someone in need and see the benefit it brings to them. There is no better reward in life.

Caitlin answered her mobile after two rings and was delighted when I told her we would cover the respite care. It was a Wednesday and she said she'd like to arrange for us to meet Jasmine and her foster carer on the Saturday, with a view to Jasmine staying with us the following week.

'I'll confirm everything as quickly as possible and let you know where the meeting will be.'

'OK. There's no rush. Erica has a dance class at nine in the morning but other than that we'll keep Saturday free and I'll make sure we've got cover in the shop.'

'Perfect.'

Caitlin was back on the phone within ten minutes and it was arranged that we would meet Jasmine and her foster carer, who was called Fran, in McDonald's in the next town on Saturday lunchtime. This was a typical time and place to meet up during term time, as it meant kids didn't need to miss school and of course the lure of fast food always helped lift the mood. It was fine for Erica to come with us; in fact, Caitlin said it might help break the ice, given that the girls were close in age.

I popped next door to give the news to Jonathan and to double-check with Barbara that she'd be happy to run the shop on her own for a few hours on Saturday, as she normally did if we had other jobs on.

'No problem,' she said. 'I don't expect it'll be too busy.'

November was always a quiet month in our florists. Jonathan flicked through the diary. We had no weddings booked in that weekend, though one of our wholesalers was due to make a large delivery.

'I'll see if Anthony's around,' Jonathan said. 'If he is, I'll ask him to help out in the storeroom when the delivery comes in.'

Barbara grinned. 'That's a good idea. He can put the kettle on too. He makes a great cup of tea!'

'What, better than mine?' Jonathan teased.

'Er, of *course* not,' Barbara replied, deliberately protesting too hard to pull Jonathan's leg.

We all knew Barbara had a soft spot for Anthony. We'd fostered him when he was a younger teenager and we used to give him pocket money for doing odd jobs in the shop, as we did with a lot of children. Anthony always made Barbara laugh, and she said he never failed to brighten up her day.

'Saturday lunchtime it is then,' Jonathan said.

Jonathan and I were really enjoying having Anthony around again, though the reason he was back was heart-rending. When he moved out of our home at seventeen he went to live with a member of his family, but promises were broken and things quickly unravelled. He found himself homeless, and lost his job when his employers found out he'd slept on the company premises overnight. When Anthony eventually told us what had happened, we invited him to stay with us until he got back on his feet. He'd been with us for three months now, and in that time had turned eighteen and managed to get a part-time job in a pub restaurant. We'd helped him with career advice and he was now saving up to start training for his HGV licence, which had been a long-held ambition.

A hard worker by nature, he was rolling up his sleeves and helping us with all kinds of odd jobs around the house and shop. We didn't want to take any money off him for keep as he was trying so hard to save, so this was his way of paying us back. It was a great arrangement as we were always glad of extra help, and Anthony could also step in and babysit if need be. He had to be police checked when he turned eighteen, just like any child we foster who reaches the age of eighteen while living with us. In those days you applied to the Criminal Records

Bureau, or CBS, which has since been replaced by the Disclosure and Barring Service, or DBS. My mum was also police checked and had been for many years, as she often babysat for us when we went out to training courses and support group meetings, or when we managed to have a night out. With their help, and thanks to Barbara being very flexible with her working hours, we could juggle most things.

I returned to the kitchen and put the kettle on. Mum appeared, looking tired and jaded.

'How are you feeling this morning, Mum?'

'Not too bad, though I didn't sleep particularly well.'

'Sorry to hear that. Are you warm enough?'

'Yes, thanks. The room is very warm and comfortable.'

'Is there anything I can do to help?'

'No, dear, not unless you have a magic sponge that can take away the pain!'

I smiled, remembering how my dad used to brandish his 'magic sponge' when I was a kid. He'd rub the invisible sponge on my bruised knee or bumped head to make me feel better, and it always worked.

I still missed Dad every day, even though he'd been gone for many years. Mum had coped so well on her own. Fiercely independent and stoical, it went against all her instincts to ask for help or appear needy in any way, despite the fact she was in her eighties now. I knew she must be finding it difficult to be in this position, staying with us while she got her strength back. It wasn't that she couldn't manage by herself – generally speaking, she was remarkably fit and well and very capable of living on her own – but the doctors had advised it was best for her to take it easy for a while and let us look after her.

'Come and sit down. The kettle's just boiled. I'll make you a cup of tea.'

'Don't you have to be in the shop?'

'Jonathan and Barbara are holding the fort. Shall I make you some porridge?'

'Only if you have time, otherwise I can manage.'

Normally Mum would get to her feet in these situations, taking over so as not to be a nuisance or cause me any extra work, but she didn't move a muscle. I'd never seen her like this, which was a bit upsetting.

'Where's Anthony?'

I told her he was out for a run. 'I don't know how he does it in this freezing cold weather,' I said.

'Me neither! He's such a good boy. What a pity things didn't work out with his family.'

I had no idea what Anthony had told Mum and I had said the bare minimum about the reason he was back with us. I felt very strongly that it was his story, not mine, and even though he was no longer in care I behaved just as I did with every child, and I didn't discuss his private life with anyone.

I made a pot of tea for us to share, set the porridge on the hob and nipped to the loo. I was surprised to see Mum on her feet when I returned to the kitchen. She was standing at the hob, stirring the porridge.

'Sit back down, I can do that.'

I chatted to Mum while I served up the porridge and fetched her some honey.

'We're going to meet a young girl on Saturday. Hopefully she'll be coming for a short respite stay.'

'How lovely. How old is she?'

'Eight, she's called Jasmine.'

'What a pretty name. I look forward to meeting her. Do you need me to sit with Erica when you go for the meeting?'

This made me feel upset all over again, as I realised that I wouldn't really want to leave my mum looking after a young child while she was still in the early stages of recovery. She was so tired from her operation, she was still wobbly on her legs and her back was sore. I wouldn't be happy leaving her in charge of a nine-year-old.

'That's kind, Mum, but the meeting is in McDonald's and she can come with us. I don't think Erica will turn down the chance of that, do you?'

'I shouldn't imagine so,' Mum laughed.

I looked out of the window and saw Anthony heading across the playing field at the back of the house. While it was fresh in my mind, I thought to myself that I must remember to ask him about helping Barbara on Saturday. *Maybe I'll ask him to keep an eye on Mum, too.*

It only seemed five minutes ago when Mum and Dad were running the shop together. Mum handed the business over to Jonathan and me in the mid-eighties, after my dad passed away. We started fostering in 1987, initially imagining we'd probably foster for just a few years, perhaps until we started a family of our own. By the time we realised we couldn't have children, fostering had become a way of life. We loved having kids of all ages coming and going and couldn't imagine life without a busy household. Of course, at the start we didn't have a clue what we were letting ourselves in for. We still laugh at how naive we were, thinking all that kids needed was love and care, a roof over their head and food on the table!

We also had very little understanding about what happens when children are old enough to leave care. Back then, kids left at sixteen (it's eighteen or older now, if they continue their education), and we imagined our job would be done and we'd have the room to take on another child. It's not that simple, of course. A well-meaning customer at our florists once remarked to me, 'At least as a foster carer you can hand them back when they are sixteen!' She said this after sharing a tale of woe about her son, who was still living at home in his late twenties. I simply smiled, as this person wanted me to. However, Jonathan and I had quickly learned that the reality is that kids leaving care need ongoing support, just like any other young people. Though our official duties as foster carers come to an end one day, we always stay in touch and help the kids we've fostered for as long as they want us in their lives.

Anthony came into the kitchen and greeted Mum with a cheery smile. 'Thelma, you didn't have to make porridge just for me,' he said cheekily, spotting the pan on the hob.

'Pardon?'

He looked at me and winked.

'He's teasing, Mum. Mind you, there's probably enough for you if you'd like some, Anthony?'

'Rude not to! Thanks.'

I felt a warm glow. It was a privilege to have Anthony living with us again. He had become like one of the family, and everybody benefited. *Who said we hand them back when they turn sixteen?* I thought, smiling to myself. *And I'm very glad we don't.*

2

'I just need a break'

'That has to be them,' Jonathan said.

I followed his gaze across the busy McDonald's and recognised Jasmine immediately from the description Caitlin had given me: 'Very long wavy fair hair, parted in the middle and held back with clips. Big blue eyes, pretty face, round and with a big, open smile.' The woman sitting beside her had dark circles under her eyes. Caitlin hadn't mentioned those, of course, but the rest of the description I had of the foster carer, Fran, fitted.

'I think you're right,' I replied. Jonathan, Erica and I began to squeeze past tables and chairs in the packed restaurant to reach Jasmine and her carer.

Fran spotted us and gave a little wave, and Jasmine looked up and smiled. She was a bit flushed in the face and looked very excited to meet us.

'She's been dying for you to get here,' Fran said.

'We've all been looking forward to it,' I replied.

Jonathan made a joke about the fact the promise of fast food might have played a part, as we were all looking forward to lunch. As soon as the introductions had been made, Jasmine started asking Fran if they could go and order their food now.

'Can we? Can we?'

Before Fran could answer, Jasmine turned to Erica. 'Do you know what you want? Do you?'

'Erm . . .' Before Erica could respond Jasmine posed the question to me, and then Fran, and then Jonathan. 'Who's having what? Do you like chicken nuggets? Do we have to get a Happy Meal or can we get what we want? What's the toy? Shall we order now, shall we?'

'How about if I go and place the order for everyone?' Jonathan said. 'If we all go, we'll lose the table.'

Fran looked extremely grateful. She seemed exhausted.

'Just a black coffee for me, thanks.' She handed Jonathan some money to cover the coffee and Jasmine's meal. Jonathan would have happily paid but he took the money, not knowing if he'd offend Fran by refusing.

'What do you want?' she asked Jasmine.

'Please can I have . . . er, what do I want?!' The little girl laughed excitedly.

'You can have whatever you want,' Fran told her. 'How hungry are you? Will you eat a whole meal?'

'Yes!'

Erica quietly told Jonathan that she would like a Happy Meal and asked if she would be allowed a pudding after, if she had room.

'No problem,' he said. Jasmine liked the sound of this and opted to do the same.

Jonathan and I were both hungry and I asked for a chicken burger and a cup of tea. 'Shall I make that a meal?' Jonathan asked.

'Well, I'm meant to be watching my weight but I suppose so, as it's more or less the same price, isn't it? And I'm sure somebody will eat my fries if I don't.'

Jonathan had heard me 'reasoning' like this many times before. He knew I would not be able to resist the fries once they were in front of me, and that a McDonald's was as big a treat for me as it was for the kids! He went off to place the order.

Jasmine continued to fire lots of questions at Erica, who was happy to provide the answers, whenever she could get a word in edgeways.

'Is there a garden at their house? Do you always live there or are you on holiday, like, I mean, respite, like me? Is it nice? Can you see that balloon stand? Can we go and get a balloon? Can we, Fran?'

I nodded at Fran who gave both girls permission to help themselves to the freshly stocked balloon stand. We kept a close eye on them as they charged off as fast as they could, pushing through the queues at the serving counter.

'Thanks so much for offering to give me some respite,' Fran said. 'I don't mind telling you, I'm finding it tough.'

'We're happy to help but I'm sorry to hear that. In what way are you finding it tough? I've not been given any background information.'

'She's not a bad kid, but it's the smirking that's getting to me. My husband says I should let it go and I'm too uptight, but I can't stand it. It irritates the life out of me. I know I'll be fine once I've managed to unwind a bit.'

The kids were back before I had the chance to find out what Fran meant by the smirking. Jasmine was beaming and it was hard to imagine her face with anything but a beautiful, big smile stretched across it.

'Look at my balloon!' she said proudly, thrusting it forward for Fran and me to see. At that moment I noticed there was a scar on Jasmine's forehead. The jagged, silvery mark stood proud of her smooth, pink complexion. I was surprised I hadn't spotted it straight away, as it was quite prominent. Jasmine's long, wavy hair was eye-catching. It bounced and bubbled all over the place, just like her conversation. In fact, everything about Jasmine seemed effervescent. *That's probably why I didn't spot the scar*, I thought. Her personality, all that pretty fair hair and her lovely big blue eyes, were definitely more eye-catching than anything else.

'Yippee! That's mine! Is that one mine? What's the toy? Open the box. You open yours! What have you got? Is yours the same? How many nuggets have you got?'

Erica had quickly cottoned on to the fact it wasn't worth trying to answer every question Jasmine directed at her. She quietly took her toy out of the box and showed Jasmine, who screamed with delight when she saw they had identical plastic Disney princesses. Jasmine tucked into her food with great gusto while Erica took ages arranging her meal on her tray and taking the lid off her little tub of ketchup before nibbling her nuggets.

'Are you sure you're not hungry, Fran?' I asked. 'Help yourself if you want some of these fries.'

'No, thanks, I'm fine. Enjoy your meal.'

She began sipping her coffee and seemed to be in a world of her own. I thought she looked as if she wanted to be anywhere but in that restaurant. Jonathan chatted to the girls and I tried to make polite conversation with Fran as I ate my lunch, but she didn't make much of an effort to engage with me. She seemed quite defeated, I thought.

'What else can you tell me?' I asked when Jonathan took the girls up to the counter to choose their desserts. 'I don't even know how long she's been with you. Is there anything in particular I need to know?'

'Not really. She's just full on, as you can see. It's tiring, looking after her. I'm shattered. I just need some rest. Sorry to moan. She's not a bad kid.'

'How long has she been with you?'

'Two months. Listen, I'm so grateful to you. I really am.'

'Like I say, we're happy to help, and it looks like she's hit it off with Erica, so that's a good sign. Hopefully you'll both enjoy the break.'

Fran nodded. 'Jasmine's a popular girl. It's just a shame she's the way she is.'

'How do you mean?'

'Sorry, there I go again. She's just full on, that's all. A handful. She keeps getting excluded from school for bad behaviour. Doesn't know when to stop, loses her temper, that sort of thing. My husband's at work all day and when she's excluded from school I can't cope with her. It's hard work, it's too much . . .'

Fran trailed off, having spotted the girls and Jonathan returning to the table.

The girls' ice creams were polished off in record time and Fran stood to leave almost as soon as Jasmine had swallowed the last mouthful.

'It's been great to meet you all,' Fran said. 'We must get going now, but haven't we had a nice time, Jasmine? How exciting will it be to spend more time with Erica next week? It'll be like a big long *sleepover*!'

Jonathan and I exchanged glances. This was not cut and dried, and this is not how foster carers are taught to handle these situations. Though we were going to agree to the respite care, we had not officially signed up to it yet. The whole point of meeting Jasmine was for us all to see if we were happy to proceed. Most importantly, it was up to Jasmine to agree to come and stay with us.

In training, we're constantly being told that it's best to avoid asking leading questions of children. Instead of saying 'How exciting will it be . . .', you need to find a way of getting the child to express how *they* feel, in their own way, and in their own time. Not only that, a sleepover is a treat to share with friends. If Jasmine agreed to stay with us, she would be coming into a strange house and would no doubt be feeling unsure of herself, however excited she appeared today. It was possible she might feel pushed out or even rejected by her foster carer too, which is a very tough thing for a foster child to cope with, having already been through the traumatic process of leaving their birth family and going into care.

Jasmine stared at Fran, the word 'sleepover' hanging in the air between all of them. She didn't speak and I'm not sure she knew what to say.

'It's probably a lot to take in,' Jonathan said jovially. 'It's been very nice to meet you, Jasmine. Fran, we'll wait to hear from our social worker.'

We said our goodbyes and parted on good terms, despite the fact Jonathan and I were taken aback by how rapidly the lunch was over, and how Fran had handled things at the end.

'Jasmine's funny!' Erica said, as she buckled herself into the back of our car.

'She seems like a very nice girl,' I said.

'Is she going to come and stay then?'

'We'd be happy to have her to stay, but it's her decision. We need to wait to hear from Social Services. I take it you'd be happy to have her too?'

'Yes. Can she sleep in my room?'

'If she decides to stay, yes she can. She can go with you in the bunk bed.' I didn't spell out that there would be no choice involved in this, seeing as it was the only spare bed in the house!

'OK. That's pretty cool.'

Erica's reaction pleased me. Being a naturally shy child, this could have worked out very differently and we would have had to think very carefully about taking Jasmine in. Perhaps the mention of a 'sleepover' had added to the attraction for Erica? It wasn't a good word for Fran to have chosen, but hopefully it would all work out for the best.

When we got home, Anthony was watching an old film with Mum. He'd lit the fire and they were sharing a pot of tea.

'This is cosy!' I said. 'Any tea left in the pot?'

Anthony sprung up and offered to top the pot up. 'Shall I make one for Jonathan and Barbara too?'

'I'm sure they won't say no. Everything all right in the shop?'

'All fine. I took in the delivery and everything's sorted out in the storeroom. Barbara said she didn't need me this afternoon – it's really quiet.'

Erica had gone up to her room and Jonathan through to the shop. 'How did your meeting go?' Mum asked.

'Really well. Erica liked Jasmine and Jasmine seemed happy to meet us all. She's a friendly girl and seems very nice. Fingers crossed she'll come to stay for a few days.'

'Do you know when?'

'No, but I expect if it all works out it will be Friday at the earliest, as her school isn't in this area.'

'Lovely.'

Mum carried on watching her film. She looked comfortable and content, and I felt relieved to see her like this. *She'll soon be back to her old self*, I thought.

* * *

On Monday morning Caitlin called first thing to see how we felt the meeting had gone and to ask if Jasmine could stay with us for two nights.

'That's fine by us and I'm pleased she's agreed to it. Fran did seem very tired. The girls got along really well and Erica's happy to share her room for a couple of nights. When do you want the respite to start?'

'Is this afternoon OK?'

'Today? I don't see why not, but isn't she in school?'

'No, I'm afraid she's been excluded. I think that is why her foster carer asked for respite. Jasmine was out of school this week and will be out of school all of next week too.'

'Oh, I see.'

Obviously, Fran had mentioned that Jasmine had been excluded from school but I hadn't realised she meant she was currently on an exclusion. I asked Caitlin if she could tell me the reason why. It wasn't unheard of for a primary school child to be excluded – several children who'd stayed with us before had been suspended or sent home from school – but a two-week exclusion seemed a long time for an eight-year-old. Naturally, I wanted to know what had happened.

'Bad behaviour,' Caitlin said. 'I'm sorry, that's not much help, is it? But that's all I know. I can try and find out more. Would you prefer me to do that before we go any further?'

'No, don't worry. I'm sure we can cope for a couple of nights. She seemed like a lovely girl. It'll be fine, I'm sure.'

'That's good. The feedback I got from Jasmine was very positive. It sounds like she hit it off with Erica straight away.'

Though I'd have liked to have known more about

Jasmine's history and the reason she was on an exclusion, I wasn't unduly worried about having such scant information. It's normal to know very little about a child's background at this stage in proceedings. In my experience, this is partly deliberate and partly accidental. Common sense tells you that if the first thing a social worker says to a potential foster carer is something along the lines of, 'This child has been excluded from half a dozen schools because she spits at the teachers', then clearly it's going to be much harder to place that child, even for a short respite stay. I don't blame social workers for focusing on getting a roof over a child's head by deliberately keeping quiet about possibly deal-breaking information. The 'accidental' element comes about because Social Services' files can be very long and, even to the trained eye, it can be extremely difficult to pick out salient information quickly. This is especially true when a child has been in care for many years and has moved between foster homes multiple times. I knew that Jasmine had only been with Fran for two months but I didn't know how long she had been in care, or how many previous foster carers she had had.

I've said for years that it would be very helpful if each child's Social Services file had a summary sheet at the front of it stating, for instance, when they went into care, how things stand with their school and their birth family, their medical background and any other relevant historical details. Unfortunately, it's not like that at all! In most cases, you'd have to pick through the paperwork for hours to compile a succinct, accurate and up-to-date summary sheet, and overworked social workers simply don't have the time and resources to do it. We understand this, and we accept that as foster carers we have to be grateful for whatever information comes our way. Also, I've learned that sometimes it's better to make up our own minds. I say this because I feel some of the things that have happened over the years should be forgotten about, and the child deserves to be given a fresh start. After all, we all make mistakes.

I agreed with Caitlin that Jasmine could arrive later that day. Her social worker, Lou, would drive her to our house at about 4.30 and Caitlin would drop in so we could complete the necessary paperwork.

I told Erica the news when I collected her from school.

'Remember Jasmine, who we met in McDonald's? She's coming over shortly and she's going to stay tonight and tomorrow night.'

'Really?' She looked surprised and screwed up her face. 'It's Monday, it's not the weekend.'

'I know. I didn't expect her to be coming to stay so soon either, but I'm looking forward to seeing her again.'

'OK. Cool! She's going in the bottom bunk, isn't she?'

I smiled, knowing what she was thinking. Erica had a large collection of cuddly toys that usually occupied the bottom bunk bed while she slept on the top.

'I'll move my toys to make space for her. I hope she likes my room.'

I was pleased about this and told Erica she was a very kind and thoughtful girl. Whenever a new child is due to arrive I normally clean their bedroom and strip their bed to have everything ready, apart from the bedclothes, as it's good to let kids choose their own duvet set. However, as Erica was sharing her room I hadn't wanted to step on her toes by moving her toys and making way for Jasmine.

'That's so thoughtful of you, Erica. When Jasmine arrives we'll get her to choose which duvet cover she wants and make her bed up. We'll also find some space for her bag and clothes, so she feels welcome. We can do that together.'

Erica looked pensive for a moment and then asked if there was school tomorrow.

'Yes, you have school but Jasmine doesn't. Her school is in another town, near her foster carer's.'

'I thought you were being her foster carer now?'

I explained again that Jasmine was only coming to stay for a couple of nights, as her foster carer, Fran, needed a little break.

'Oh yeah, I remember. That's good!'

Erica accepted the arrangement happily, as I knew she would have done had I told her Jasmine was moving in with us permanently. I loved her for that. She was an accommodating child and had only looked on the positive side of sharing her bedroom. She didn't question me about Jasmine being out of school, which I was relieved about, as I wouldn't have broken Jasmine's confidence by telling Erica about the exclusion. Thankfully, the conversation moved on.

'What are we having for tea?'

'Bangers and mash.'

'Can we have beans?'

'If you like. Jonathan likes peas with sausage and mash but I can do both. And gravy. You can't have bangers and mash without gravy, can you?'

'Yes you can, if you have beans.'

'Good point. I wonder what Jasmine will choose?'

'Beans.'

'I say peas, and gravy.'

'I bet I'm right! Beans, beans, beans!'

We didn't have long to sort out the girls' bedroom before Jasmine arrived. Erica lined all her teddies up on the carpet, against the back wall. She also tidied some clothes away so that Jasmine had a bit of wardrobe space and somewhere to put her bag, and she moved all her things to one side of the wide dressing table so they could share it.

When the doorbell rang, we went to answer it together. Erica seemed excited to see Jasmine again but, understandably, Jasmine was in a different frame of mind from the one she had been in at McDonald's.

'Hi,' she said flatly, half raising her hand to give a little wave, then thinking better of it.

It's very normal for a child to feel nervous and intimidated when they arrive for a placement, however long they may be staying. I always try to put myself in their shoes, thinking back to when I was their age and trying to imagine how I would have felt if I'd had to go into care and stay with people I'd only met once. I know I'd have been scared and miserable and riddled with homesickness. It must have been very tough for Jasmine.

'Come on in,' I said, smiling at her warmly and introducing myself to Lou, her social worker.

'Thanks,' Lou said, sounding as lacklustre as Jasmine, and also slightly irritated, I thought.

'Was the traffic OK?'

'Not too bad.'

'That's good. Jonathan will be here shortly. Come through into the kitchen. Can I get anyone a drink?'

As it was cold and already dark I offered the girls hot chocolate, hoping that it would cheer Jasmine up.

'Yes please!' Erica said. 'Can we have some of those mini marshmallows?'

'I don't see why not. How about you, Jasmine? Would you like a hot chocolate, or something else?'

'No thanks,' she muttered, 'I'm fine. I'm not thirsty.' As she spoke she looked blankly around the room, making no eye contact. I wanted to give her a hug and tell her we'd look after her and that she didn't need to be anxious, but I had to hold back. After all, I was still a virtual stranger and I understood that she would need time to settle.

Lou declined the offer of a drink. She said she didn't have long, looked at the clock on my cooker and asked if our support social worker was coming.

'Yes,' I said, just as the doorbell rang. 'That will probably be her now.'

Caitlin introduced herself cheerfully, praised Erica for sharing her room and told Jasmine she was very pleased to meet her. Caitlin had never met Lou before but commented that it was 'nice to put a face to a name.' Lou gave a half-smile. 'Thanks for helping us out. As if we all haven't got enough to do without having to place kids an hour down the motorway.'

Caitlin gave a polite smile. Efficient as ever, she began dealing with the standard paperwork straight away, beginning by making sure I had all the contact numbers I needed.

'Have you got any other notes for Angela?' Caitlin asked Lou. It's usual for the child's social worker to hand over basic details about the child's religion, say, or any important dietary and medical requirements. Lou gave me a single sheet of paper that looked like a multiple-choice questionnaire. There was a tick in every box that said 'n/a' or 'no' or 'not known'.

'There you go. As you'll see there's nothing to flag up really.' Lou told us that she had not been Jasmine's social worker for very long but assured us that everything was 'pretty standard'.

'Why the rush?' Caitlin asked Lou, as discreetly as she could. 'We weren't expecting this to happen so soon.'

Erica had started giving Jasmine a tour of the kitchen and I could hear her explaining that Jonathan and I ran the florists next door, and you could get into the shop through a 'secret door' that was 'so cool'. In fact, this was simply a connecting door that took you from our house into the storeroom at the back of the shop.

'Fran was desperate for a break, simple as that,' Lou explained with a shrug. 'Needed respite immediately. You know how it is.'

She looked at me knowingly and I gave a slight nod of

the head to acknowledge I understood. Foster carers can sometimes suffer from what is known today as 'secondary trauma' or 'transference'. We didn't use those terms back then, but we certainly knew that looking after troubled children could be a strain on those looking after them and cause stress and even illness in foster carers.

'We hope the respite will stop the placement breaking down,' Lou added confidently.

When a carer wants to stop fostering a child they are required to give twenty-eight days' notice to Social Services, so that other arrangements can be made. I thought back to how disillusioned and weary Fran had seemed in McDonald's and it occurred to me that she may be nearly reaching this point.

'Can I ask,' I said very quietly, 'is the placement actually breaking down?'

Lou shook her head and told me forcefully, 'No. As I've said, we're hoping the respite will give Fran the breather she needs and then the placement will continue. That is the aim.'

Lou made no attempt to lower her voice and said this a little too loudly, in my opinion. Jasmine was still in the kitchen, and within earshot. She spun her head around when she heard this. 'It's make or break,' she said nonchalantly, to nobody in particular.

We were all alarmed.

'Who told you that?' Lou asked fervently.

'Fran,' Jasmine shrugged. 'Can I see where I'm sleeping?'

'Yes, sweetheart,' I said, 'of course you can. Erica, why

don't you show Jasmine up to the bedroom? I'll make your hot chocolate, I haven't forgotten, and I'll be up shortly.'

'Have I got my own room?'

'No, you're sharing with Erica. There's bunk beds in her room.'

Jasmine didn't react to this and I had no idea how she felt about sharing a bedroom.

'Where's my stuff?' She looked from Lou to Caitlin to me.

'Didn't you bring your holdall in?' Lou asked, unable to disguise the fact she was frustrated by this.

'No.'

'Why not?'

'You didn't tell me to. Er, shall I go and get it?'

'No, *I* will,' Lou huffed.

I wondered if Lou and Jasmine had had words during their hour-long car journey because the atmosphere between them was unmistakably fraught.

The girls trooped upstairs together while Lou went back out to the car. Unfortunately, she returned looking like thunder. It had started to pour down and her face and clothes were splattered with large wet blobs of rain.

'I'm going to head off now, I've got a long drive back,' she said, setting the holdall down in the hall. Lou had been in the house for a very short time and had not even met Jonathan. I was surprised she hadn't wanted to meet him, given that he would be as responsible for Jasmine's care as I was. He was only next door and was due in any minute, which I'd mentioned, but Lou clearly wasn't going to hang around.

'Bye Jasmine,' she called up the stairs, not seeming to

care if she was heard or not. She got no reply, bobbed her head around the kitchen door to say goodbye to Caitlin, and promptly left.

'Well, that was a quick handover,' I commented.

'The pressure some social workers are under is ridiculous,' Caitlin said diplomatically. She was too professional to make any criticism of Lou and too humble to realise the irony of what she had said, as in my opinion Caitlin was also under a ridiculous amount of pressure, thanks to her heavy caseload and the fact she always seemed to give one hundred and ten per cent to her job. Not only that, but she had been obliged to take on more work as one of the other social workers in her team was on long-term sick leave, which meant that the extra caseload had been shared out with the rest of the team. Whenever a social worker was off on long-term sick leave it seemed no replacement staff were ever taken on, which left the rest of the team over-burdened, in my opinion.

'Are you done for the day now?' I asked Caitlin. 'I hope you are.'

Caitlin said she was going to call in on another foster carer who lived nearby. *Typical Caitlin*, I thought. She was such a dedicated social worker and seemed to squeeze a mind-boggling amount of work into her busy days. Although she was expected to visit all the carers on her caseload every six weeks, I imagined this was not an essential visit and Caitlin was probably maximising her time in our neighbourhood.

'Is there anything you need from me, before I go?' she asked.

'No. I think we're fine, thanks. You get going.'

I'd wanted to ask how long Jasmine had been in care and how many other foster homes she'd lived in, but it didn't really matter. She was here for two nights, that was all. We could manage with the extremely sketchy history we'd been given.

Jonathan came through from the shop just minutes after Caitlin left.

'Jasmine's upstairs with Erica. You've missed both social workers.'

'Really? Have I misread my watch?'

'No. Lou was in a hurry to get going. I expect she's got at least another hour's drive back in the car, in rush hour too.'

He asked why I hadn't fetched him. I explained about the tension in the air between Lou and Jasmine, and added, 'I hadn't realised how short the visit would be until Lou was practically heading out of the door. And there was no need for Caitlin to stay. Lou had given me all the info she wanted to share, which doesn't amount to much. I'm guessing Lou's only been involved with Jasmine since her move to Fran's, two months ago. She said she hasn't known her for long. Caitlin was going to make another visit and I didn't want to hold her up. I'm not sure there was much more she could have told me in any case.'

Jonathan nodded and said that he understood. 'How's Jasmine?'

'A bit subdued, but that's understandable. She seems to be OK with Erica. I was just about to take her bag up.'

Jonathan said he'd carry it and we both went upstairs, so

he could say hello and I could help Jasmine choose a duvet set for her bed. Erica heard us coming.

'I win, I win!' she sang, running onto the landing.

'What?'

'Jasmine likes beans! Jasmine likes beans! I win! I knew it!'

I started to laugh and Jonathan scratched his head.

'Doesn't everyone like beans?'

Erica explained about our little wager on whether Jasmine would prefer beans or peas with her bangers and mash.

'Oh I see! Well everybody's entitled to their opinion, but I'll stick with peas and gravy. That's the best.'

Jasmine appeared at the bedroom door. 'Can I have my bag?' she asked, without looking at Jonathan.

'Of course,' he said, passing her the holdall. 'It's good to see you again. Here you go.'

It was a very small holdall, but big enough for her short stay.

'Shall I help you unpack and we can get your bed made up?' I asked. 'We've got loads of different covers you can choose from.'

'OK!' Jasmine seemed to brighten up at this suggestion and she enjoyed picking out the brightest duvet cover, pillow cases and bed sheet she could find. None of them matched, but it didn't matter at all, and I let her choose whatever she wanted. Jonathan left us to it.

'Your bed looks like an explosion in a paint factory!' Erica said. 'You're funny!'

Jasmine said her pyjamas were like rainbows and they would match her bed.

'Hang on, hot chocolate!' Erica suddenly remembered.

'Oops, I almost forgot. I'll go and make it. Do you want one now, Jasmine?'

'Yes please.'

'Do you like mini marshmallows too?'

'Yes. I love them!'

Progress! I thought.

3

'I didn't dream it!'

I woke with a start. Someone was hammering on our bedroom door. Jonathan was already on his feet and pulling on his dressing gown before I'd lifted my head off the pillow.

'Whoa! Hang on!'

He opened the door and found Erica standing there in her pyjamas. Her face was contorted into a ball of temper and confusion.

'Can you stop her?' she demanded.

I was on my feet now, too. My bedside clock told me it was gone midnight.

'What do you mean?'

'That, that *girl*! *Her!*'

Erica pointed up towards her bedroom and started rubbing her eyes furiously. She didn't look fully awake, yet there was no mistaking how cross she was.

'What's the matter, sweetheart?' I asked softly.

Jonathan stepped past Erica. Our bedroom was on the first floor of our town house, along the landing from the lounge, and hers was on the second floor, at the top of the house. The two bedrooms Mum and Anthony were using were also on the top floor. Jonathan headed towards the stairs, leaving me to soothe Erica.

'Can you tell me what's happening?'

'I can't sleep! She's doing it on purpose!'

'Doing what?'

'Kicking me!'

'Come on, let's go up and sort this out, shall we?'

Erica had already calmed down a little. She nodded and followed me up the stairs, where we found Jonathan standing on the landing outside the girls' room. Their bedroom door was wide open.

'Jasmine's fast asleep by the looks of it,' he said.

He hadn't been in the room. If there had been any sign of danger or trouble he would have gone in, but for obvious reasons he avoids going into girls' bedrooms on his own, or being alone with them in any scenario, for that matter. It's not just that the girls might not like it or might feel vulnerable – we can never know everything that's gone on in their past – but there's a danger they might make accusations against him. Of course, boys can react in the same way as girls towards male foster carers, and female foster carers aren't immune to false allegations from both sexes, but it's well documented that male foster carers and female foster children make the riskiest combination, and we have to limit the potential for upset and trouble whenever possible.

'She can't be asleep!' Erica bellowed.

'Hush, sweetheart. Don't forget, Mum and Anthony are sleeping just along there. Let's not wake them.'

I crept in and, sure enough, Jasmine appeared to be fast asleep. Erica shadowed me and glowered at Jasmine in her bed.

'Look, Erica, we'll talk about this again in the morning. You need to get back into bed as you have school in the morning. Whatever's happened, Jasmine's as quiet as a mouse now, and fast asleep.'

'She's pretending,' Erica hissed.

'I tell you what. You climb up the ladder and get back into bed and I'll stand on the landing for a while and make sure everything is OK. How does that sound?'

'OK,' she said suspiciously, letting out a long yawn.

'Night night, love.'

'Night, Angela.'

I waited for several minutes before peeping in. All was quiet, and I could detect the gentle rise and fall of both girls' duvets as they slept soundly. Erica must have been shattered, bless her.

'What was all that about?' Jonathan asked as we settled back into our own bed.

'Perhaps the bunk bed frame was creaking or something. Maybe it made a noise when Jasmine turned over?'

'Possibly. Erica's not used to having anyone in the bottom bunk.'

'That would make sense, but she told me Jasmine was kicking her.'

'Kicking? Seems odd. Maybe Erica woke and got a bit

confused. Who knows. We'll have to find out in the morning.'

I couldn't get back to sleep straight away. Erica wasn't one to make things up. Did she mean Jasmine had been kicking her mattress from underneath? I had a sketchy memory from my childhood of mucking about at a friend's house and doing just that, as she stretched out on the top bunk and I was on the bottom. I was teasing her and it was harmless fun; I don't think there's a kid alive who's not done the same when sharing bunk beds, and I've seen kids doing similar things when we've taken them on holiday and they had to bunk up in the many caravans we've had over the years.

Jonathan eventually nodded off. He's generally a better sleeper than me. I lay in the darkness thinking back over our evening, trying to work out if I'd missed any red flags.

As far as I could see, it had been a pleasantly uneventful evening. Everybody had enjoyed the sausages and mash I'd served up, and the girls loved it when Anthony decided he wanted peas and gravy as well as beans. He had a tremendous appetite and ate a huge meal, as always.

'Are you training to be a wrestler?' Jasmine had asked him.

'A wrestler? No! Why do you ask?'

She said Fran's mum liked to watch the wrestling on telly and all the wrestlers had big muscles like Anthony. She added that Fran's mum had told her that wrestlers did nothing but eat 'gigantic mountains of food and work out in the gym.'

'I like doing weights and running,' Anthony told her. 'And I love Angela's cooking. So maybe I should take up wrestling. Do you reckon I'd be good at it?'

He flexed his biceps, which were the size of a small rugby ball. Even Mum looked impressed.

'Wow!' Jasmine said. 'You could knock someone out good and proper. You could flatten them and they'd never get up again!'

Anthony laughed. I don't think he knew quite what to say in response to such fighting talk from a little girl. He changed the subject back to food.

'Talking of Angela's cooking, what's for pudding? And where's my washing-up bowl?'

Erica groaned, as she'd heard this joke before. 'Don't worry, he doesn't *really* eat his pudding out of a washing-up bowl,' she told Jasmine. 'He's just being *silly*.' Jasmine burst out laughing.

Anthony was such a friendly teenager and he seemed to be able to make himself popular with anyone. He was a breath of fresh air, and I was so pleased he was staying with us again and getting his life back on track.

We had all played cards after dinner and Jasmine threw herself into several different games, which was great to see. She appeared remarkably relaxed given that she had only been with us for what amounted to a few hours, and I noticed she became more and more chatty as the evening wore on.

When we'd said it was bedtime she did everything she needed to without having to be asked twice. I left both girls reading in their beds before lights out, and when I went back to say goodnight they were chattering and giggling away, talking about a TV show they liked.

I would never have anticipated that Erica would be knocking on our door after midnight complaining about her new companion. I couldn't imagine Jasmine kicking Erica on purpose, to make her as angry as she had been. I wanted to get to the bottom of it. It took me a very long time to get to sleep as I just couldn't get Erica's cross little face out of my mind.

Predictably, I had a hard job getting Erica up for school the next day. She was grumpy and sulky and complained bitterly about the fact Jasmine didn't have to go to school.

By contrast, Jasmine was already awake when I went upstairs. In fact, she was running up and down the top landing in her pyjamas, flapping her arms up and down as if she were trying to take flight. I suggested she go down to the kitchen as I was worried she would wake Mum and Anthony and antagonise Erica still further.

'OK!' she said, making a 'zoom-zoom-zoom' noise as she rushed towards the stairs.

'Don't run!' I cautioned. 'Those stairs are steep, please be careful.'

She didn't respond and continued to flap her arms and make her 'zoom-zoom-zoom' noise, but thankfully she did slow down to a fast walk before going down the stairs.

'I'll come and sort breakfast out in a minute,' I told her.

I got no response. Jasmine seemed to be in a world of her own.

There was a frosty atmosphere around the breakfast table. Erica had entered the kitchen wearing her school uniform, her hair neatly brushed and with a look of disdain on her freshly washed face. She didn't look impressed by Jasmine, who was lounging around, still in her multicoloured pyjamas and with her long hair tumbling messily over her shoulders and down her back. Jasmine looked Erica up and down. She had a look of smug amusement on her face.

'Why did you keep on doing that?' Erica squeaked, folding her arms crossly.

'What?' Jasmine said sweetly, as if butter wouldn't melt. She set her big, blue eyes on Erica and stared at her, unblinking. Her wide forehead was smooth and untroubled, save for her scar, which in the morning light looked like the silvery shadow of an exclamation mark hovering above one eyebrow.

Erica scowled and pursed her lips. 'Kicking me, of course!' she snapped. 'You kept on waking me up. You're stupid!'

Despite being a year older, Erica was shorter and what my mother would have described as 'smaller boned' than Jasmine. Her small brown eyes and chiselled little nose suited her neat, square-jawed face. With her black, bobbed hair and grey uniform she looked like an angry little storm cloud bumping into the fluffy, bright rainbow that was Jasmine that morning. It must have been so frustrating for

Erica and I felt quite sorry for her, but I couldn't let her get away with name-calling.

'Erica!' I said. 'Please don't call Jasmine stupid. We don't call each other names, you know that.' This was one of our basic house rules. I'd shown Jasmine a copy of the rules, as I do with all new arrivals, no matter how long they are staying. The list states that children should be kind and polite and treat others with respect. It also instructs them not to wear shoes in the house, take food upstairs or leave wet towels on the floor, and we ask all children to do chores appropriate to their age, like setting the table or emptying the dishwasher.

Jasmine began to smirk and she continued to stare at Erica. She had a superior look on her face and her eyes said 'don't mess with me'. I found this unnerving and remembered what her foster carer had said: 'She's not a bad kid, but it's the smirking that's getting to me.'

'Jasmine, please can you tell us what happened last night? Erica was awake very late.'

Had Jasmine been going to school with Erica I probably would have left this conversation until later, but I was focused on the fact Erica was the one who had to go to school. She had brought it up, and I didn't want her to leave the house feeling frustrated or not listened to. I chose my words carefully, so as not to accuse Jasmine of waking Erica, in case that was not the truth of it.

'Was she? Was she awake very late?' Jasmine said this in a fey voice, her eyes flashing randomly around the room like a couple of blue torchlights.

'You know I was! You were booting my mattress and rattling the whole bed.'

'Did I? Was I? I must have done it in my sleep. Or maybe you had a bad dream?' Jasmine yawned slowly, tossed her hair about and made puppy-dog eyes at nobody in particular.

'No. I didn't dream it! You did it! You knew what you were doing! Nobody does that in their sleep!'

I intervened, suggesting we eat breakfast and deal with this later. It sounded to me like Erica was the one who was telling the truth and she was getting wound up all over again, which wasn't a good way to start the day.

Erica had plenty of issues linked to her dysfunctional family background, but telling lies was not one of them, as far as I knew. In the six months she had been living with us, we'd had no problems either with her inventing stories or getting up in the night.

I decided I'd have a word with Jasmine later on that morning. I hoped that maybe she'd open up to me after we'd spent some time together, doing something she enjoyed.

Both girls studiously ignored each other while they ate breakfast. I put the radio on and listened to a phone-in about whether it was too early for shops to put up their Christmas trees, which neither child seemed to pay any attention to.

'Jasmine, please go and get dressed,' I said when she'd finished her cereal.

'Do I have to?'

'Yes. You need to come with us on the school run.'

'Do I have to?'

'Yes, you do.'

She got up, tossed her hair again and left the room smirking. At least she did as I'd asked. In fact, she was dressed and ready to go before Erica had brushed her teeth.

Jonathan joined us on the school run. Though the primary school was within walking distance and we liked to go on foot whenever possible, we had decided to go in the car. 'The sooner we separate them the better,' I said.

Ideally, it would have been better if one of us could have stayed at home with Jasmine while the other did the school run. However, we're advised by Social Services not to be alone in a car with a child if we can help it, which is another way of reducing the risk of false allegations being made by kids. Given that the clock was ticking – Erica's tiredness had meant she had dragged her feet and we were behind schedule – walking to school was not an option in any case.

You could have cut the atmosphere on the back seat of the car with a knife.

'Why are we all going?' Jasmine started to complain as we drove off. 'What's the point? Why couldn't I stay at your house? I'm not going to *do* anything. Where's your mum? What about Anthony?'

'Safety in numbers,' Jonathan said, tapping the side of his nose as he pretended this was some kind of dangerous spy mission. 'We need to stick together.'

'Who do you think we are?' Jasmine snorted. 'Like, we're only going on the school run. It's not like we're going into a jungle or a forest or a desert or on a scary roller coaster or flying to the moon or . . .' She ran out of examples and, amusingly, went down another route, one which didn't make a lot of sense. 'You're not Scooby Doo or Mr Incredible or Spider-Man or Superman or Ace Ventura or SpongeBob SquarePants!'

Erica sniggered at this, though I could tell she had tried not to, and I laughed too. I felt some of my stress evaporate and gave Jonathan an appreciative look. He has a knack of knowing when I need a smile, and when to inject a bit of playfulness or a silly distraction into the day. In that moment, as I have done so many times over the years, I felt incredibly grateful that we work as a team. Even Jasmine looked appeased, having got that load off her chest!

After dropping Erica at school we drove straight home and Jonathan went into the shop. I asked Jasmine what she fancied doing.

'Have you got a computer?'

'Yes. I've got loads of CD ROMs. Is there anything you're doing at school that you're enjoying?'

'I'm not in school.'

'I know you're out of school at the moment, but I mean what do you enjoy most on your timetable? What are you interested in?'

'Lots. I like art and we did a project on Australia and that was good. Do you know, they don't eat Marmite, they have Vegemite? Have you been to Australia? Do they, like, feed you on the plane or do you have to wait?'

'Oh yes, you'd get food on a long flight like that. No, I've never been to Australia. I think you might be able to buy Vegemite in some supermarkets here. I'm sure I've seen it, but I've never tried it. Maybe we could try to buy some? There's a huge supermarket in town.'

While I was talking we'd walked into the dining room and I was fetching out a box of educational games for Jasmine to choose from.

'What do you think? Shall we try to buy some Vegemite?'

There was no response and I realised Jasmine wasn't listening to me. In fact, now I was looking at her, I realised she appeared to be in a trance.

'Jasmine, are you OK?'

There was no reply. She was standing as still as a statue, next to the dining table. She had a vacant look in her eyes and her face was rigid and completely expressionless. Unfortunately, I've seen many foster kids react this way. It's a common response in a child who has been traumatised, and it's something I've learned more about over the years. Most people are familiar with the 'fight or flight' reaction to a stressful or threatening situation. It's the human body's way of coping with danger, flooding the body with energising adrenalin to help you tackle a threat, either by fleeing or confronting it. Both are tools for self-preservation, of course. The 'freeze' response often comes into play when a child feels overwhelmed or just needs to 'shut down'. It can be misinterpreted as rudeness or disobedience, when in fact it is nothing of the sort. The child has no control over the response, and they may not hear you or even see you clearly when they have frozen. You have to give them a moment, stay calm and understand that they are not doing it on purpose. 'Jasmine? Can you hear me, sweetheart?'

It took a few moments before she reacted, during which time I smiled at her encouragingly and didn't press her. Eventually, I saw her shoulders drop a little and the muscles in her face soften.

'You know, right? You know, don't you? *Because I think you do.*'

I didn't know what she was talking about. It certainly wasn't anything to do with our conversation about school subjects or Australia, and somehow I didn't think it had anything to do with whatever had gone on the night before with Erica.

Jasmine looked very serious and perhaps even a little scared.

'What is it you think I know? I'm not sure what you mean, sweetheart.'

I started stacking up the table mats, just to give myself something to do. It's generally easier for kids who are disclosing if you don't make a fuss or look them in the eye. It's far better to carry on as normal and not let them know that you are waiting with bated breath in case they want to share important information that might help them deal with past traumas.

'I bet you know. I bet that social worker told you. I don't like her. Did you know?'

I gently told her again that I wasn't sure what she thought I knew or had been told. I added that she could tell me anything she liked. She looked sceptical.

'You sure?'

'Yes.'

Gently, I added that I was not allowed to keep secrets, and that I might have to tell Social Services anything she told me that could be important. Normally I'd try to have this conversation before I found myself in a situation where it appeared a child was about to disclose, but I had not expected this to happen so soon, as it's unusual for things to progress so quickly.

I left a pause but she didn't fill it, so I spoke again.

'All I know,' I explained, 'is that Fran, your foster carer, needed a little break and you are staying here for a couple of nights so she can have a rest.'

'She says I'm off the wall. Off the wall? What does that even *mean*? I've heard her talking on the phone. She tells people, like all her friends and everyone, that my *behaviour* is, like, *so* bad, *so* bad she can't cope and it's off the wall. She tells *everyone*! She's not allowed. She should be reported. She talks about me behind my back and she thinks I don't know. She doesn't care, does she? She doesn't care about me. I know she doesn't. She just wants to make money from me.'

'I'm sorry you feel that way about Fran,' I said, leaving space for her to answer. This was a phrase I'd used so many times over the years. You have to be careful not to say something like 'I'm sorry she's like that', because of course that gives credence to the child's story, which might not be an accurate portrayal of the situation.

Jasmine said nothing in response.

'I'm here to take care of you,' I continued. 'If you want to talk to me, you know you can tell me anything you want to.' She thought about this for a moment and narrowed her eyes as she looked at me, as if slowly sizing me up.

'My dad used to hit me, *real* bad.'

She narrowed her eyes further still, as if she was analysing my reaction.

'He used to hit you?' I spoke evenly and began to re-arrange some flowers in a vase on the table, even though I felt a sharp pain in my heart and wanted to scoop Jasmine into my arms.

'Beat the living daylights out of me.'

'Beat the living daylights out of you?'

That sounded like a phrase she'd heard from someone else. Again I left a pause, hoping she would fill the gap but she didn't. 'I'm very sorry to hear this.'

Jasmine walked out of the dining room and into the kitchen. I followed her and observed quietly as she began reading some of the slogans on our collection of fridge magnets before studying a picture on the wall.

'Did you paint that?'

'No, sweetheart. It's a picture my parents used to have on their wall when I was growing up. Mum got fed up of it and gave it to me.'

'Where is he?'

'Who?'

'Your dad.'

'My dad died a long time ago. Mum lives on her own normally, her house isn't far from here.' I'd already explained to Jasmine that Mum had just had an operation and that's why she was staying with us at that time. I gently reminded her of this.

'How long ago? Was he nice or was he horrible? Did your mum hate him or did she like him? Were you grown up or little when he died?'

My heart sank. I was sure some of those questions would not have entered my head when I was eight years old.

'We lost my dad more than twenty years ago. He was a good man and Mum loved him.'

A memory flashed into my head, of Mum telling me how my father had had problems with alcohol when I was young. He eventually conquered his addiction, largely thanks to my mum's dogged devotion. I took a deep breath. 'I must have been, let me see . . . I was in my late twenties when my father died.'

'I wish my dad was dead.' Jasmine said this in an emotionless way and started counting on her fingers. I had a good idea what she was doing, and a wave of sadness washed over me. 'Late twenties, is that, say, twenty-nine?'

I said it was and she went back to counting, starting at eight.

'Twenty-one more years until that day,' she said eventually. 'I hope he dies before I'm *that* old or I'd rather be dead.'

'Sweetheart, I'm sorry to hear you say these things. I'm so sorry you feel like this.'

I was very shocked and I wanted to tell her not to talk in this way, but of course I couldn't. It was important for her to be able to talk freely and disclose anything she wanted to about her feelings, her father and whatever she had endured in her earlier childhood.

'So . . .' she said, leaving a dramatic pause, 'can I have a go on the computer now? What games do you have? How long can I play?'

I took her back into the dining room, where the computer was set up on the desk in the corner and showed her the box of computer games. There was also a large selection on the shelf above. She chose an educational game called Spooky Manor and was soon engrossed in searching the various rooms in the haunted house for puzzle pieces that would enable her to escape.

While she played I fetched my notebook and wrote down what Jasmine had had said to me, so I could pass it on to Social Services. From the way she spoke, and because she'd said this so soon after her arrival, I didn't think it was the first time she had said such things. Social Services may already have been aware of what she'd said about her father, but nevertheless I'd write a note and pass this information on.

4

'Do I have to go back to hers?'

For the rest of the day we stayed in and played games, made some leek and potato soup and watched a film. The weather was awful and when it came to school pick-up time Mum and Anthony were both around, so we left them in charge of Jasmine, playing the board game Guess Who?

Jasmine had been well behaved all day. She was bubbly and enthusiastic in fact, just as she had been when we met in McDonald's, and Mum had remarked on what a lovely girl she was.

I'd noticed Jasmine had a habit of talking over people and not always answering when spoken to, and it wasn't always clear what she was trying to say, but nobody seemed bothered by this. When Anthony had lived with us previously we'd had another child staying who had ADHD and suffered from various communication problems, so he was quite used to taking this kind of thing in his stride. As for Mum, she was very patient and just seemed to let it all wash over her. 'How interesting!' she'd say when Jasmine came out with a baffling

list of sentences that perhaps contained only one compre-
hensible fact or anecdote. 'How funny! Aren't you a clever
girl!' Though Mum had not undergone any of the extensive
fostering training Jonathan and I had over the years, you
would never have guessed it as she very rarely put a foot
wrong. I always admired the way she dealt with the children
who lived with us. She had a natural knack of talking in an
encouraging, non-judgemental way and the kids always
warmed to her and usually ended up adoring her.

Jonathan and I drove down to school together to collect
Erica. It was tricky to park nearby, especially when the
weather was bad, so it was useful to have both of us there.
Jonathan dropped me at the gate and drove off to find a
parking space while I went to collect Erica outside her classroom door, which opened onto the playground. Thankfully,
she came out beaming. She told me she'd won a pen as a
prize in a quiz, and she was clearly delighted with herself.

'It's the first time I've ever won anything,' she said. 'Except
once when I won a raffle but it wasn't allowed.'

'Wasn't allowed?'

'No, see, I was the one who was pulling the tickets out
of the tin.'

'Oh. That's a shame, but it's better to win a quiz than a
raffle, isn't it? You've done really well, Erica. I'm proud of you.'

Erica brought her good mood into the house. She showed
off her new pen and willingly did her homework before
watching some TV with my mum and Jasmine. The problems of the previous night, and the resentment Erica had

shown this morning, seemed to have been forgotten. I'd given Jasmine a couple of opportunities during the day to tell me anything she wanted to about the bunk bed incident, but she had stuck with the line that she didn't know what Erica was talking about. Unfortunately, it meant we were none the wiser about the truth of the situation and there were questions left unanswered.

'I think we'll have to take a leaf out of the girls' books and simply move on,' I said to Jonathan. 'Hopefully it won't happen again tonight.' He agreed that this was the best tactic. After all, Jasmine was only staying one more night and we didn't want to ignite any trouble.

Dinner went well, with the girls discussing the previous week's *X Factor* at great length. I was a big fan of the show too – it was only on series five then – and I had plenty to say, but when I offered an opinion on one of the singers the girls didn't engage with me. In fact, they simultaneously flicked their eyes in my direction with a look that said 'yeah, whatever!' and carried on talking to each other!

Jonathan winked at me. I knew this meant 'Leave them to it', and he was right. Kids often think 'old people' (and that's anyone in their late twenties onwards!) can't possibly know anything about pop music, and I wasn't offended. It was great to see the girls getting on.

Being the younger girl, I sent Jasmine upstairs first to have her shower and get ready for bed. She didn't complain. When I went up to check on her, before sending Erica up, I found her dancing around the bedroom to a Sugababes CD, which was one of Erica's favourites.

'I've had a lovely day with you, Jasmine,' I told her.

She carried on dancing, completely ignoring me.

I turned the music down, as it was a little loud, and this got her attention.

'I said I've had a lovely day with you. You've been a pleasure to have around.'

'This is my last night, isn't it? Two nights of spite? Do I have to go back to hers? Do I? It's boring in her house and she doesn't even want me there, I can tell.'

'Two nights of respite,' I said, gently correcting her misuse of the word 'spite'. 'Yes, that's what we all agreed to.'

She had stopped dancing and now stood as still as a stone. 'He hates me.'

'He hates you?'

'Her husband. What's his name? I forget now. He's never in anyway. He's always at work or moaning about work. Why doesn't he change his job if he hates it so much? Grumpy, grump, grump!'

I made a mental note of this. It was something I'd need to mention in my log for Social Services. I had no idea if Jasmine was correct in her summing up of Fran's husband, but it was not my job to make a judgement. 'Grumpy?' I said quizzically, to give Jasmine the opportunity to tell me more, but she didn't expand. I decided to leave the conversation there. Sometimes kids come out with so many things it's difficult to know what you should be picking up on. She hadn't given me an example of why she thought her foster carer's husband hated her and I wondered if it was more a case of her not liking him, or not engaging with him, which seemed possible, given her scathing description.

I hadn't yet heard what the arrangements were for Jasmine's pick-up the next day. Caitlin was due to ring me in the morning to tell me who was coming and at what time. I assumed it would be Jasmine's social worker, Lou, and that she'd arrive towards the end of her working day, but I wasn't sure so I didn't say any of this to Jasmine.

'I'll talk to my social worker tomorrow morning, sweetheart. We'll find out what's happening. It's been great to have you here. And it's been lovely to see you and Erica getting on so well this evening.'

'She's OK,' Jasmine shrugged. This was somewhat ungenerous, I thought, given how the two girls had been getting along, but I was well used to kids who've been traumatised having trouble expressing themselves or even recognising their emotions. Problems forming relationships with peers are very common, and a child's understanding and evaluation of social interactions can be impaired when they have a dysfunctional, stressful background.

As tactfully as possible, I had a last go before bed at trying to resolve 'bunk bed gate', as Jonathan and I had referred to it between ourselves.

'I hope everything works better this time,' I said to Jasmine. 'It was a pity Erica was woken up last night.'

'I didn't do anything.'

'Well, I'm not really sure what happened, but just to be on the safe side, can you do your best to keep still and quiet in bed, so she doesn't get disturbed?'

Jasmine didn't reply. She looked like she'd stopped listening and had completely disengaged.

'And if you have any problems, please come and find me. You know where my bedroom is if I've gone to bed. Just give me a knock if there are any problems at all. Is that a deal?'

There was no reply.

'Jasmine, is that a deal?'

'Deal,' she said, but I wasn't convinced she had listened to half of what I'd said and it looked like her mind was already on the next thing, whatever that was.

Erica came upstairs to get ready for bed and Jasmine didn't argue when I asked her to turn the CD player off after one more track.

'You can read while Erica has her shower and gets into her pyjamas. I'll come up and see you both at lights out time. Did you remember to brush your teeth?'

Jasmine nodded at me and looked very thoughtful as she scanned the bookshelf for something to read.

'I bet Jonathan's never hit anyone,' she said, just as I was heading out of the door.

'Jonathan? No, sweetheart. He wouldn't hurt a fly.'

Jonathan had a rough time as a kid and grew up avoiding violence and any form of physical conflict like the plague. The youngest of four brothers, he was beaten by his father, who saw him as a clumsy weakling on account of the fact he was the thinnest and smallest of the boys and also had poor eyesight, which made him accident-prone. Occasionally, Jonathan had shared this information with some of the older teenagers who'd lived with us, when it seemed appropriate, perhaps to help them see that it's OK to talk about bad things that have happened in the past. I wished Jasmine was old enough to have a conversation like that, especially in the light of what she'd said about her own dad, but it wouldn't have been right. It might have upset her to think of Jonathan being beaten, or it might have raked up memories of her father when she wasn't in the right place to talk about him.

'Beat the living daylights out of me.' That's how she'd described her father's treatment of her, wasn't it? I certainly didn't want to trigger any bad memories and, besides, I always try to avoid discussing anything upsetting with the kids directly before bedtime. I don't believe it's good for anyone to have sad or negative thoughts going around in their head before they go to sleep, myself included.

'He wouldn't hurt a fly?' she said. 'Does that mean he would hurt a bee or a ladybird or a spider?'

'No, not at all! It's an expression meaning he wouldn't hurt any living creature at all. Anyhow, talking of flies, I've got another game similar to the Spooky Manor one. It's called Creepy Jungle and you have to catch bugs and insects so you can escape. Maybe you could have a go on that tomorrow?'

She looked at me a bit oddly. I'm not sure she saw the connection between me saying 'he wouldn't hurt a fly' and 'talking of flies'. Perhaps it was a little contrived, but it did the trick in terms of getting her to think more positive thoughts.

'Yeah. That sounds very cool. Do you like ladybirds? I love ladybirds. And caterpillars. But ladybirds are the best.

Once I had an umbrella like a ladybird. Or wellies. Was it wellies? No, it was an umbrella.'

'Did you? I think I had an umbrella like that, once upon a time.'

She stared at me as if waiting for me to carry on. 'Once upon a time what?' she asked impatiently, looking a bit bemused.

'Oh, it's another phrase. "Once upon a time" just means in the past, years ago. I can't remember when exactly.'

'So you are not telling me a story? Because one of my teachers used to always say, "Once upon a time" when we had story time in little school.'

I smiled. It was heartening to know Jasmine had good memories like that, as all small children should. 'No, sweetheart, I'm not going to read to you, unless you want me to? You can read your book for a while.'

'Good!' She looked relieved that I wasn't telling her a story, which I could understand at her age. 'I can read all by myself,' she said confidently.

She'd chosen an illustrated book of poetry and made herself comfortable in bed and began to read it.

The girls slept soundly and nobody was up in the night. The school run also went off without a hitch the next morning. Jasmine beat me to it and told Erica she might have left before she got home.

'OK,' Erica said. She sounded disappointed. 'Maybe see you around.'

'Yeah,' Jasmine said. 'Thanks. I liked your Sugababes CD and stuff.'

I felt a pang. The care system could be a confusing, disrupting world. In the six months she'd been with us, Erica had settled in well. Given the dysfunctional background she had, we'd worked very hard to make her world as stable and secure as we possibly could. As I've said before, we were passed by Social Services to take in up to three children and we always do our best to help every child who needs a home. Inevitably, during her time with us Erica had seen several other children come and go. She'd been indifferent to some, glad to see the back of others and once or twice had told me she missed one of the other kids who'd come for a respite stay. I'd have a talk to her after Jasmine left, I thought, to make sure she was feeling OK about the latest shift in the household.

We had a couple of errands to run after dropping Erica off at school and it was gone ten o'clock by the time Jonathan, Jasmine and I returned home. I'd made sure my mobile was switched on in case Lou or Caitlin were trying to get hold of me. Caitlin was generally extremely efficient and called first thing when we were waiting for news, as we were today, but I heard nothing.

Unexpectedly, she arrived at the door.

'Come on in,' I said. 'I've been wondering what the plan is with Jasmine's pick-up today.'

'Yes, sorry to keep you hanging on. I didn't phone earlier as I have to do an unannounced visit today, so it wouldn't have been appropriate for me to speak to you earlier. I thought we could kill two birds with one stone.'

Jasmine was standing behind me, having followed me to the front door.

'What?' she said, open-mouthed.

'What is it, Jasmine?'

'What does she want to kill birds for?'

I explained about the expression. Jasmine looked unimpressed, or maybe I just didn't explain it well enough and she didn't understand.

'Can I go on the computer? Where's that game? What was it called?'

'You mean the Creepy Jungle game? I'll set it up for you.'

An unannounced visit is exactly as it sounds – your support social worker drops in without warning to check everything is as it should be. This happens at least once a year.

Caitlin came with us into the dining room while I got Jasmine started on the game.

'Is this computer used only by the children?' Caitlin asked, taking out some paperwork and a pen from her bag. I understood this was the kind of check she had to make on an unannounced visit and, as I knew the drill, I tried to be as helpful as possible.

'Yes. It's got all the parental controls set up. Jonathan and I have our own laptop that we store in the bedroom.' Anticipating Caitlin's next question, I added, 'It has passwords that only we know, and we don't write them down.'

'Thanks,' she said appreciatively. 'Anyone would think you'd done this before, Angela!'

We left Jasmine working on her puzzle game and went into the kitchen. Jonathan was taking washing out of the tumble dryer in the adjoining utility room, which was one of his regular jobs.

'Morning, Caitlin', he nodded through the open door. 'Good to see you, though I wasn't expecting you to come today. I'll be through in just a second.'

I put the kettle on. 'Tea or coffee?' I asked Caitlin.

'Coffee would be lovely.'

Jonathan finished his job and came and sat down at the kitchen table with Caitlin while I made the coffee.

'How's your day going so far?' he asked.

'Busy busy. I've just been explaining to Angela, this is my unannounced visit. As if we haven't got enough to do!'

'Oh, I see. Well, it's not bad timing, is it? What's the plan for Jasmine later? Is Lou picking her up?'

There was a pause.

'Now I've got you both, the first thing I need to ask is whether you could keep Jasmine for another night.'

Jonathan and I caught each other's eye and nodded. 'Yes, of course,' I said. 'Why?'

'Fran's requested it. Said she just needs a bit more time. Just the one extra night.'

This request had apparently been passed to Caitlin via Lou. I wondered why Lou herself had not talked to us about it.

It was Wednesday so I also thought about what we had to do and what Erica had on after school. Everything was manageable.

'It's fine. No problem at all.'

Jonathan nodded in agreement.

'You're lifesavers,' Caitlin said. 'Thank you.'

She took a cup of coffee from me gratefully, added two sugars and drank for a moment before asking, 'So, I take it everything is going OK? Jasmine certainly seems happy enough. Getting on OK with Erica?'

I told Caitlin about what had happened on Monday night with the bunk bed but explained that last night had been trouble-free. 'Jasmine does have a habit of talking over people and interrupting and she sometimes seems to go into a trance. Also, she's made a few remarks about her dad. They're quite strong – they shocked me, to tell the truth. I've made notes.'

I passed a copy of my notes to Caitlin, who quickly scanned them. Had Jasmine been moving in with us, at this point I would have pressed for more background information. There was no point in asking for this now, however, as Jasmine would be gone before the process had even got started.

Caitlin finished her coffee before continuing to run through her checklist for the unannounced visit. This included having a chat in private with Jasmine, having a look at the girls' bedroom, having first asked Jasmine's permission, and asking me to demonstrate that we fulfilled basic health and safety requirements, such as having a first aid kit and keeping sharp objects and anything potentially poisonous, like bleach, locked way.

Ideally, Caitlin would have also chatted to Erica in private to ask her views about the care she was receiving, but she had done this very recently and was satisfied everything was in order.

Before she left, Caitlin signed and dated my log book to show she'd read my latest notes and to record the time and date of her unannounced visit.

'Lou will call you about the arrangements for pick-up tomorrow,' she said.

She'd checked with Jasmine that she was happy to stay an extra night and reported that she'd agreed without hesitation.

'Perfect,' I said. 'I think Erica will be pleased they'll get another night together too, she seemed quite sorry to see Jasmine go.'

Caitlin was delighted to hear this and thanked us both profusely. 'Fran is very appreciative of what you're doing. Lou said to pass that on.'

After Caitlin left I wondered if she had asked Jasmine how she felt about returning to her foster home. I'd logged Jasmine's remarks about Fran supposedly not caring and only doing the job for the money, and the very negative comments she'd made about Fran's husband. Caitlin must have seen them when she scanned my notes, though of course it's not uncommon for kids to make complaints and criticisms like that. Had Caitlin asked Jasmine about them when she spoke to her privately, or was she going to leave that to Lou to deal with, given that she was Jasmine's social worker? I imagined Caitlin would be hoping, as we all were, that things would be so much better after Fran and Jasmine had spent time apart and Fran had had a rest. I really hoped that would be the case. Maybe Jasmine would benefit from a fresh start and slot back in. I crossed my fingers.

5

'She just put that in her mouth!'

Unfortunately, things went a bit pear-shaped after Erica came out of school on the Wednesday afternoon. She had seemed happy to see Jasmine and said she was glad they would have another night together, so I wasn't anticipating trouble. However, problems started when I was cooking dinner and the girls were supposed to be taking it in turns playing a game on the computer. One would be in charge of the mouse while the other watched, and vice versa. They'd agreed to swap over every time they went into a new section of the game and this worked well for a while, but a heated row broke out after about fifteen minutes. I dashed from the kitchen into the dining room to see what was happening.

'What's going on?' I asked, looking from one to the other.

Both girls started blaming the other and Jasmine began shouting louder and louder. Jasmine looked so mad I was afraid she might lash out. Recognising this, I wheeled her computer chair away from Erica's and stood between them. It seemed that Jasmine was refusing to let Erica take control of the game when it was her turn, as they'd agreed, and Erica had said to Jasmine, 'I wish you'd gone to your own foster home like you were meant to!'

I told Erica she must not speak to Jasmine like that, as it was unkind.

'Sorry,' she muttered. 'I didn't mean it.' I could tell she felt bad and the apology was heartfelt.

'If you don't share, you can't play,' I told Jasmine. She grumbled and shouted and refused to let go of the mouse. I had to repeat myself three times before I got through to her.

'Suit yourself!' she shouted, standing up and pushing her chair into the wall in anger as she did so. 'It's a rubbish computer anyway. That game sucks. When can I go back on?'

'Which is it, Jasmine? Do you want to have a turn or not?'

'Yes! Of course I do!'

'Then please don't behave like this. You and Erica have to share and take turns. If you can't take turns at being in charge of the game then you won't get to play at all.'

Jonathan and I were only just starting to learn about therapeutic parenting, which we're now very familiar with and are staunch advocates of. In hindsight, I realise I shouldn't have started out by asking the girls 'What's going on?' Kids who have suffered childhood trauma are unlikely to know why they are behaving in a certain way and they find it impossible to explain why they are playing up or having a row. It's therefore not helpful to ask for an explanation, as they genuinely can't give you an answer and this

ANGELA HART

only frustrates them further. It would have been better if I'd tried to distract the girls, and particularly Jasmine, who was the one refusing to play fair. Instead of threatening that she wouldn't get a go at all if she didn't take turns, I should have said, 'Come into the kitchen with me, Jasmine, and we can play a game of cards while Erica has a turn on her own, and then you can have a turn on your own.' This is because studies have shown that kids who've been traumatised need 'time in' rather than 'time out', as it helps them to calm down and control their emotions. By contrast, sending a child to their room, for instance, or excluding them from an activity is akin to pouring petrol on the flames. The child feels punished for behaviour they probably had no control over and didn't understand in the first place. The result is that they feel isolated, misunderstood and even more angry than they did before the blow-up.

As I've said, I was just starting to learn all this, and it's only looking back that I can see how I could have done things better. Setting a timer up next to them and giving the girls an equal amount of time in charge of the mouse instead of leaving it up to them to swap after each different section of the game was something else I could have done, to make it fairer and therefore reduce the chances of a row breaking out.

As it was, I suggested the girls choose another game each and take turns at the computer, rather than trying to play the same game together and arguing about whose turn it was to be in charge. I said Erica was to go first because Jasmine had refused to let her take over when her time was up.

Jasmine scowled and Erica looked quietly smug as she took her place at the computer.

'You can have ten minutes each and then swap.' I'd keep an eye on the kitchen clock, I thought.

We had a well-stocked bookcase, colouring books and pens and a few boxed games in the dining room. I encouraged Jasmine to read or do something on her own while Erica played on the computer. She reluctantly picked out a dot-to-dot book. It was for a much younger child but I didn't say anything. I had a pan of potatoes simmering on the hob and needed to get back in the kitchen, which I did as soon as both girls were occupied.

I'd started draining the potatoes when I heard Erica scream. I splashed boiling water on my hand in my hurry to put the pan down quickly.

'What's the matter?' I asked, dashing into the dining room once again.

Jasmine was smirking.

'She just put that in her mouth!'

Erica looked shocked and was pointing at my phone charger.

'I thought she was going to get electrified!' Erica had one hand over her mouth as she stared in horror at Jasmine.

I always kept my phone charger on the bureau next to where the computer sat, unplugged when it wasn't in use. However, it was plugged into a socket on the wall on the other side of the room and Jasmine was standing beside it.

'What's going on?' I asked her.

'Nothing. I always do that. And it's electrocuted not

electrified.' She spoke in an emotionless voice yet carried on smirking, which I found unsettling.

'Jasmine, let's get this right. Did you plug in my phone charger?'

'Yes.'

And did you put the end of it in your mouth when it was switched on at the wall?'

'Yes.'

Nonchalantly, Jasmine explained that she liked it when she got a little electric shock, and that this sometimes happened when she put the end of a plugged-in charger on her tongue and stuck her fingers in her mouth at the same time.

Erica was staring at her in disbelief. I wasn't surprised she'd screamed – I think I might have done the same if I'd seen Jasmine do that.

I explained to Jasmine, forcefully, that this was not a good idea, and told her why and that she must never do it again. She looked nonplussed, sat herself back at the table and picked up her dot-to-dot book. Erica resumed her game on the computer, rolling her eyes and tutting as she did so.

I took my charger away and made sure there were no others lying around the house. I had no idea if Jasmine had actually had the electric shock she'd described or was simply trying to scare or impress Erica. The only way to find out would have been to try it myself, which obviously I wasn't going to do.

By the time I returned to the kitchen the potatoes had gone soggy, having been abandoned in half a pan of boiling water. I also had an angry red scald mark on my thumb. It was too late now to run it under a cold tap so I just got on with making the dinner.

It'll have to be mash again, I thought, looking at how the spuds had started to mush and fall apart.

Anthony came in from a shift at the pub restaurant just as I'd started to mash the potatoes. 'Oh good, are we having mash again?'

'Yes, Anthony, we are now!'

I didn't bother explaining that I'd been planning to serve boiled potatoes with the baked fish we were having. At least Anthony didn't mind, I thought, though I had a private bet with myself that Mum would remark on the fact we'd had mash once already this week!

'Want me to do anything?'

'Yes, please. Can you take the salt and pepper through to the dining room and check on the girls while you're at it?' Noticing the time, I told him Jasmine should be having her go on the computer and asked him to supervise the switch over.

'I've just had to have words with them about sharing so come and tell me if there's a problem.'

'Sure thing.'

Thankfully, despite the fact my timings were a little inaccurate as I was doing two or three things at once, there was no more bickering and the girls each had two turns on the computer before dinner.

Jasmine helped Anthony set the table, and by the time we all sat down to eat the girls seemed to have forgotten their differences. Moving on quickly and putting arguments behind them was a strength of character both girls had, I'd seen.

'Didn't we have mash potato on Monday, dear?' Mum remarked.

'Yes,' I smiled. *At least Mum's getting back to her old self*, I thought, before explaining we were meant to have boiled but I 'overdid' them.

'Oh I see,' she said, sounding relieved that I hadn't intentionally tried to feed everyone mash on a Wednesday as well as a Monday. Heaven forbid!

When I was a child Mum used to cook more or less the same meals in rotation. We'd have a roast on Sunday, leftover cold cuts with pickles and chips on Monday, chops and boiled potatoes on Tuesday, cottage pie on Wednesday, casserole or stew on Thursday, fish on Friday, and sausages, burgers or something 'exotic' like risotto on Saturday. I grew up understanding that no 1950s or 1960s housewife worth her salt would have served up mash twice by Wednesday! I thought everybody had the same ideas about food and ate the way my family did, until I moved to the city for work in the 1970s and discovered a whole new world of Chinese takeaways, frozen dinners, Vesta curries and boil-in-the-bag rice.

Jasmine had a very good appetite and I could see she appreciated the meal I'd prepared. Having Mum and Anthony around the table also helped keep the mood light, which I was thankful for.

Anthony entertained us all with stories about things that

had happened in the pub, and there was a great atmosphere in the house all evening. The girls went to bed without a problem. I let them listen to a CD while they took turns in the shower and got their pyjamas on, and there were no arguments about lights out.

After congratulating ourselves on a successful evening, Jonathan and I watched some TV and headed up the stairs to bed a few hours later. Anthony had popped out to see a friend and Mum had gone up an hour earlier, after watching the news.

'Whatever are you doing?!' I suddenly heard Mum shriek. 'You gave me such a shock!'

We dashed up to the top floor to find Mum looking startled in her nightdress. Jasmine was standing right in front of her, smirking.

'What happened?' Jonathan asked. 'Everything OK, Thelma? Jasmine?'

'Yes, dear. Sorry to make a fuss. I just didn't expect to see Jasmine flapping up and down the landing. It gave me quite a start.'

Jasmine froze and said nothing. Mum explained she had used the bathroom and was going back to her bedroom when Jasmine apparently flew at her 'from nowhere'. She said Jasmine began charging along the landing flapping her arms up and down furiously, as if she were a bird trying to take off.

'You weren't making any noise, Jasmine,' Mum said. 'It really took me by surprise to see you there like that.'

Jasmine continued to smirk, said nothing and stood

statue-still. She offered no explanation when we asked her what she was doing getting up in the night like this. We sent her back to bed, which she did without a fuss, thankfully. I made sure Erica had not been disturbed and Mum was OK before Jonathan and I finally turned in.

'Probably just as well this is her last night,' Jonathan commented. 'She's got bags of personality, but she's got an unpredictable streak, hasn't she? At least she's got on with Erica tonight, but we can't have your mum getting spooked like that, can we?'

I agreed. I liked Jasmine. She was a spirited little girl who must have had a really rough time, but we had a full house and my mum was still getting her strength back. It would be best all round if Jasmine could start afresh with her placement back at Fran's.

We knew by now that Jasmine was the only child being fostered by Fran, whose own children were grown up and had left home. I didn't know if Social Services had specifically wanted to put Jasmine in a single placement or if it was just chance that Fran wasn't fostering any other children at the same time, but I could see how a single placement would work well for Jasmine. She needed a close eye to be kept on her, and from what I'd seen, she was better behaved when she had your full, undivided attention.

It was quarter past midnight when Erica thumped on our door. I could have only been asleep for half an hour and I had that horrible, heavy head-fog you get when you're jolted awake very suddenly.

'She's woken me up again!' Erica cried. When I say cried, I really mean it. Erica was in tears. Her face was white and had that wrung-out look that kids get when they are exhausted and emotional. She seemed distraught with tiredness and the injustice of it all. I gave her a tissue and helped her dry her eyes.

'What happened?'

It took Erica a couple of attempts to explain what had gone on – she was just too tired and cross to think straight, but we got the gist. Jasmine had been banging on the wall and rattling the bed frame, Erica said.

'Can I give you a cuddle?' I asked. She willingly agreed and started to calm down.

Once her tears had stopped we repeated the routine from Jasmine's first night, taking Erica calmly back to bed and checking if Jasmine was asleep. As anticipated, when we got to the girls' bedroom Jasmine was either fast asleep or doing a very good job of pretending to be. There wasn't a peep from her. Erica gave me another hug and climbed gratefully into her bed.

The phone rang while I was eating my breakfast on Thursday morning. Jonathan and I had just been patting ourselves on the back for getting Erica up for school on time; she was looking remarkably bright-eyed and bushy-tailed after her disturbed night.

I was expecting to hear from Lou that morning, to let us know what time she'd be collecting Jasmine later that day, but it was before office hours so that would have been unusual.

'Angela?'

'Oh! Good morning, Caitlin. Is everything OK?'

'Yes, I mean . . . Sorry it's so early but I wanted to catch you before the school run.' She sounded rushed and stressed.

'Is there a problem?'

'Well, I hope it isn't a problem, but I've just spoken to Lou, actually. Can you have Jasmine for one more night? Sorry to ask again.'

'You mean keep her again tonight, so she'll go back to Fran's tomorrow instead of today?'

The plans had been changed so much I wanted to make sure I had the facts straight.

'Exactly. Fran needs another night's respite, apparently. Sorry to mess you around. Lou says she will do the pick-up tomorrow, Friday.'

It didn't sound like we had much choice. I hesitated momentarily before saying I'd need to quickly check with Jonathan.

'No problem. I'll stay on the line.'

'What d'you think?' I said to Jonathan, swiftly explaining the situation.

'It sounds like Fran's made her mind up to be honest so, yes, of course Jasmine can stay. It's only one more night. She'll go home tomorrow, you say?'

'Yes.'

'Fine. I guess that makes sense, seeing as Fran finds it hard to cope with Jasmine when she's not in school. This way she'll return for the weekend and then she'll be back at school on Monday.'

Social Services would never force you to continue to care for a child against your will, but if Jasmine couldn't return to Fran's as planned and we refused to keep her until Friday, then the only alternative would be for her to go into another foster home for the extra night, possibly miles away. If there was no place available, which was a distinct possibility, given that the fostering service was completely over-stretched, she might end up in a children's home. Obviously, we wouldn't let that happen.

'It's fine, Caitlin,' I said, returning to the phone. 'I'm sure we can manage for one more night.'

I could tell she was up against it so I didn't bother mentioning the issues we'd had the previous afternoon and evening. It would have taken too long and, more to the point, it would not have made any difference to the plans for Jasmine.

'Thank you *so* much, Angela,' Caitlin said. She sounded incredibly relieved. 'I can't tell you how helpful that is. I'll talk to Lou again and I'll be in touch later about the arrange-ments for pick-up tomorrow.'

'Perfect. Have a good day and we'll talk later.' I took out my diary.

'It'll be fine,' I reasoned, turning to the relevant page. I looked at my notes. First Jasmine was only staying Monday and Tuesday. Then it was last night too, and now she was with us until Friday.

'Maybe it'll work out for the best,' I said to Jonathan. 'Yesterday didn't end well, did it? Hopefully the girls can end things on a better note.'

Just as I had done the previous day, I crossed out 'Jasmine pick-up' on that date and wrote it on the next one.

Jonathan watched.

'Bit like *Groundhog Day*,' he mused.

Despite the fact Jasmine had been with us for just three nights, and two of those had been disturbed, I really was hoping for an end to the disruption.

'Bless her,' I said. 'I don't like to wish any child away, but it hasn't been particularly easy, has it? Let's hope the change has done Jasmine and Fran some good, and will give them both the new start they need.'

'Let's hope so,' Jonathan said. 'And I've got everything crossed for us to end things on a high. I hope we'll have served our purpose.'

6

'I left the bad Jasmine under my pillow this morning'

Jasmine didn't turn a hair when I told her she wasn't going back to Fran's until Friday.

'I thought she was going today,' Erica said.

'No, it's changed.'

Erica didn't seem bothered, despite what had happened the afternoon and night before. As I've said already, she was the type of girl who could forgive and forget easily, and Jasmine also seemed to start each new day afresh, with a blank slate. The girls weren't exactly chatty on the way to school, but the atmosphere was cordial between them. After we'd dropped Erica in the playground I explained to Jasmine that Erica had an after-school club that evening.

'She does gymnastics at the leisure centre. How about we go and have a swim later, while she's in her club?'

'I like swimming. Yes, I'm good at swimming. What's the pool like? Is it big? Are you allowed to dive?'

I told her that the pool in this particular leisure centre was average-sized and there was one small diving board.

'Cool. What can I wear? I didn't bring my swimming stuff.'

I'd thought of this. 'We can walk into town and buy a costume,' I told her. 'Do you want to do that?'

'Yes! Yes!'

Erica had recently outgrown one of her swimsuits and it possibly would have fitted Jasmine, but I thought it would be better to buy a new one. As a child I wore all kinds of hand-me-downs, passed on by my older cousins and neighbours, and sometimes friends of friends I didn't even know. My parents weren't short of money, but that's how their generation was brought up, having lived through the war and rationing. I saw it as normal and never questioned it or felt hard done by, as that was what everyone did in those days. In fact, I used to look forward to opening the bag and seeing what I was getting, but times had changed. Not only that, I'm sensitive to the fact that a child in foster care is likely to have issues about self-worth. Giving them 'cast-offs' might upset them and make them feel even less valued as a person, or inferior to other children. For this reason I try to avoid offering them hand-me-downs or even getting them to borrow another child's clothes. Lots of foster carers have a cupboard full of clothes for emergency placements, which is a good idea, but I've generally managed without one as we have rarely taken emergency placements out of hours.

I told Jasmine we'd walk into town and pick out a swimsuit. I knew there was a good sale on in the department store and, failing that, there was an ex-catalogue shop where I loved to browse and always found bargains. There was an excellent sports shop in town too, which stocked all the best brands. I was sure she'd find something she liked, and she was absolutely thrilled at the prospect of shopping for something new.

'How long now?' she asked me about half-a-dozen times that morning. 'How long until we go shopping? Is it nearly time yet? Can we go now?'

We finally set off after lunch. The weather was cold but dry and we wrapped up warm and walked into town together.

Jasmine had done all sorts of arts and crafts at the kitchen table in the morning, as well as having a lesson from my mum in how to knit. She was very polite and patient, despite chattering non-stop, and I complimented her on her behaviour.

'It was a lovely morning,' I said, as we waited at the zebra crossing. 'You've been such a good girl and I've enjoyed spending time with you. It was great to see you working so hard on your painting, and Mum said you're going to be a good little knitter. Did you like learning how to knit?'

'Yes. I left the bad Jasmine under my pillow this morning.'

This comment took me by surprise. Jasmine said it in a matter-of-fact way, as if it were the kind of thing any little girl might say every day.

'You left the bad Jasmine under your pillow?'

She'd already moved on to another topic. 'Is it far? How much further do we have to walk?'

'Not far now. We'll soon be inside and out of the cold. It's only a couple of minutes from here.'

Even though it was still early November, the department store was already decked out for Christmas. There was a sparkling, silver tree beside the escalator in the centre of the store and next to it was Santa's grotto. I thought they'd excelled themselves this year, as everything was shimmering with glitter and fake snow and looked fabulous. At the entrance to the grotto was a model of a red-brick fireplace with knitted stockings hanging from the mantelpiece. Red, yellow and orange cellophane flames danced and crackled in the hearth, which glowed realistically.

Jasmine gasped and then stopped in her tracks.

'It all looks fantastic, doesn't it?'

I turned to look at her and realised she wasn't gasping in awe at the wonderful decorations. She was having one of her moments when she froze and stared into space. It seemed the sight of the tree or the grotto – or maybe something else? – had triggered this reaction. I stood beside her, talking to her gently.

'Jasmine, sweetheart, I'm right here. We'll go and find the swimming costumes, when you are ready . . .'

She was back in the room moments later. 'What?'

'Are you OK, sweetheart?'

She looked pale and her breathing was more rapid than normal.

'What? Yeah.'

'Shall we go and find the right department? For your swimming costume?'

She looked at me blankly and narrowed her eyes. I noticed that with some of the colour drained from her face, the scar on her forehead was once again more noticeable than usual. Not for the first time I wondered how she'd got it. I wouldn't ask, though. I didn't want to trigger a bad memory. I hoped she'd maybe tell me about it herself but I guessed that was unlikely, given the limited time she was staying with us.

'Swimming costumes? What do you think – children's section or sportswear?'

'Can we go in the lift?' She pointed to the signs.

'Yes, of course. They're at the back, over there. Come on.'

I looked around to see if anyone was looking over, in case Jasmine had spotted someone who'd frightened her, but I didn't see anyone looking in our direction. I did this because I'd cared for another child who was terrified of seeing her father in town and had panic attacks whenever she saw someone who looked like him.

I also considered whether Jasmine was afraid of escalators, but I didn't want to ask and put any ideas in her head. I thought that at eight years old she was definitely still young enough to visit the grotto, but it seemed quite obvious this wasn't on her agenda. She made a beeline for the lifts and seemed to relax only when the escalator, tree and grotto were behind us and out of sight.

There wasn't a great choice of swimming costumes – I guess late autumn was not the best time of year to be shopping for one – and I suggested we go over the road to the catalogue shop. We took the lift down and I guided us out of the department store on a route that avoided the grotto and tree as much as possible.

Jasmine walked around the catalogue shop wide-eyed, taking in all its treasures. 'Look at that! Ooh, what does this do, Angela? Can I touch that? What's that for?'

The household goods, toys and sundries were at the front of the shop and we had to snake past baskets of bath towels and various random items such as giant garden gnomes, Chinese lanterns, toilet seats and plastic golf clubs in order to reach the clothing section at the back. It was much more orderly in this part of the shop and we soon found the rails of children's clothes. Again there wasn't a huge choice, but thankfully Jasmine found one swimming costume she liked in her size. It had a palm tree on the front and looked more suited to a beach than the local council leisure centre, but that didn't matter one bit. She was thrilled with it and couldn't wait to wear it later that afternoon.

Jonathan came with us on the school run. We'd arranged for Barbara to close up the shop for us that night so he could come swimming too.

'How was your shopping trip?' he asked.

Jasmine completely ignored him and stared out of the car window.

'Jasmine, I was asking about your shopping trip?'

He looked at me and I looked at Jasmine.

'Sweetheart, Jonathan is talking to you.'

She cranked her head round ever so slowly, until we made eye contact.

'Are you coming in the water because my dad never took me swimming. My dad . . .' she broke off.

'It's OK,' I said. 'Tell me what you want to say.'

Jasmine clamped her mouth shut. She looked nervous, as if her words might get her into trouble.

'You can tell us anything you like, sweetheart.'

'I don't want to. You're all the same! Just nosy, nosy, everyone asking questions. Leave me alone!'

She sat in silence all the way up to the school and was monosyllabic when we collected Erica.

'How was your day?' I asked Erica.

'OK.'

'What did you do in class?'

'Er, I forgot.'

'Lunch? What did you have for lunch?'

'Thursday is *always* roast dinner day,' she said somewhat impatiently, annoyed that I was asking a question I should already know the answer to.

'Oh yes, I forgot it was Thursday. This week has flown. Did you have beef or chicken? Or something else?'

'They didn't tell us,' she said.

I wanted to ask how she couldn't tell from the taste, but decided it was best to change the subject. 'By the way, we're all going to have a swim while you do your gymnastics.'

'Oh.' Now it was Erica's turn to stare out of the window.

Jonathan looked at me and raised his eyebrows. The end of the school day can go one way or the other. Often kids are tired and non-communicative like Erica, because they've been working hard to be polite, focused and sociable all day and need some quiet time, but just as often they race out of school babbling and bubbling with energy, letting off steam after reining themselves in for hours in the classroom. We found that their mood at home time doesn't tally with how they've behaved in school, which means we've got used to going to parents' evenings and having teachers describe children in ways we don't always recognise. For instance, we'd had a young lad staying with us for a short placement. Every afternoon he came charging out of school at top speed. I was surprised he didn't have steam coming out of his ears. I had a word with his teacher, to make sure he was not being too boisterous in the classroom, and she looked at me with a puzzled expression on her face before saying, 'He's the quietest little boy in the class.'

The girls studiously ignored each other on the way to the leisure centre. When we arrived Erica went off to do her gymnastics and Jonathan and I took Jasmine to the pool. She did as we requested in the changing room and I was pleased to see she was a really confident swimmer. She asked us to time her doing widths and enjoyed having a few races with Jonathan and jumping off the diving board.

'Look at me!' she said over and over again. 'Can you do this?' She did handstands on the bottom of the shallow end and demonstrated how to do forward rolls under water. Naturally, we never took our eyes off her, despite the fact she was a strong and capable swimmer. It's second nature to track kids constantly when they're in water and we were well used to doing so. If Jonathan went off to do a length on his own, I was on duty, and vice versa. Jasmine seemed to be in her element, having so much attention from both of us.

'I think it's very good that she's in a single placement

with Fran,' I commented to Jonathan as we both watched her walk up to the diving board. 'I think she thrives when she has one-to-one attention.'

Jonathan agreed with me; it was something we'd talked about already.

'Look!' she called. 'I'm going to do a pike jump this time!' Jasmine took her place in the queue for the diving board and made sure we were both watching before launching herself into a perfect pike jump. She was having so much fun I dreaded having to tell her it was time to get out.

'D'you think she'll play up?'

'I hope not,' Jonathan said, looking at the clock. 'We've got to collect Erica soon.'

'Jasmine, it's time to get out now,' he told her after agreeing to 'one last jump'.

She pulled a face.

'I thought we could have a drink and a snack in the cafe,' I added.

'OK, I'm starving!'

'I think you cheated, Mrs Hart,' Jonathan whispered as we all got out of the water. 'You've bribed her.'

'I might have done, but it's worked. And I'm dying for a coffee, I don't know about you!'

Jonathan was showered and dressed before Jasmine and me so he went to collect Erica from her gymnastics class on the other side of the leisure centre. As we dried our hair, Jasmine looked at her reflection in the mirror. 'I could bang my head on that mirror and kill myself.'

'Jasmine, please don't say that. It's not nice at all.'

She continued to look at her reflection.

'My dad didn't take me swimming. My dad hit me with a stick. Did you know?'

She was looking at herself so intently in the mirror that she didn't seem to be aware of two teenagers standing nearby, listening. One of them nudged her friend and they both giggled and walked away. I saw the other one holding her forefinger up to her head and spiralling it round as she looked at Jasmine, as if to say, 'That girl's round the twist.'

'He hit you?'

'Yes. He hit me. And he tried to drown me.'

'He tried to drown you?'

Now Jasmine looked at my reflection. I was trying not to look shocked because I didn't want to put her off saying any more. 'Yes. He tried to drown me. I told him I would smash my head into the mirror and kill myself.' She snapped her head round to look me in the eye. 'I wish he'd drowned me. *Then I'd be dead.*'

Jasmine ran a brush through her hair, slung her bag on her shoulder and said, 'You don't know what I had done to me.'

She made to walk away and I gathered my things together.

'Sweetheart, is there anything else you want to tell me? Because you know you can tell me anything you like, don't you?'

'I'm hungry. Do they sell doughnuts in the cafe? Can I get a hot chocolate?'

The girls greeted each other like old friends at the leisure centre cafe, which was heartening to see. Erica started chattering about which of her friends watched *X Factor* and this sparked a long and animated discussion about all the various acts. The troubles of the previous night definitely seemed to be forgotten, thank goodness.

Jasmine didn't rattle the bunk bed that night. I think she was tired out from swimming and went out like a light, and Erica was also fast asleep within minutes of her head hitting the pillow.

Unbelievably, on Friday morning I got another early call from Caitlin. Fran had asked if the pick-up could be put off for yet another day. As it would be a Saturday and Lou would not be working, Caitlin explained that Fran had offered to collect Jasmine herself, or meet us halfway, in the McDonald's where we first met. Once again, we agreed. We felt we had little choice. Luckily, Jasmine was happy to stay and didn't seem unduly troubled, so we didn't mind.

'Please just let us know what the plan is as soon as you know,' I asked Caitlin. 'I'll need to know today so I can make arrangements to cover the shop.'

Friday was what I'd describe as 'so-so'. Like a lot of kids, Jasmine seemed to be better behaved when she was busy and active and burning off energy. Anthony was around first thing in the morning and the weather was dry. He volunteered to take Jasmine over to the play area and fields at the back of our house, before he went for his run.

'I'll come with you, I could do with some fresh air,' I said. The truth was I'd rather have stayed in the warm house and had ten minutes to myself while Jonathan was at the wholesalers and Mum was still in bed, but I didn't know Jasmine well enough to allow Anthony to take sole responsibility for her. A little voice in my head was telling me that we all needed to be careful. Jasmine had told me quite a few worrying things about her dad and had seemed very willing to offer up this information. As I've said before, most children take longer to disclose such disturbing details. One explanation could be that she was saying things for effect, perhaps things that weren't entirely true, but who knows? I didn't want Anthony to find himself being blamed for something he didn't do, or to be accused of upsetting or hurting Jasmine in any way.

I wrapped myself up in a big anorak, scarf and bobble hat, and sat on the bench in the playing field.

Anthony had brought a rugby ball and was teaching Jasmine how to throw it properly. She was squealing and dashing around like an excited puppy, blowing white clouds of hot breath into the cold morning air.

What a shame I can't trust her to play a simple game of throw and catch on a field with Anthony without worrying about what might happen, I thought.

I found myself wondering once again how Jasmine had got the scar on her forehead. She'd never mentioned it and there had never been an opportunity for me to raise it, without feeling I might be opening up a memory that would most likely be bad, if only because of the physical pain it must have caused her.

There were so many questions I would like to have had

answers to. What exactly did her dad do? Where was he now? How long did she live with him? Did he ever face any charges? There had been no mention of siblings, or of Jasmine's mother. I felt that knowing more about her background might have helped me care for her better.

Jonathan often said that short-term respite fostering is like trying to drive a new car with one hand tied behind your back. Not only that, you've been given no manual or service history, despite knowing the car has been involved in several bumps along the way. It's not easy, that's for sure.

I felt my phone vibrate in my pocket. I was wearing woollen mittens and pulled one off quickly in order to answer the call. It was Lou.

'Morning, Angela,' she said. It sounded like she was driving. 'OK if I arrange for Fran to collect Jasmine at ten o'clock tomorrow, at your house?'

'Yes,' I said. 'I thought we'd maybe be meeting at McDonald's like last time, but that's fine. I'll let Jasmine know. We'll have her ready.'

The line crackled and went dead. I waited for Lou to call back but she didn't.

Despite the negative things Jasmine had said about her foster home, all things considered I felt it was best that she was returning to Fran's. Not only was she a child who needed a lot of one-to-one attention, but our circumstances were not ideal. We'd already agreed that Mum would be with us until after Christmas, and Anthony was probably going to be around for many more months, as his savings account wasn't growing as fast as he would have liked (a common problem in teenagers, I've found!). This meant Erica would have to continue sharing her bedroom, which had not exactly worked out brilliantly.

On the Friday afternoon Jonathan and I had lots of jobs to do. We needed to buy a new Venetian blind for the bedroom Mum was using, as one of the children who had previously lived with us had damaged the rod you twisted to open and close the slats. It was just about usable, but Mum had arthritis and was struggling to operate it, so it was time for a replacement. We also had to pick up some food shopping and go into the bank. 'Can you help me write a shopping list?' I asked Jasmine.

'Sure.'

I gave her a piece of paper and a pencil.

'What do you want?' she asked.

I dictated a short list which she put in her pocket.

'Do you want me to look after that?' I offered.

'No, I can.'

'OK, great.'

Unpredictable kids have a habit of playing up in supermarkets and I was thinking that if Jasmine had been involved in writing the list and then I asked her to find certain items, it might limit the risk of her getting bored and misbehaving.

When we arrived at the supermarket I asked Jasmine to give me the list. She smirked and handed me the piece of paper. 'Here you are,' she said, putting on a sweet and innocent baby voice.

'Let's see what we have here,' I said. I'd cottoned on to the fact something was going to be awry. 'Jonathan, let's see who can go and get what.'

I opened the list and showed it to him. Jasmine had her eyes trained on us and continued to smirk.

This is what the list looked like:

eggs

bum

milk

bum-bum

cotton wool

bummer

brown rolls

poo

stock cubes

wee

dog, cat, ginnee pigs, hampster, goldfish

We both knew full well that Jasmine's aim was to provoke a reaction, so we didn't give her one.

'Eggs,' I said. 'Let's find the eggs first.'

Jonathan asked her to help him pick out a dozen eggs. She looked at him suspiciously but did as she was asked. He let her decide which size and colour, knowing that kids like to have some control.

'Oh dear, there seems to be a few items on the list that the shop won't stock,' he said, giving a shrug. 'Never mind. Let's get the milk next.'

Neither of us cracked a smile, though we were both dying to laugh.

Eventually, Jasmine couldn't take this anymore.

'Bum, bum-bum, bummer!' she shouted.

'No, there's none of those here,' Jonathan said.

'Poo and wee! Poo and wee! Poo poo poo. Wee wee wee!'

She shouted this in my face while blocking the trolley. People were starting to stare.

'No,' I said, 'they don't stock those.'

'I hate you!' she shouted.

'That's a shame. As it's your last night I was going to make a cake for you. I've just seen some lovely cake decorations, but I don't suppose you want me to make a cake . . .'

'Yes I do! Yes I do!'

I looked her in the eye. 'Good. So let's have no more silly business. Move out of the way of the trolley and let's finish this shopping.'

She was as good as gold after that. She was also an

absolute angel when we had to pay a very boring visit to the blinds shop and bank some business cheques.

Once home, the evening went well. Jasmine loved making the cake and clearly enjoyed being the centre of attention when Jonathan made a little speech at the dinner table to say goodbye to her. We'd discussed this before he did it, by the way, and had both agreed that, with Fran herself collecting Jasmine, coupled with the fact Jasmine was due back at school on Monday, we did not expect another extension to her respite stay.

'To Jasmine!' Jonathan said, raising his glass. We were only drinking water or squash, but everybody chinked their glasses. 'It's been very good to meet you!'

Erica said 'cheers' with a big grin on her face, which I was delighted to see, and Jasmine looked happy and relaxed. I felt very thankful that both girls were 'in the moment' types, which had helped no end this week.

There was a good vibe in the air all evening and the girls went to bed on time, without any hitches.

'All we've got to do now is get through Erica's dance class run in the morning and we'll be on the home straight,' Jonathan said, as we turned in.

Erica's regular dance class took place every Saturday morning at nine o'clock during term time, in the school hall. I wanted Jasmine's stay to end on a positive note and I asked Jonathan if he had any ideas about what we could do for her last hour with us, before Fran collected her at ten.

'How about calling in on George?' he said. 'I bet Jasmine would love that.'

'Great idea.'

George was a good neighbour who kept guinea pigs and rabbits for his large brood of grandchildren. He was nearly always at home and encouraged us to call in any time with children we had staying with us. We'd kept various different pets over the years but didn't have any at the time. I knew Jasmine was an animal lover and would enjoy this. We'd talked about her love of animals on several occasions, and it hadn't gone unnoticed when she listed 'dog, cat, ginnee pigs, hampster, goldfish' on the shopping list!

We had a quiet, trouble-free night on Friday and, before we dropped Erica at her dance class, the girls parted on good terms. This was in spite of the fact that Jasmine was being quite grumpy and had dragged her feet getting ready that morning. Troubled kids often muck about when it comes to doing basic things like taking a shower or cleaning their teeth. It's a way of regaining some kind of control. We knew that, and we cut her as much slack as we could. Fortunately, Erica didn't seem to notice and got ready for her class with no fuss, totally unruffled.

'We've just got time to call in on George,' I said to Jonathan quietly after we'd dropped Erica off. 'Everything packed up and ready to go.' I'd helped Jasmine pack her bag and checked that she hadn't left anything in the bedroom.

Luckily, one of our foster carer friends was going to drop Erica home, as her daughter was in the same class and one of her teenage foster children helped the teacher with the younger kids. This was a big help, as the class finished at ten, which was the exact time Fran was collecting Jasmine. We hadn't mentioned our idea about dropping in to see George's pets, just in case he was out, but Jonathan and I were hoping he'd be in and that she'd have a lovely time.

My phone rang just as we got back into the car in the school car park.

'It's Caitlin,' I said, recognising the number. Most social workers don't call at weekends. If you have an issue you need to call the out-of-hours number, but having said that, it wasn't unusual for Caitlin to phone outside office hours. I don't think she ever switched her phone off, in fact. She often double-checked arrangements and I assumed this was what she was doing.

'Hi Caitlin! We're all set for ten o'clock. I spoke to Lou yesterday.'

There was a momentary pause.

'Is that why you're calling?'

'No, Angela, not exactly.'

Caitlin's voice sounded strained. I got out of the car because I knew this was not going to be good, and I didn't want Jasmine to overhear the conversation.

'What is it?'

'I'm afraid Jasmine can't go back to Fran's.'

'What? Why not?'

'I don't know. I've had a message from Lou. She just said Fran can't have her back and therefore she won't be collecting her.'

'Do you mean today, or not at all?'

'My understanding is that Fran isn't going to take Jasmine

back, full stop. We are looking at other options.' I caught Jonathan's eye through the car window and gave him a wide-eyed look, as if to say, 'You won't believe this.' Thankfully, Jasmine was flicking through a picture book that had been left on the back seat of the car and wasn't aware that anything was going on. 'In the meantime, can she stay with you?'

'Can you hold the line a second? Jonathan's here. I need to tell him what's going on.'

I signalled to him to get out of the car and quietly gave him the news.

He blew out a long, slow stream of breath. 'I guess we should have seen that one coming. We really should have worked that one out.'

'No, I don't think so. Jasmine's supposed to be going back to school on Monday. We couldn't have predicted this. I mean, what about school? It's not really fair, is it?'

We both looked towards the car and just at that moment Jasmine looked up and gave us both a big smile. Our hearts went out to her. This was very unfair on Jasmine, we thought. Extending her respite stay by three nights, each one at short notice, was one thing, but this was completely different. This was potentially life-changing. What would happen next?

We smiled back at Jasmine.

'I'll tell Caitlin it's fine,' I said.

Jonathan nodded. 'Of course. We'll manage, we don't have any choice.'

In theory we both knew we did have a choice. As I've

said, Social Services could not force us to keep Jasmine, but there was no way we were going to turn her away and risk her going into a children's home or being moved miles across the country. Our home was the only one she had right now, and we'd take care of her for as long as necessary.

7

'I want to live with Dad'

We drove straight home after taking the phone call from Caitlin. George's rabbits and guinea pigs could wait and, besides, it looked like we'd have plenty of time for that now. The priority was to talk to Jasmine and explain what was happening; we decided it would be best to do this when we got to the house, rather than talking to her in the car, as we were only a few minutes away from home.

I saw Jasmine's holdall as soon as I opened the front door. It was packed and standing in the hallway, all ready for her pick up. The sight of it saddened me. I couldn't imagine for one moment what it must be like to be eight years old, in care and in this predicament. As a young girl I found it difficult to cope if one of my parents was away overnight, or if I stayed at a relative's home without Mum and Dad, as I did only now and then.

'Can I play on the computer before I go?' Jasmine asked enthusiastically. 'There's time, isn't there?'

'Jasmine, sweetheart, come into the kitchen for a moment, we need to talk to you.'

She followed us both without saying another word. She seemed to know something was about to happen, and perhaps not something good. This saddened me, as I could tell she had been given bad news before.

'The thing is, we've had a message from Social Services. You're not going back to Fran's today, after all.'

Jasmine considered this for a moment and then smirked. 'Good. Can I go on the computer?'

'OK, yes,' I said, wondering what my next move would be. 'You can play an educational game.'

Had Jasmine quizzed me about the arrangements I would have had to be as truthful as possible. I probably would have explained to her, gently, that it was unlikely she would be going back to Fran's, but that I needed to find out exactly what was going on. After so many changes of plan, I would not have said categorically that she wasn't going back to Fran's, as by now I clearly couldn't trust that what I was being told was definitely going to happen.

I was grateful that Jasmine had apparently taken this in her stride, without question, although I suppose her reaction wasn't too surprising, given the complaints she had made to me about living with Fran and her husband. It gave me time to get more information before having another conversation with her – the last thing I wanted to do was make any promises that would be broken or cause her unnecessary stress or confusion. I think she'd already had her fair share of all of those things.

I decided to call Fran direct, and Lou. Optimistically, I reasoned that as the plans had changed so many times already that week, perhaps Fran was just having another bad day and would have Jasmine back after all, perhaps in a couple of days?

I took out the paperwork I'd been given when Jasmine had arrived, looked up Fran's phone numbers and, once Jasmine was set up on the computer, went into the kitchen and called Fran's home number.

A man answered.

'She's not here at the moment. Who's calling? I can get her to ring you back?'

'Thanks, it's important. It's about Jasmine. My name is Angela Hart and I'm the foster carer who's doing the respite care.'

'Oh, right. Like I said, she's out but I'll give her the message.'

'Shall I give you my number?'

'What? Oh yeah, hang on. Let me get a pen.'

I assumed this was Fran's husband. He tutted as he hunted for a pen and sounded uninterested and a little vacant; I wondered if I'd woken him up. He rushed me off the phone before I could ask what time Fran was likely to be back, and I didn't feel one hundred per cent confident my message was going to be passed on.

I tried Fran's mobile but it went straight to answerphone. The same happened when I called Lou's mobile immediately afterwards, although this was understandable, as it was a Saturday and she would not be on duty. Normally I wouldn't bother a social worker out of hours like this, but it was urgent and her number was on Jasmine's emergency contact sheet. I left messages for both Fran and Lou to call me back as soon as possible.

I had given Jasmine half an hour on the computer and reminded her when she had five minutes left.

'Time's up now,' I said, looking at my watch. I suggested she could unpack her bag and I offered to help her. I wished I could do it for her, as it seemed so unsettling for her to be unpacking a bag she'd only just packed, but kids should always do their own unpacking, whatever the circumstances. It generally helps them to settle in, or in Jasmine's case, to settle back in.

'What? I'll do it later. I've only got one piece left to collect in this section.'

'No, Jasmine, you've had your time on the computer. Switch it off now, please.'

'Please, Angela,' she pleaded, putting on the baby voice I'd heard before.

'No, Jasmine. I told you that you had half an hour and I gave you a five-minute warning before your time was up. If you come off now without a fuss you can have another session later, otherwise there'll be no more computer time today I'm afraid.'

'I want to live with Dad,' she said, speaking robotically.

'You want to live with Dad?'

'Yes. Because I'd be dead now if I'd been allowed to live with him. If he dies I'm going to do a dance on top of his grave, did you know?'

She was staring at the computer screen when she said this and showed no emotion. I noticed that she was in a part of the Spooky Manor game where you had to work out riddles that were written by ghosts in a creepy cemetery. I considered what she'd said. 'I want to live with Dad.' It took me a moment to take it in. 'I'd be dead now if I'd been allowed to live with him.' I repeated this back to her, with a questioning tone in my voice. 'Sweetheart, I heard what you said.'

I waited for her to reply.

'Suit yourself,' she said, in a rude, brusque manner. This time she sounded more like a stroppy teenager. I found her shifting mood and tone disturbing. She'd gone from putting on a baby voice to talking like an expressionless robot, and now she was behaving like a cheeky adolescent.

'Come on then,' she said. 'Let's go and unpack my bag seeing as you're so worried about it!'

I didn't respond to that. I'd learned that you can't take on every battle. Sometimes you have to let things go and accept that the child can't help their behaviour. They've learned to react in certain ways in times of trauma and it's going to take a long time for them to learn new ways. Offering them support is a much better solution in the long run, because then they start to trust you. Only then will they listen to you and follow your example and, hopefully, begin to make positive changes for themselves.

'I don't like it when you're rude,' is all I said, in a way that made it easy for her not to respond.

I carried the holdall up the stairs and Jasmine unzipped

it. Inside was a note written in different coloured felt tip pens. She looked at it curiously, clearly not having put it there herself.

To Jasmine. Good luk back at your foster mum's. I wish you a happy life!!! Luv Erica. PS I wont miss you ratter-ling the bunk bed, ha ha ha.

My heart swelled. I had no idea Erica had done this, and I thought what a very kind gesture it was. Though the girls had had their differences, neither of them seemed to bear a grudge. This might prove very useful going forward, I thought.

I helped Jasmine to put some clothes back in the wardrobe and then left her to it, because the phone rang downstairs. I hoped it might be Fran returning my call, but it was Lou, sounding impatient and tetchy.

'Look, I'm sorry about the change of plan. I've been up to my eyes with it all, I really have.'

'What's going on?' I explained to Lou that I didn't want to say too much to Jasmine until I was sure I had all the facts and was confident that nothing was going to change again.

'Well, there is no danger of that happening,' Lou said flatly.

'I'm not sure what you mean?'

'What I mean is, Fran is definitely not going to change her mind. She won't have Jasmine back I'm afraid. There is no chance of that. I'm going to pick her things up on Monday and I'll bring them straight to you.'

'I see. What shall I say to Jasmine? Will she get to say goodbye to Fran?'

We're taught that however difficult a placement has been and even if it's broken down like this one had, it's good practice to try to leave things on a positive note, with a so-called 'good goodbye'. Usually you have the twenty-eight-day notice period leading up to this, but it seemed this rule had been effectively overruled by Fran's last-minute refusal to take Jasmine back.

'No, I'm afraid she won't get to say goodbye. Unfortunately, the respite has had completely the opposite effect to the one we'd hoped for. Fran doesn't want to see Jasmine again.'

Lou went on to say that Fran had decided she was going to stop fostering, full stop. I can't lie; I was very cross with her for making this decision so rapidly, and at Jasmine's expense. I had plenty of questions. I wanted to know why Fran had allowed this situation to unfold in the way it had. Would it not have been better for everybody if she had given the required twenty-eight days' notice to Social Services, informing them that she wanted the placement to end? That way Jasmine would have had time to adjust and perhaps she could have been placed in a more suitable home than ours, ideally as a single placement, as she had been used to.

I didn't say any of this to Lou, of course. It would have been unprofessional and, if this job has taught me anything, it's that you never know what goes on in other people's lives. I took a very deep breath and told myself that, for all

I knew, Fran could have had personal problems that made it impossible for her to continue fostering. Right now, I had to focus on Jasmine and what was best for her.

'What shall we say to Jasmine?'

Jonathan was scratching his head and was still trying to take on board what had just happened.

'We'll have to tell the truth, as tactfully as we can. We'll have to try to focus on the fact that Fran has decided not to continue fostering.'

I had the conversation with Jasmine before Erica was dropped back from her dance class.

'I'm not surprised,' she said, with a couldn't-care-less look on her face. 'I don't think she was a good foster mum. She wasn't kind enough and her husband didn't want me there, I could tell. He was never in a good mood. Always grumpy, grump, grump.'

Erica took it on the chin with even less of a reaction.

'Oh,' she said. 'That's a bit annoying, isn't it?'

I didn't know if she meant *she* was annoyed by it, or if she thought it was annoying for Jasmine to have her plans changed at the last minute. Either way, the good news was that Erica accepted without question that Jasmine had moved back into her room, and neither of them asked me how long Jasmine would be staying for.

The weekend passed quietly. One of Jonathan's brothers visited on the Saturday evening and we all had a takeaway together, and Sunday went by in a flash of homework for

Erica, while Jasmine helped me make the roast dinner and played games with Mum. In the afternoon, I suggested we could walk down to our neighbour George's, to see his rabbits and guinea pigs before it got dark. It was a good excuse to get some fresh air on a cold wintry day as much as anything. Both girls wrapped up warm and were very excited by this idea. I parcelled up some raw cabbage leaves and carrots I'd put aside when preparing the vegetables for lunch and the girls carried a little newspaper package each.

'George might not be in,' Jonathan warned. 'Don't be disappointed if not, we can call another day.'

Happily, not only was George in, but he was about to feed the animals.

'What have we got here? Cabbages and carrots? They're all going to think Christmas has come early!'

The girls thoroughly enjoyed feeding the pets and loved it when George made them sit quietly on his garden bench so they could have a turn petting the animals.

Erica wanted to put her guinea pig back after a couple of minutes, but Jasmine looked like she would have sat there all afternoon if she could. 'He's so cute, isn't he the best? He's the cutest animal I've ever seen. Angela, can we get one? Can we? Feel how soft his fur is!'

I explained that we were a bit busy at the moment. Privately, I was extremely pleased that she was talking about 'we' in this way, so soon after everything that had gone on with her irregular departure from Fran's. Against my better judgement, I added, 'We've had guinea pigs before though and I wouldn't say never.' Jonathan gave a gentle roll of his eyes. He knew I wanted to make Jasmine as happy as possible, but he also knew that I didn't particularly want to have any pets right now. When we'd had rabbits and guinea pigs in the past Jonathan and I had nearly always been the ones who took responsibility for their care once the novelty wore off with the kids. I'd do it all again, though, if I thought it would benefit a little girl like Jasmine.

I was making some sandwiches for lunch when Lou turned up early on Monday afternoon. Jasmine was helping me and was busy squirting mayonnaise into a bowl of tinned tuna.

'Sorry it didn't work out at Fran's,' Lou said to her briskly. 'Your stuff's all out there.'

Lou had dumped three bulging bin bags full of clothes, toys, shoes and other belongings in the hallway. Jasmine didn't say anything and carried on mixing up the sandwich filling.

'Would you like a cup of tea, Lou? We can make you a sandwich if you like?' I was hoping she would say yes and stay and chat for a while, so I could glean as much information as possible, but she seemed to be in a hurry. Not only that, she appeared rather jaded and irritated, as she had done when she first dropped Jasmine off.

'No thanks, Angela. I'll have a chat with Jasmine and I'll have to be off. I'm already behind as it is.' She looked at me as if she expected me to leave my own kitchen. I understood that she wanted to talk privately to Jasmine, which is standard practice in situations like this. She'd need to ask Jasmine if she was happy to stay with us, and of course it was best not to do this in front of me. Over the years I've become accustomed to social workers treating our home like their office – we've been informed many times, for example, that a meeting is taking place at a certain time, with certain people, and that the venue is our living room! I've come to accept that, but Lou wasn't being particularly friendly or polite and I didn't really like the blunt way she'd told Jasmine her 'stuff' was in the hall.

'If you want to talk privately, feel free to go up into the lounge,' I said. 'I'll finish making the lunch. You can show Lou the way, can't you, Jasmine?'

Jasmine ignored me but looked at Lou and said smugly, 'I told you it was make or break.'

Lou rolled her eyes, with no attempt to do so discreetly. Jasmine gave her a triumphant look and led her out of the kitchen and up to the lounge. I heard Jasmine exchange a few words in the hallway with Mum, who had been reading in her bedroom and was on her way down for lunch. Mum knew all about the fact Jasmine was staying with us for longer than originally planned, but still, she was taken aback by the sight of the bin bags.

'What on earth is going on with those black sacks?' she said, a look of horror on her face.

'I told you, Mum. Jasmine's not going back to her foster carer's. That's her belongings. Her social worker has dropped them off.'

'Yes I know that, dear. What I mean is, why in the world

would you put a child's belongings into bin bags? Surely they had something better than that? How awful!'

Mum had a knack of making common-sense observations and she rarely held back in sharing her views when she felt strongly about something. I told her that, unfortunately, it wasn't uncommon for children to arrive with their life in bin bags. 'It happens all the time, Mum, but I guess you've just never seen it.'

'Really? That's just awful, awful!'

'It's far from ideal,' I agreed, going on to explain that it's most common when kids have just been taken into care, especially if they've been removed from the family home in an emergency situation. 'When that happens it's a question of filling whatever bags you have to hand, and unfortunately that often means bin bags.'

'Yes, but Jasmine has come from another foster carer,' Mum said, a note of incredulity in her voice.

I reasoned that when Jasmine had originally gone to live with Fran she probably arrived with bin bags, or maybe carrier bags, as a lot of kids do. Seeing as the placement had ended as abruptly and unexpectedly as it had, Fran had obviously just packed up Jasmine's belongings into whatever she had to hand – and that was bin bags. No doubt the only piece of luggage Jasmine owned was the holdall she'd turned up with for her respite stay.

'It's not what foster carers are trained to do, but there you have it,' I replied. 'Needs must. Right Mum, do you fancy a tuna sandwich and some tomato soup?'

I was putting on a brave face, but really I was as upset

and offended as Mum was by this turn of events. Over the years I've given away all kinds of bags, backpacks, suitcases and holdalls of my own to avoid scenarios like this. Kids in care need their self-esteem building up, not dragging down, and Mum was proof that you didn't need foster care training to work that one out. Having said that, I didn't want to be openly critical of Fran. I knew precious little about her circumstances and it wasn't fair to pass judgement.

Lou and Jasmine must have only spoken for a matter of minutes before returning to the kitchen.

'All sorted,' Lou said breezily. 'I'll be off. Thanks, Angela.'

'Hang on, can I have a word?'

She looked at her watch. 'Yes, of course.'

I said I'd walk her to her car as she was clearly in a rush, and that way we could talk privately too.

'I'd like some more background information. I was given nothing, as it was only respite. Jasmine's already come out with a lot of worrying remarks, especially about her dad. Now she's here to stay for longer, I'd like to know what I'm dealing with.'

Lou promised she would fix up a core meeting as soon as possible.

'That's good,' I said. 'I'll feel happier when I know what's what.'

I wanted to say that my instincts were telling me that Jasmine would be better in a single placement, but I'd see what was said at the meeting first. I'd known Jasmine for just one week, and the poor girl must have been feeling incredibly insecure after all that had happened. Whether she liked Fran or not, she had been rejected by another adult in her life. Her mum had never been mentioned and all I'd heard were extremely worrying details about her dad, or what she thought of her dad and how he made her feel. Jasmine needed some stability, compassion, support and loving care. She also needed a school place, as it was too far to take her to the school she'd attended when she'd lived with Fran. The core meeting couldn't come soon enough.

8

'A turn for the worse? Please explain.'

'It's lovely to see you again, Jasmine. Tell me, how are you settling in with Angela and Jonathan?'

We were at a Social Services office in town. Jasmine was with us along with Lou and Caitlin. A Social Services manager called Mrs Hutton was running the meeting. It was Thursday now, and we'd had a dreadful few days since Lou had dropped Jasmine's belongings at our house in the bin bags on the Monday.

Unfortunately, today didn't look to be shaping up any better. Jasmine had been in an argumentative and aggressive mood all morning, shouting at me at every turn and threatening to smash her head on the window of the car when Jonathan asked her to buckle herself in.

Now she refused to look at Mrs Hutton or answer her question. Instead, she started to grunt and growl and kick the legs of the table we were sitting around.

'Jasmine, can you hear me? I'd like to know how you're getting on, living with Angela and Jonathan?'

Mrs Hutton was an intense-looking woman in her mid-thirties. She had two deep vertical lines etched between her black, wing-like eyebrows, which had the unfortunate effect of making her look permanently cross.

Jasmine started whining and wailing and shaking her head from side to side. Jonathan and I looked at each other in alarm. Though she'd displayed some very challenging behaviour over the past week or so, we hadn't seen her whine and wail like this.

'We're all here to help you. This meeting is for your benefit, Jasmine. Can you please stop that noise? I want to know how things are going at Angela and Jonathan's. Can you tell me?'

Cue more animal sounds, kicking of the table, grunting and head-shaking.

Jasmine had begun playing up as soon as Mrs Hutton walked in the room, and she got worse and worse the more the manager tried to communicate with her.

Lou offered to take her outside to 'cool off' and Jasmine couldn't get out of her chair quick enough. She bolted to the door with Lou in tow before Mrs Hutton spoke again.

The core meeting was a chance for us all to exchange information and work out some practicalities going forward. Everybody present was given photocopies of notes that summarised key points about Jasmine's placement, going back to our initial meeting in McDonald's, and including bullet points taken from my log.

Mrs Hutton turned her attention to me.

'Let's start again,' she said, clearing her throat. 'How is

Jasmine settling in, since the change of plan last Saturday morning?'

It was my turn to clear my throat. I felt slightly intimidated under Mrs Hutton's gaze. She was clearly not impressed by Jasmine's behaviour and this made me want to defend her, but I knew I had to give a balanced, accurate summary of how Jasmine had been behaving.

'When Jasmine was with us for respite we had a few issues and concerns, which you can see I logged, but we also had periods when she was well behaved and a pleasure to be with. Unfortunately, things have taken a turn for the worse since we found out she wasn't going back to her foster carer.'

Mrs Hutton arched one eyebrow. 'A turn for the worse? Please explain.'

I glanced at Jonathan who gave me a look of encouragement. We'd discussed what we were going to say and had spent time making notes together, so as to make the best use of the time at this meeting.

'We've had so many problems we've made a list.' I was glad we'd done this, as the tension in the room might have thrown me and made me forget things. I sat up tall and, reading from the list, I began trying to paint a picture of what had happened over the last few days.

'Aggravating other child in placement by rattling bed/ kicking mattress every night, keeping Erica (age nine) awake. Banging on walls. Banging her head into mirrors, saying she wants to kill herself. Knocking on my mum's bedroom door and running away. Mum is recovering from an operation. Flapping arms and making noises like a cow, seems in world of her own when she does that. Refusing to shower/clean teeth/get dressed when asked, as if deliberately trying to hold everyone up. Chewed a piece out of a cushion in the lounge while watching TV. Ran off and tried to hide from us in supermarket and said, "I could get you done for losing me." Told Jonathan to "f— off" when he told her he was more worried about the fact she would be putting herself in danger if she got lost in town.'

Caitlin gave me a sympathetic smile while Mrs Hutton looked increasingly agitated. She began rapping her pen on the desk and seemed to be deep in concentration.

I ended by describing an incident that had happened the night before. 'There was a big bonfire on the fields at the back of our house. It was not long since Guy Fawkes night. I asked Jasmine if she wanted to walk over and see it, as lots of the kids from the neighbourhood were out with sparklers and glow sticks and so on. She froze when I asked this question. She looked completely terrified and then she started talking really fast, not making any sense. It was as if something had triggered her and she completely lost control. She was wide-eyed, babbling and getting louder and louder. She was in her bedroom and she picked up her teddies and shouted at them. "You know who did it! You know who started it!" Erica was scared and found it very disturbing to see Jasmine like this. We felt at a loss as to what to do as nothing we said or did seemed to get through to Jasmine. Like I say, it was as if she had completely lost it and was in a world of her own.'

Jonathan took over, as he could see I was feeling stressed

and upset. 'The truth is, it is not just Erica who has been disturbed by Jasmine's behaviour. We are disturbed too. We want to help her but we're not sure we are the right carers for her, given our other commitments at the moment, and the fact she is sharing a bedroom with Erica.'

Mrs Hutton's response was to nod sagely and suggest it was 'very early days'. 'I know you have Jasmine's interests at heart and I do appreciate your concerns. We need to monitor the situation, that's clear. Jasmine has been through a lot of change and I'm hopeful that once she has settled in, we'll see an improvement in her behaviour.'

She told us that Jasmine had 'regressed' when she'd first gone to live with her previous foster carer, but said it wasn't long before she 'found her feet and turned a corner'. I was not convinced by this, given what Jasmine had told me about how she felt about Fran and her husband, and the fact Fran had decided she couldn't cope with her.

Caitlin explained we had virtually no background infor-mation on Jasmine and asked Mrs Hutton to provide any details that may be helpful to Jonathan and me.

Mrs Hutton began to thumb through a folder of notes contained in an A4 binder. Silence fell in the room and it took several minutes before she located the details she was looking for. During this time I heard Jasmine growling in the corridor, and the sound of Lou trying to hush her.

'Jasmine was taken into care three months ago. EPO issued. Her dad was physically abusive and neglectful. He is an alcoholic. She is an only child. Mother absent since Jasmine was, let me work this out . . . six years old.'

An EPO, or Emergency Protection Order, is used in exceptionally serious situations, when a child is at risk of physical, mental or emotional harm and needs immediate protection. It gives Social Services the right to enter a child's home and remove them into care. I felt my heart ache for Jasmine. We already knew she'd suffered, but hearing this detail somehow made it more real and more alarming. She had been in grave danger, the poor little girl.

'Two foster placements,' Mrs Hutton continued. 'The first one was emergency respite cover. She spent twenty-four days in that placement, then she moved to the placement with Francis that has just broken down. She was with Francis for just over two months. Her first foster carer could not take her back and there was no other suitable carer available in that neighbourhood.'

Jonathan reached across and gave my hand a squeeze. He knew how I'd be feeling, having heard the upsetting details about Jasmine's life and move into care. With the sounds coming from outside the door, the whole experience was distressing, to say the least. My brain was working over-time. If Jasmine was an only child and had been taken into care just three months ago and her mother had left when she was six, did that mean she'd been alone with her father for the best part of two years? Had he neglected and abused her for all that time, from the age of six to eight, before the abuse came to light?

I asked if there was any more information that could be shared, perhaps about Jasmine's mental health or education. I wondered aloud how she'd got the scar on her forehead. Caitlin supported me by saying it would be helpful to know if Jasmine had received any kind of therapy or if we should look into having her assessed in any way. 'We know she isn't statemented and we know she was excluded from school, but what else can you tell us? Are there any special needs we should know about?'

There was another silence while Mrs Hutton scanned the file again. My heart had already sunk. I realised that if Jasmine had only been in care for such a short time, it was odds on that she had not received any psychological assessments. Often they are requested by carers or social workers after a child has been brought into care, but this takes time and there are always long waiting lists to access services like CAMHS (Child and Adolescent Mental Health Services).

'No reported health problems, either mental or physical. No records of any psychological assessments or therapy. As for the scar, no. There is no medical record about the injury. She has some special needs. On that note, we need to find her a school place as quickly as possible.'

It was clear that Mrs Hutton's aim was to keep Jasmine in placement with us; there seemed no viable alternative, at least not one that was readily available.

'Why was she excluded from school at the end of her stay with Fran?' Jonathan asked.

'Poor behaviour in class,' Mrs Hutton said unhelpfully. We all looked at her, waiting for further explanation. 'Let me see. It seems she was refusing to do any work and began "throwing pens like darts" at other children. When she was asked to stop she tried to kick the teacher.'

Caitlin said she had already put a call in to our local primary, the one Erica attended. She was waiting to hear back from the head teacher and was hoping to arrange a trial visit.

'What special needs does she have, as I'll have to let the head know?'

'I can't see any details on that. I'm afraid I don't know. There's nothing here about that.'

I'd had Mrs Hutton down as an extremely efficient manager. The way she spoke and composed herself made me think she would have all the answers, but that was not the case at all. In fact, I was starting to feel quite surprised at how unprepared Mrs Hutton seemed to be. She'd made it clear she had met Jasmine prior to this meeting, but she didn't seem to know her at all. I wondered if perhaps Mrs Hutton had only seen Jasmine at the emergency meeting that would have been held when she was first taken into care. Lou would hopefully be able to tell us more. I assumed she'd been Jasmine's social worker for the three months she'd been in care, so perhaps she would know her better than anyone else in the room.

There was no sound coming from the corridor now. Mrs Hutton asked Caitlin to go and check how Jasmine was, and to invite her and Lou back into the room, if possible.

I didn't think Jasmine would come back in, and I was right. Lou came in on her own, leaving Caitlin outside, in charge of Jasmine.

'I managed to calm her down,' Lou said, 'but she was adamant she wasn't coming back in here. Sorry.'

We didn't glean much from Lou. She told us she had only seen Jasmine on a handful of occasions since she was brought into care in August. All she knew about her special needs was that Jasmine was often taken out of class with a small group of other children who were either given some one-to-one tuition or were allowed to do arts and crafts when the class teacher thought they wouldn't cope with some of the more academically challenging parts of the curriculum. When asked by Mrs Hutton to elaborate about the breakdown of the placement with Fran, Lou said, 'Fran was finding it increasingly difficult to cope with the challenging aspects of Jasmine's behaviour, such as her refusal to get ready for school on time and the fact she sometimes disengaged, refused to answer questions and seemed to smirk a lot, which Fran found particularly hard to deal with.' Lou added that the placement broke down not only because of Jasmine's behaviour, but because 'there were things going on in Fran's personal life that made it extremely difficult for her to carry on as a foster carer.'

This fitted. Fran had never returned my call from the previous Friday. I'd assumed she must have been embarrassed by the way things had turned out, what with all the changes of plan and then not even saying goodbye to Jasmine. I know I would have been mortified if I were in her shoes. I'd also imagined Fran might feel guilty about leaving Jonathan and me with very little choice about keeping Jasmine on. Hearing that she had some personal problems made sense, I supposed.

Mrs Hutton began to wrap up the meeting after Lou had

spoken. She did this by praising our 'generous understanding' of Jasmine's predicament and thanking us for continuing to care for her. We glanced at one another. If you could have read the thought bubble above our heads it would have said, 'Have we got any choice?'

It seemed to both Jonathan and me that this was a fait accompli. Jasmine was staying with us for the foreseeable future, whatever that meant. The wheels were already in motion for her to start school in our town. Whatever concerns we'd raised about her behaviour, the disturbing comments she'd made and the impact on Erica were not going to prompt Social Services to find her a more suitable placement, at least not yet. I had intended to discuss the fact we thought Jasmine might be better off in a single placement, but there didn't seem much point. I reasoned that it was very early days for me to be making that judgement, and Social Services would no doubt be quick to tell me that. The fact Jasmine had been growling like an animal in this meeting room and in the corridor was duly noted in the minutes of the meeting, but even that was not going to change how Social Services intended to deal with Jasmine right now. They wanted us to keep her on and do our best. Only if the placement began to break down would they look at other options. I understood that, and I was certainly not going to argue or refuse to keep her on.

After years of fostering I've accepted that this is how our overstretched Social Services have to operate. The phrase 'if it ain't broke, don't fix it' is probably the best way of describing the system. There simply aren't the resources available to seek out and provide a perfect, tailor-made placement for every child in care. It's a case of making do with whatever's available at the time, hoping for the best and clinging on to that hope for as long as possible. We were that hope and, despite the concerns we had, we would not let Jasmine down and would try to deliver the best possible care for her.

I was relieved to find that Jasmine was in a good mood by the time the meeting ended. Caitlin had distracted her by playing memory games in a small waiting area along the corridor. We found them playing 'I went to the shops and bought . . .' taking it in turns naming a food item beginning with a, b, c and so on. Jasmine was slowly recounting the shopping order. 'I went to the shops and bought an apple, a banana, a carrot, dog food, eggs, erm, erm, fish fingers and . . .' There was a pause while she thought up a word beginning with g. 'Jelly!' she yelled out triumphantly.

'Very good try,' Caitlin said. 'But jelly starts with a j not a g. It's j-e-l-l-y. Have another go.'

'Gin!' Jasmine shouted. 'Can I have that? Can I?'

'Yes, well done.'

Mrs Hutton said a bright 'goodbye' as she walked past the waiting area. She looked pleased to see Jasmine was in a much better mood; from her point of view, I imagined, the meeting had gone well. Jasmine was happy to stay with us – Lou had fed back this information – and we were willing to keep her. Not only that, but a school place was already in the offing. For Social Services, this was a job well done.

Again, Jasmine refused to look at or speak to Mrs Hutton,

and when the manager walked away down the corridor I saw Jasmine blowing out air very slowly, as if she was trying to deal with a difficult situation. This made me think once again that Mrs Hutton might have played a part in the original child protection proceedings, when Jasmine was first brought into care. I wasn't sure how – it's the child protection social work team who would be in charge, not a manager like Mrs Hutton – but somehow I felt their paths had crossed. It would have been a traumatic time, especially as an EPO was issued. Whatever Jasmine thought about her father, it would still have been an ordeal to be removed from the family home and placed with a foster carer. I didn't know the details, but this would have happened very quickly, possibly with no warning whatsoever for Jasmine, because that is how EPOs work. Was this why Jasmine was so ill at ease in Mrs Hutton's company? Perhaps she associated the rather stony-faced manager with her memories of being at home one minute and being driven away by a social worker the next? Or maybe she simply reminded her of somebody else? Of course, I had no idea how Jasmine's dad had reacted to the EPO, but from the picture I'd started to build up of him I couldn't imagine it would have been a peaceful scene.

As we were leaving the building, Jasmine asked Lou if she could still see her grandparents.

'Oh, yes, of course,' Lou told her. 'I was going to mention that, thanks for reminding me.'

Lou informed us that she'd already given our phone

number to Jasmine's grandparents, Lenny and Pearl. 'I hope you don't mind. They're lovely people. Think the world of Jasmine. They've been taking her out at weekends.'

This was something that perhaps should have been mentioned in the meeting but, for whatever reason, Lou had forgotten. She became a bit flustered as she brought us up to speed. 'Yes, really nice, they are,' she said, speaking very quickly. 'Sorry, should have told you I'd passed on your number.'

'No, not at all,' I said, not wanting to stress her out any more. 'Do you have your grandparents' phone number, Jasmine?'

She said she didn't. Lou rooted through her large, extremely messy bag, found the number in her diary and wrote it out for us, after asking me for a pen that worked.

'Great. We'll give them a ring. Thanks for that.'

'Can we do that as soon as we get in? Can we, Angela, can we ring them today? Can we do that? I want to talk to Granny!'

'Yes, of course, Jasmine. No problem at all.'

We said goodbye to Lou in the car park and she checked her watch before walking away. As she did so, Jasmine chimed up, 'I'm going to ask them if I can live with them.'

Though she was in a hurry and walking quickly, Lou must have heard this, but she continued striding towards her car and didn't look back. I didn't really blame her. Her job with Jasmine was done for the day and she no doubt had a stack of other appointments to keep.

'Tell me about your grandparents, Jasmine,' I said. 'I'd love to hear all about them.'

On the journey home Jasmine painted an appealing picture of Lenny and Pearl. They were 'older than you but not *really, really* old' (we were both in our early fifties). Lenny was good at building walls and doing DIY, while Pearl played in a darts team and was crazy about her two ginger cats, Stan and Ollie. 'They take me nice places. They take me out for lunch and stuff in lots of different restaurants. They're kind and Granddad tells the stupidest jokes! Granny pretends to fall asleep when he tells long stories. They have a fish that sings on the kitchen wall when you press a button, and Granddad has a big beard and pretends he has mice living in it!' She laughed, and we did. They sounded like a breath of fresh air in Jasmine's life.

Naturally, I was interested to know if they were her dad's parents or her mum's. Or maybe only one was a blood relative and the other was a step-grandparent? You can never make assumptions and you always need to check the facts, but it's usually best not to ask a child direct questions about such things. They need to tell you about their families in their own way and in their own time.

As soon as we got home Jasmine wanted me to show her how to use the phone.

She was clearly very excited as she dialled her grandparents' number, which I was pleased to see.

'Granny! Is that you?'

Jasmine started giggling at whatever her granny said. 'Yes. No. Didn't you know? I'm not living with that one anymore.'

I'd asked Jasmine if she wanted me to leave her to talk in private, as I do with all the children when they are calling relatives – unless Social Services has asked me to supervise calls, that is – but she said no, she wasn't bothered. Nevertheless, I busied myself by pairing up a pile of socks, so she didn't feel I was listening to her every word.

'Angela's nice,' she said. 'I've been living with her for more than a week, I think, and I'm going to stay.' There was no mention of Jonathan or anybody else who was living in our home. 'I'm going to a new school. Yes, I didn't like the old one, it sucked. Yes, hang on.'

She called me over. 'Can you talk to my granny?'

'Of course,' I said, taking the phone and introducing myself to Pearl.

She sounded friendly and down to earth, and straight away I felt a good vibe. She told me she had been given our number by Lou earlier that day and had been about to call us. 'I'm very pleased to speak to you,' she said. 'Before I realised Jazz was with you, I'd left a message with Fran about the weekend, but she didn't return my call. I was wondering what was going on, but I guess it makes sense now. We've already made plans for this weekend but we'd love to take Jazz out next weekend, for something to eat and maybe a drive out somewhere. Does that fit in with what you're doing?'

'Yes, of course, it'll be good to meet you. Either day is fine. My husband Jonathan will be very pleased to meet you too.'

I told Pearl a little bit about us, explaining how long we'd been fostering and that we ran a florist shop, and she told me that she and Lenny had retired recently but 'liked to keep busy'.

'What exactly happened with Fran?' she asked.

I told her I really didn't know. As Jasmine was standing next to me I added, 'One minute Jasmine was here for respite for a couple of days and then . . .' I paused and gave Jasmine a big smile, '. . . the next thing you know, she'd moved in! Aren't we the lucky ones?'

We picked a day and time for Pearl and Lenny to take Jasmine out – a week on Saturday – and I explained where we lived. I also told Pearl we were fostering Erica, who was nine, and that my mum and Anthony – 'who's a former foster child but like a lodger now' – were also living with us.

'Gluttons for punishment,' Pearl chuckled. 'I'm always in awe of foster carers like you. Are you sure you can manage with our Jazz too? I've told Social Services we'd have her, you know, but they're not having any of it. Seems daft to us. We're family, after all.'

My ears pricked up at this. We'd got the impression that if we didn't look after Jasmine, Social Services would have a problem on their hands. I didn't want to pry, but of course I wanted to find out more, and hear the reason Social Services had ruled out Pearl and Lenny as guardians for their granddaughter.

'Really? I didn't know that. I think there's a lot I don't know, but that's not unusual.' I added light-heartedly, 'Mind you, foster carers are always the last to know.'

Happily, Pearl seemed in no rush to get off the phone. 'We feel like we're kept in the dark too,' she said sympathetically. 'We love our Jazz. She's the light of our lives and we'd love to have her. You'd think it would be an easy fix, wouldn't you? But life is never simple. They have to have rules I suppose, these social workers. Still, seems ridiculous. We don't let him anywhere near us. Never will again. We've told them all of this but it doesn't seem to make any difference. They've turned us down flat. It doesn't matter that we have nothing to do with him; Jazz is not allowed to live with us because he's our son.'

Pearl told me they had disowned their son because of how he had treated Jasmine. 'But that's not good enough for those people,' she said with a sigh, explaining that Social Services had concerns that Jasmine's father might contact her through them. 'I think the authorities need to look at what they're doing. With all due respect, the money would be better spent on sending *him* away, not our Jazz. But will they listen to us? No, they won't. We've been told it's not even worth applying as we stand no chance. We might get a solicitor involved, if it comes to it.'

Pearl took a breath, apologised for 'going on' and said she looked forward to meeting us.

'Not at all. It's very good to talk to you. I look forward to meeting you next Saturday. I'll put Jasmine back on and I'll tell her you're taking her out.'

Had Jasmine not been in the room I might have told Pearl what a relief it was to finally get some more background information, having been drip-fed precious little from Social

Services. I wanted to ask about Jasmine's mum, but of course I didn't.

'Am I seeing them on Saturday?' Jasmine asked excitedly. 'How many days is that? Can I talk to Granddad? Can I?'

'Not this Saturday, next Saturday,' I explained.

'How many sleeps?'

'Nine. That's not many! Just nine days and you'll have a lovely day out with your grandparents.'

I put Jasmine back on the phone and listened to her telling her granddad that yes, she would love to go and see the street that had been on the telly, where all the houses were lit up with fairy lights and Christmas decorations. 'And can we have pizza like last time?'

She cheered.

'Bye, Granddad. I love you to the moon and back too!'

9

'I know who started the fire'

'How many sleeps now?' Jasmine asked.

It was the following Thursday, a week after our core meeting and the phone call to Pearl and Lenny.

'Two,' I said somewhat wearily. 'Just two.' Little did Jasmine know that I was also counting the days until she went out with her grandparents, because I felt we all needed a break.

Unfortunately, Jasmine's happy mood had evaporated very quickly after that upbeat phone call. We'd gone up to the lounge, where Mum was sitting quietly, doing her cross-word. I was hanging up strings of card holders between the two pictures on the wall behind the sofa, so we could display the Christmas cards that had started to arrive. Meanwhile, I'd asked Jasmine to set out the pieces in a wooden nativity scene that I brought out every year. All the kids loved it and I hoped it would keep her occupied for a little while.

'I like the donkey the best,' she said. 'And who are you? Where shall we put you? No, naughty donkey, you can't go there! Silly donkey! Move it! Go there.'

It was good to hear her chattering away unselfconsciously, as young children do.

'Have you ever taken part in a nativity play at school?' Mum asked, looking up from her crossword.

Jasmine had a think. 'No. I was going to be an angel but then they wouldn't let me.'

'What a pity. I remember Angela being an angel.'

I cringed, remembering the old family story of how I'd accidentally tucked my white dress into my pink knickers when I went to the toilet before the show, and then walked out on stage. Thankfully Mum didn't recount it on this occasion.

'What did you play instead, Jasmine?'

'Nothing.'

'Oh! Never mind, there's always next time.'

Mum left it there. She was starting to get to know Jasmine and understood she had 'issues'. I hadn't shared any of her private or confidential information of course, but Mum had seen Jasmine in action. The night I'd mentioned at the core meeting, when Jasmine had knocked on Mum's bedroom door and woken her, was just one example. My poor old mum had got out of bed and found Jasmine running up and down the landing and flapping her arms even more wildly than she had seen her do before. This time it was even more alarming, because Jasmine started making noises like a cow, mooing wildly.

'Angela, I don't think the young girl is right in the head,' Mum had said to me the next morning. It wasn't language I would use, but I knew what Mum meant: Jasmine's behaviour was disturbing and, as Jonathan and I had told Social Services, this was concerning us. We weren't sure we were equipped to deal with her mental state, which we had no information about whatsoever.

Now, Mum went back to her crossword and Jasmine continued to play with the nativity scene. It was cold and very windy and there was a gale picking up outside. I felt a draught blowing down the chimney, so I asked Mum if she wanted me to put the fire on before going to collect Erica from school.

'That would be lovely, dear.'

Out of nowhere, Jasmine grunted loudly and tipped the nativity scene upside down, scattering all the neatly laid-out pieces across the rug in front of the hearth. Then she started rampaging round the room, flapping her arms and growling.

'Jasmine, what's the matter?' I exclaimed.

'I know who started the fire,' Jasmine chanted, in an eerily emotionless voice. 'I know who started the fire.'

Mum thought she meant the fire in our living room. She told Jasmine that nobody had started the fire and said she needed to stop racing around like that.

'You don't know anything!' Jasmine screamed. She was very animated now, and the scar on her forehead had become red and angry. 'You didn't see! I know who did it. I know who started it.'

It was very obvious to me that Jasmine was not talking about the fire in our living room, but of course I didn't know if she was talking about a real experience she had had or if she was randomly ranting.

'Jasmine, please calm down.'

She screeched at the top of her voice now, making Mum and me jump. Mum covered her ears, it was that loud.

'I KNOW WHO STARTED THE FIRE! I TOLD HIM WHO STARTED IT! I TOLD HIM! I TOLD HIM!'

'Jasmine, sweetheart, please stop. Please don't scream like that.'

She completely ignored me and then started charging in circles around the coffee table in the middle of the room, her eyes staring wildly at nothing in particular. Mum looked at me in shock and confusion.

I went to stand in front of the hearth. 'Jasmine!' I spoke as forcefully as possible without shouting. 'Please stop this, right now. You're going to break something or, worse still, hurt yourself.' Again, she totally ignored me.

'I know who started it, I know who started it,' she chanted over and over, thankfully at a much lower volume now. 'Zoom! I know! Zoom! I know!' She was getting faster and faster and now she seemed to be pretending to be an aeroplane.

I thought about what we were learning at our therapeutic training classes and tried to put it into practice. I stepped forward purposefully, to try to get Jasmine's attention but without looking threatening. I also tried not to look alarmed or flustered, but unfazed and in control.

'Jasmine,' I said as calmly as I could manage. 'Why don't you and I go into the kitchen and we can have a go with the felt set?'

The felt set was one of those creative kits, where you made

different pictures by sticking felt shapes on a fuzzy board. Jasmine had played with it the day before and really enjoyed making a beach scene and choosing which shells to stick on the sand and what colour bikinis to dress the girls in.

'Grrr!' She grunted in my face, but at least she stopped running in order to do so.

'Did you hear me, Jasmine? Let's go and play with the felt set, just you and me.' Finally, she seemed to engage with me. Her expression softened and she looked me in the eye.

'OK, if we have to!' She was out of breath from all her exertion. 'Come on then, what are you waiting for, Angela?'

That evening we had a repeat performance of 'bunk bed gate'. This time Erica didn't come and knock on our door as she had done previously. She simply screamed over the bannisters, 'Angela! Jonathan! She's doing it again!' This inevitably woke Mum and Anthony as well as us.

It was one in the morning this time. I took Jasmine down to the kitchen and made some hot milk in the hope it would make her sleepy and the rest of the household could settle down again before she went back to bed. It worked, but inevitably this and the other disruptions did nothing to quell the growing doubts Jonathan and I were having about whether Jasmine was in the right placement.

'We can't carry on like this, can we?' Jonathan said later that night, albeit through bleary eyes. We were both cranky and irritated and were finding it hard to get back to sleep.

'I know. I've tried to tell Jasmine that it's not fair on Erica to keep waking her like this, but it doesn't get through. It's not fair on anyone. I wish we had a better understanding of how Jasmine's brain works.'

We conceded that it was early days and we had to keep doing our best. Social Services clearly wanted us to make a success of this placement and even if it turned out that Jasmine didn't stay with us in the long term, we knew that she would not be moving out any time soon. The system simply didn't work that quickly, unless there was an emergency situation.

'Hopefully she'll settle down,' Jonathan sighed wearily. 'She's been through a lot of change and upheaval.'

'Let's hope so. Things can only improve, can't they? We have to keep going. I'm sure we'll turn a corner.'

Unfortunately, our hopes were quickly dashed. The next couple of days brought so much aggravation I filled three sheets in my notebook. Jasmine threw stones at a child on the playing field at the back of the house. She chewed a hole in her bedspread. One of Erica's school polo shirts was scribbled on with black pen, though Jasmine vehemently denied having anything to do with it. Every time we needed to leave the house Jasmine dragged her feet, making us all late for no good reason.

'It seems like she's trying to derail the placement,' I said to Jonathan.

'You're right. Do you think it's because she's about to see her grandparents? It could be that she knows they've been trying to take her in. Maybe she thinks if this placement fails, she can go and live with them?'

'I hadn't thought of that. Maybe you're on to something.'

This theory seemed to hold water, but it didn't help us in any way. We knew Social Services had refused to let her grandparents take her in. From what Pearl had said, she and Lenny might have to take legal action in order to overturn the decision, and of course even that might not work. Therefore, if moving in with her grandparents any time soon was what Jasmine was angling for, she was going to be disappointed and, possibly, even more difficult to deal with.

I was relieved when the Saturday of the visit finally came around, and I don't mind admitting I was very much looking forward to spending a few hours without having to worry about what Jasmine might do next. For her part, Erica's eyes had lit up when she found out Jasmine was going out for the day with her grandparents, which was discouraging to see. There had been moments when I thought the two girls were getting on so well, such as when they watched TV and talked about their favourite shows and music, and they giggled together when Anthony told them stories and played games with them.

However, I had noticed that Erica had begun to withdraw from Jasmine, even when there was no immediate reason to. That was Erica's default position whenever she sensed danger. She withdrew into her shell, not wanting to risk being involved in any conflict whatsoever. This is a common behaviour pattern in children who have been traumatised. They display increased sensitivity to stress and often try to snuff out the merest hint of a spark of conflict, sometimes unnecessarily.

'I'll just go to my room,' Erica had said much more frequently than normal. 'You can go on the computer, Jasmine. It's OK, I'm going to read my book.'

Poor Erica, I thought. She didn't want any trouble, and it hadn't taken her long to work out that Jasmine could be trouble with a capital T.

As they'd promised on the phone, Pearl and Lenny were taking Jasmine out for pizza and afterwards they were driving out to see the display of Christmas lights and decorations on the street her grandfather had mentioned, which had featured on the local TV news. They were collecting Jasmine at twelve o'clock, and she was ready and waiting with plenty of time to spare.

Talking in her baby voice she asked me sweetly, 'Can you help me with my laces please, Angela?'

She knew how to tie the laces on her trainers. 'Let me remind you how to do them. You did them yesterday, remember?'

Now she was staring into space. 'Ooh, did I? I can't remember. I'm sorry.'

'Right, watch me show you again.'

When I had her attention, I demonstrated how to do the laces and then asked her to have a go herself. I watched as she fumbled with the laces theatrically, giving me a swift look to make sure I was still watching. Then she appeared to get herself in a tangle deliberately.

'Please can you do it?' she said, continuing to use her baby voice. She chewed her finger and looked at me doe-eyed.

I showed her again and again but she continued to behave in a babyish way and claim she couldn't do it.

'Why don't you just leave your trainers by the door for now and, when your grandparents arrive and you're ready to leave, I'll help you tie your laces?'

She seemed very pleased with this and ran into the kitchen. I had no idea what was going on in her head.

Jonathan was outside the house looking at a loose drainpipe when Pearl and Lenny arrived. I heard them all chatting and Jasmine ran to the door.

'Where's my gorgeous girl?' Pearl said, throwing her arms wide. Jasmine ran to her, allowing herself to be enveloped in her granny's thick lilac anorak.

Lenny winked and offered Jasmine a high five.

'Granddad!' she said, going to give him a high five. He pulled his hand away just at the last minute and she jumped in the air to try to grab it.

'Gotcha!' he said, chortling with laughter. Jasmine laughed too.

Once the introductions were done I offered Pearl and Lenny a cup of tea.

'I'd love one,' Pearl said, 'but I don't want to hold you up?'

'It's no trouble, none at all. I don't want to hold you up either.'

We all looked at Jasmine. 'We'll have a cuppa before we get going, Jazz,' Pearl said. 'That OK with you, sweetie-pie?'

'Yes! I can help. I know where the cups are, and the milk, and the sugar. Granddad has two sugars. Sometimes three.'

'Did someone say *three*?' Pearl said teasingly, looking at Lenny.

'Oops! Secrets aren't safe with you, are they Jazz?'

Jasmine threw her head back and laughed. I hadn't seen her looking this happy and relaxed before. Her eyes were shining and she looked like she didn't have a care in the world.

The men started talking about the drainpipe. Jasmine had told us that Lenny was good at DIY and, sure enough, he offered Jonathan some advice about how to fix it. He suggested that Jonathan get a certain joint that you could buy in any hardware store. 'If you can wait until next time we come over – I reckon it'll hold up for a few weeks yet – I've just fixed a drainpipe of ours and I've got a spare one of those bits. I can bring it and show you how it fits on, if you like?'

Pearl was equally friendly, just as she had been on the phone. She was one of those people who fit in effortlessly and within five minutes I felt I'd known her for ages. She was interested in how we combined running the shop with fostering and asked lots of questions. When I talked about Anthony she looked at me in admiration.

'I think it's fantastic that this lad is staying with you even though you're not fostering him anymore.'

'Well, we've kept in touch with a lot of the children we've fostered over the years. We always tell them we are here for them if ever they need us and there's been several who've come back to stay with us again while they find their feet. It's not easy leaving care and we're always happy to help.

We feel like we've got a huge, extended family now. It's very rewarding to hear how they are all doing.' Pearl looked quite moved. I wasn't sure if she was thinking about the fact Social Services would not let her look after Jasmine, or about her own son, from whom she was estranged in such awful circumstances. I felt a pang of sorrow for her. To have an alcoholic son who abused his own little girl was unimaginable. Jasmine's father was their only child, she'd told me. Pearl and Lenny must have been through hell.

'I think you're marvellous, Angela,' she said. 'Come on Jazz, let's get going shall we?' She spoke chirpily, getting to her feet.

'Yes!' Jasmine exclaimed before running into the hall, putting on her trainers and lacing them up at lightning speed. She smirked at me when she saw me noticing this. I said nothing and waved her off with a smile.

'What a lovely couple,' Jonathan said. 'And they're smitten with Jasmine, aren't they?'

'Yes, they love her to bits and she's a different girl around them. Obviously, we don't know all the ins and outs, but it really doesn't seem right that they can't even apply to look after her. She's their only grandchild, it's so sad for them.'

'It is a great shame,' he replied, 'but you know how strict Social Services can be. Remember the hoops we had to jump through when we started the process?'

'How could I forget!' I said, thinking back to the long-winded application process Jonathan and I had gone through in order to become foster carers. It took more than a year for us to be passed, and we were amazed at how thorough the vetting process was.

Mum appeared. 'Jasmine sounded in a good mood when she went out with her grandparents,' she commented. 'I heard her giggles from all the way up the stairs!'

'She was. It was lovely to see.'

'It's a pity she's in foster care at all, with family like that.'

There she goes again, I thought. *Good old Mum. Hitting the nail on the head!*

Jonathan and I are not quitters and we've always persevered for as long as we possibly could to help every child who has come into our lives. We didn't want to push Jasmine out, but meeting Pearl and Lenny certainly made us question her placement with us once again. Surely living with her grandparents, in the area where she had grown up, instead of being one of two placements in our crowded house, would be a much better option for Jasmine? Social Services had apparently made a final decision and weren't going to budge, but I'm not one to take no for an answer. This was too important a decision to accept without a fight.

'There could be other reasons, things we don't know,' Jonathan cautioned.

'I know that, but I also know that sometimes Social Services can get decisions wrong. I want to find out more. It could change Jasmine's life for the better.'

10

'Is he a nice man or a horrible man?'

'I'm going to have to move, aren't I?' Erica asked quietly.

We'd been sitting at the kitchen table together. I was writing some Christmas cards while Jasmine was out with her grandparents, and Erica was getting on with some art homework.

'Move? No, not at all. What makes you say that?'

I could see her steeling herself before speaking again, in her thin, meek voice. 'Well, Jasmine keeps waking everyone up and there isn't enough room for us both, is there?'

'Sweetheart, you certainly do not have to move. I think you've been very good sharing your bedroom with Jasmine. I know it hasn't been easy but you definitely do not have to move.'

Erica bit her lip.

'*She* said there wasn't room for us both and she's going to break up the placement.'

'Who said she's going to break up the placement?'

'Jasmine. She said it this morning and she said it the

other day. She keeps saying it. You know when there was pen scribbled on my school top? I know she did that. I think she wanted to get me in trouble. I think she wanted you to think it was me, and then I would be in big trouble and I'd have to move out.'

Erica looked at the table.

'Sweetheart, come here. Can I give you a hug?'

She stopped to think about this before saying, softly, 'No, it's OK.'

One of the sad legacies of her dysfunctional childhood was that she had difficulties recognising her own emotions and dealing with certain social interactions. I always asked Erica if it was OK before giving her a hug, as we're taught to do with all children. I suspected she would have benefited from a cuddle right then, but she couldn't see that. She hadn't been used to hugs when she lived with her family and the result was she always had to think twice about them, rather than having an instinctive reaction and following her gut.

'I'm very sorry you've been upset like this,' I said, being careful not to lay any blame at Jasmine's door, just in case Erica had got this wrong or wasn't telling the story accurately. As I've said, I hadn't known her to tell fibs, but I couldn't rule out the possibility she may have been stirring the pot.

She shrugged and I saw the flicker of a smile. 'I don't want to move out. I like you, Angela. You're kind to me.'

My heart ached with love for this little girl.

'I like you too, Erica. You're a great girl and we love having you living with us. Please don't worry about your placement, nothing has changed.'

I would have liked to have told Erica that we hoped she would stay with us for a long time, but I couldn't, as we didn't know what the future held. Like a lot of children, she had come to us for an initial three months and had simply stayed on when things had worked out. I hated to think of her worrying about having to move to another foster home when that was certainly not on the agenda.

I told Jonathan about this conversation later on, when we were alone in the kitchen, preparing the evening meal. Erica was watching Saturday afternoon telly with Mum, and Anthony was at work at the pub.

In a thoughtful tone, Jonathan repeated back what I'd told him Erica had said to me: 'She said there wasn't room for us both and she is going to break up the placement.'

He considered this carefully. 'You know what? You could take that two ways. Understandably, Erica has taken it to mean Jasmine is trying to push her out. However, Jasmine could be saying she is going to break her own placement up, because there isn't room for both of them.'

'I didn't think of that. But it's not how I took it, and it's clearly not how Erica took it.'

'Well, who knows? As we've said, maybe Jasmine has her eye on going to live with her grandparents, and who could blame her?'

We caught each other's eye. We both had furrowed brows as we stood there, trying to make sense of what two damaged little girls may or may not have said and meant. Jonathan sighed and pointed out how impossible this was.

'We have no idea, do we?' he said. 'What we do know is that Jasmine's behaviour is unpredictable. We have to keep our eyes peeled and make sure we have Erica's back covered.'

'You make it sound like a minefield!'

Jonathan widened his eyes and gave me a look that said, 'And you don't think it is?'

Pearl and Lenny were due to drop Jasmine home any time soon and, as the clock ticked towards five o'clock, I could feel myself getting stressed. 'Unpredictable is definitely an accurate word to describe Jasmine's behaviour,' I commented. 'I'm wondering which Jasmine is going to come back tonight.'

By now we both knew full well that it could be baby-voice Jasmine, or happy, smiley Jasmine, or stroppy teenager Jasmine or the Jasmine who spoke robotically and didn't show any emotion at all.

'I'm placing my bet on Happy Jasmine,' Jonathan said optimistically. 'And we're all going to have a great evening, eating this delicious feast and watching Saturday night telly.'

I smiled, and as I did so I felt some of my stress subside. When I'm feeling the pressure or expecting the worst, Jonathan always tries to lighten the mood with his positivity, and he very often succeeds. There is no way I could have fostered so many children over so many years without his support.

'Let's hope you're right,' I said. 'She was so thrilled to go out with her grandparents. I'm sure she's had a ball.'

I could feel my shoulders relax and the tension in my

neck slip away as I carried on chopping peppers, tomatoes and onions. We'd decided to make a Mexican meal for a change this evening. Everything smelled delicious and I was really looking forward to tasting the various dishes and dips we were preparing.

The doorbell rang. 'Here's one of our dinner guests now,' Jonathan announced grandly as he went to answer the door.

'Jasmine!' he exclaimed. 'How was it? Have you had a good time?'

She bounced in, bobbing her head and shaking her hair. And when I say 'bounced' I really mean it. She was jumping up and down as if she was on a pogo stick. *Oh dear*, I thought. *Someone's had a sugar hit!*

As far as we knew, Jasmine had no food allergies and she hadn't been diagnosed with any degree of ADHD, but that has never stopped any young girl from becoming hyperactive after an overload of sweets and fizzy drinks.

'Had a good time?' I asked.

'Yes!' she said. 'The best! Can I watch *X Factor*? What are we having for our tea? Guess what? I had five slices of pizza and an ice cream with fudge sauce and free sweets and marshmallows. I could do my own sprinkles and everything. And I had topless lemonade, that's the best, that's so cool! No! Not topless, bottomless. That's what we had, wasn't it, Granddad? What are we having for tea, Angela? What are you cooking?'

'We're doing a Mexican meal, if you've got any room left,' I told her, which made her even more excited. 'Wow!

Mexican! What is it? Can I see? Where is it?' She poked her head into the kitchen to investigate.

Pearl and Lenny stepped into the hallway, closing the door for a minute – 'to keep your heat in' – but said they were not stopping as it would take them about an hour to drive home.

'Truth is, we're worn out!' Lenny laughed. 'We've had a lovely day. Those Christmas lights are worth seeing, if you get the chance.'

They both said goodbye, promising to phone Jasmine in the coming week to fix up another trip out.

'Don't know how you're going to manage to eat a Mexican,' Pearl said, as they turned to leave. 'You must have hollow legs like your granddad, Jazz.'

'We're not eating a Mexican man or a lady, Granny! It's a Mexican dinner!' Jasmine threw her head back and let out a raucous laugh. She was bouncing on her tiptoes as the door closed behind them and then she raced up to the lounge, singing 'Santa Claus is comING to town!'

'Told you,' Jonathan said, giving me a wink. 'Happy Jasmine. Or should I say happy, hyperactive Jasmine. I'll settle for that!'

We had a terrific evening. Everybody enjoyed the meal and Jasmine's hyper mood settled by the time *X Factor* started. The girls were glued to the show and Mum unwittingly provided extra entertainment, coming out with line after line that made them groan and giggle behind their hands.

'What on earth is that young woman wearing? Why would

147

anybody do that to their hair? I don't understand why such a handsome young man would want to have a *tattoo*. What is it supposed to be?'

The girls slept like logs, neither of them making a peep.

On the Sunday we took the girls swimming with some other foster carers and the children they were looking after. This was something we tried to do every once in a while. We knew the group of carers well, having attended a lot of the same training sessions and support meetings together for years, and it was always a good opportunity for us to catch up outside the formal setting of the Social Services meeting rooms. Swimming was an activity all the children loved, and our Sunday meet-ups generally worked really well.

The swim was good fun. After the success of the previous evening the girls were still getting on well, which was very good to see. Jasmine encouraged Erica to go on the diving board, which she didn't normally like to do, and they both played well with the other children, some of whom were a few years older.

'Can we go in the cafe again?' Jasmine asked.

'Yes,' I said. 'We can have a snack to keep us going. I'm doing a roast dinner this evening.'

'Yummy, yum-yum YUM!'

We pulled two tables together and the girls shared some cheesy chips, which was a speciality of the leisure centre cafe. They also had hot Vimto, which for some reason was another stalwart on the menu and had been for as long as I could remember, though I never saw it on sale anywhere else!

'It's great to end the week on a high,' I said to Jonathan at home that evening. All six of us had sat around the table and enjoyed a lovely roast dinner and the girls were now getting ready for bed. There had been no trouble or tension – save for a small altercation about the fact Erica had a bigger slice of apple pie than Jasmine, which was easily rectified.

As we'd discussed at the core meeting, Caitlin had arranged for Jasmine to have a trial visit at the same primary school Erica attended. This was happening the next day, and Jasmine had been very willing to listen when I talked through the arrangements.

'I like some schools and others I don't,' she said. 'Hopefully this will be one of the good ones.'

'That sounded slightly ominous,' Jonathan commented later, when the girls were in bed.

We were in the kitchen, and I was stripping the meat off the chicken. This was one of my Sunday night rituals; I was going to use the bones to make a soup and Jonathan loves cold meat sandwiches.

'We haven't been told how many different schools she's been in, have we?' I said.

'No, we haven't. Oh well, she's in a great mood, and let's hope it lasts.'

'Indeed. Erica was more relaxed around her too this weekend, which is very good news.'

I'd just finished putting the cold meat into Tupperware tubs when the phone rang. It was one of our foster carer friends, Sara, who we'd been swimming with earlier.

'Sorry to bother you, Angela,' she said. 'It's just that one of my boys told me that Jasmine said something quite worrying, at the pool.'

'Oh dear, did she?' I can't say I was entirely shocked by this, given that Jasmine had said so many alarming things to me in the short space of time she'd been living with us. However, when I asked 'What did she say?', I was really hoping it was nothing too serious.

Sara explained that Jasmine had 'bragged' that she once took a razor blade into school. She said this to Sara's teenage son, who was in secondary school.

'Maybe she was just trying to act cool and grown up,' Sara said. 'But I thought I'd better let you know.'

'Thanks, you did the right thing.'

'No problem. See you soon, and good luck at the school tomorrow.'

'Thanks. I hope we don't need it!'

I felt grateful that I had a friend like this, who was in the same boat as us and could discuss difficult issues without any fuss or judgement. It could have been very different if Jasmine had said this to a child whose parent was not an experienced foster carer, and who might have been much more disturbed by this than Sara was.

When I put the phone down I thought about the head teacher at the primary school and wondered what he would have made of my conversation with Sara. Mr Weatherstone had a reputation for running an extremely tight ship, and he was very strict on discipline. Kids had been sent home for wearing the wrong footwear. What would he do if a child actually did take a razor blade in? I shuddered to think, and

I hoped to goodness this was just a silly boast of Jasmine's. Later, I wrote down what Sara had told me in my notes. It would be up to Social Services to decide if this information should be acted upon in any way. The story could be true, it could be a complete fabrication, or it might be a red flag. When I closed the file I felt some small relief that it was not my job to make a call about what to do with information of that nature. That word 'minefield' came into my head again. You certainly did have to keep your wits about you, and your eyes peeled for danger.

The next morning, Jasmine's eyes were everywhere as we waited in reception for the head teacher to come and meet us.

'What's that for? Why is that there? Is he a nice man or a horrible man? Do you have to play football?'

'That's the trophy cabinet and they are all the cups and trophies children from the school have won. I'm sure you don't have to play football if you don't want to, at least not unless it's a PE lesson. I know Erica doesn't play football. As for the head teacher, oh, here he comes now!'

'Mr and Mrs Hart, good to see you again,' Mr Weatherstone said. 'And you must be Jasmine?'

She looked at him suspiciously and gave a nod. 'Pleased to meet you,' he said briskly.

I'd met Mr Weatherstone on a few occasions but didn't know him well. The handful of children we'd looked after who'd attended this school in the two years since he took over hadn't given us any reason to meet with him, other than for an introductory visit like this one. I'd always found Mr Weatherstone to be quite businesslike in his manner, even when talking to the children, and I knew that plenty of parents didn't like his strict rules on uniform and discipline, which created a lot of gossip at the class doors. However, the school was getting good results and its recent Ofsted report had shown an improvement under Mr Weatherstone's headship, so he was obviously doing something right. Erica was happy here, and I liked the ethos of the school, which was to encourage kindness as well as to work hard and do your best every day.

Mr Weatherstone invited us into his office, where there were three chairs positioned in front of his large, tidy desk. Once we were all seated, he spoke to Jasmine.

'Do you enjoy school?' he asked directly.

'Erm, well, I'm not sure yet. I haven't started . . .'

'Forgive me, what I meant was, do you enjoy going to school generally? Did you like going to your last school?'

He scanned some paperwork on his desk, presumably to remind himself where she'd come from. I didn't know exactly what Caitlin had told the school about Jasmine's educational history or the fact she'd been excluded from her previous primary school, though she would have been required to pass the basic details on when she'd contacted the school asking for a place. I was grateful Mr Weatherstone was prepared to give Jasmine a chance, and that he was treating her in the same way as he did any potential new pupil.

'Erm, yes. I liked my teacher and, erm, they had new gym

bars put up in the hall.' She stalled there, as if she'd run out of things to say.

'I see. What is your favourite subject?'

Jasmine thought about this very carefully but didn't come up with an answer.

'Perhaps it's PE? Did you like using the gym bars?'

'I never got to use them. But I liked the science topic. I like animals and learning about different places and landscapes.'

'Landscapes? That's an excellent word. Excellent! I enjoy science and geography too.'

Mr Weatherstone smiled and now looked less stiff and serious, I was glad to see. He went on to talk about the school facilities, which included a new greenhouse and allotment area he was clearly very proud of. Then he asked Jasmine if she liked any particular sports.

'I like swimming and I like running around, like, doing rounders or something like that. I can play football but it's not my favourite. And I'm learning – what's that thing Anthony does?' She looked at Jonathan and me.

'Rugby,' we both replied.

'Very good!' the head teacher exclaimed. 'Very good indeed. I'm a huge fan of rugby, but we don't play it here.'

'Oh,' Jasmine said.

Mr Weatherstone showed us around the canteen, the assembly hall and finally the playground area, which Jasmine told him she'd already seen, when we'd taken Erica to and from school. After that we were all introduced to Miss Dowden, who would be Jasmine's form teacher.

Miss Dowden stepped out of her classroom to greet us

in the corridor, at which point Mr Weatherstone excused himself, saying he had another meeting to go to. He told Jasmine it had been a pleasure to meet her and he looked forward to seeing her soon. This was a good sign, I thought. The meeting was as much for Jasmine to have a look around as it was for the head teacher to meet her and make a final decision on whether he would take her on.

'Hello!' Miss Dowden grinned. 'We're in the middle of some role play. It's quite lively in the classroom at the moment!'

We all peered through the window to see children dressed as Vikings.

'I have a lovely class this year,' she said, addressing Jonathan and me. 'And I'm very lucky to be assisted by Miss Jenson. She helps some of the children with SENs. I'll get her to pop out and say hello.'

I was pleased the teacher had been made aware of the fact Jasmine had special educational needs (SENs). It's not always the case that key information gets passed to the relevant members of staff, but this time the system seemed to have worked. I took it that Caitlin had passed on what we'd been told at the core meeting – the fact that Jasmine had had some one-to-one tuition at her old school and was taken out of class in a group sometimes, when the teacher felt certain parts of the curriculum would be too academically challenging for those with special needs. Exactly what she had told them about the fact Jasmine had been excluded we didn't know.

Miss Jenson joined Miss Dowden in the corridor, leaving

a teaching assistant in charge of the class. Miss Jenson was equally smiley and welcoming and I was impressed that both teachers seemed very keen and enthusiastic. This rubbed off on Jasmine, who became quite excitable as she asked lots of questions about pets in the classroom, playtime, which house group she would be in and, finally, what the school dinners were like.

'Let's start with the dinners,' Miss Jenson said. 'They are delicious! Especially fish and chips on a Friday. That's my favourite.'

Jasmine grinned. 'When can I start?' she asked wide-eyed. 'Can I come on Friday?' I explained that we had a few things to sort out first and then Miss Jenson chatted for a while to Jasmine, before Miss Dowden answered a few more of Jasmine's questions and escorted us back to reception.

'I hope you enjoyed your visit,' the receptionist said warmly as we signed out.

'I did,' Jasmine said. 'It looks a lot better than my old school; that sucked.'

The receptionist couldn't help giving me a subtle smile as she caught my eye.

'Come on, let's go,' I said. 'Thanks for having us.'

I knew the system. We'd receive a phone call from the school to let us know what would happen next.

Jonathan and I smiled at each other as we walked to the car. The visit had gone very well, and with a bit of luck this would be the start of a very positive new phase in Jasmine's life.

11

'She's a very welcome addition to the class'

Within a few hours of our visit the school receptionist called, telling me that the head teacher was happy to offer Jasmine a place. She talked through the formalities and said she'd pop some paperwork in an envelope for me to collect when I picked up Erica.

'If you and Jasmine are happy, we can arrange a half day later this week?'

We agreed on Wednesday morning, which would give us time to sort out Jasmine's uniform and buy her a book bag, PE kit and the regulation sweatshirt, which they sold at the school office.

We knew from experience that kids often moved on before a term was out and others, sometimes unexpectedly, stayed for years. However unpredictable the timeframe, of course we always do our best to give each child as much support and stability as possible when joining a new school. This means kitting them out with the right uniform, bag, shoes, sports kit and so on, and never forgetting what a big deal it is for a child of any age to start a new school, especially midway through a year, when friendship groups have already been established.

The next day, Jonathan and I took Jasmine to the out-of-town retail park to buy her some new shoes and underwear as well as polo shirts, trousers and a school skirt in the correct shade of grey. We chose the retail park as the smaller shops in the town centre only tended to have uniform on sale at the start of the school year. It proved to be a good decision. Not only did we get everything we needed, but Jasmine loved the experience. There was an ice rink set up in the car park and we took her on it once we'd finished shopping.

'This is magic,' she said, holding on to a plastic penguin as she skated between Jonathan and me. 'Can we come here again? I like it here. Can we come ice skating again? Can we?'

There was a charity tombola stall set up next to the ice rink and Jasmine won a key ring with a small polar bear on it, which she named Snowy. All the way home, she chatted to Snowy.

'Did you know, I'm starting a new school? Yes, I did! No, I didn't! Did you know, I got a new skirt and shoes? No, silly! You don't need shoes! He doesn't need to know. No, no, no. I'm not telling! I like my new tights. Did you know? I like ice-skating, I don't know, I'll ask. I can ask. No, I can do it. She wouldn't like it.'

She lowered her voice to a whisper when she said, 'No, no, no.' Some of her chat left us feeling a little curious and slightly concerned. What was the other half of her invented conversation with Snowy? Who didn't need to know, what was she not telling and who wouldn't like what?

'Hopefully it's all innocent make-believe,' Jonathan said, when we had the chance to talk in private. 'After all, it was quite magical, the way they'd done up the ice rink. Maybe it fired up her imagination.'

'I hope so,' I said. 'But I think there's a lot we don't know about Jasmine and her past.'

To our relief, Erica responded well to the fact Jasmine was joining her school. She commented that it would be good not to be the only one in the house who had to get ready for school in the morning and she told Jasmine she would show her around, if she wanted.

'Maybe,' Jasmine said. She was talking in her baby voice again. 'You won't be bossy, will you?'

Erica laughed awkwardly; she was not a bossy kind of child at all. 'No, I won't be bossy.'

Lou called round on the Tuesday afternoon, after our shopping trip. Apart from receiving a brief phone call asking us to make this appointment, we hadn't heard anything from Jasmine's social worker since she walked hurriedly away from us in the car park after the core meeting.

'How are you feeling about starting school?' Lou asked Jasmine in a very matter-of-fact way. As she spoke she was filling in some paperwork and giving no eye contact.

'Erm, good,' Jasmine told Lou. 'I've got new stuff. I'm going to be in Christopher Columbus.'

All the houses at the primary school were named after explorers so this made perfect sense to me. I wasn't sure if Lou knew what Jasmine meant, but she didn't ask.

'Good, and I hope you're going to be well-behaved.'

I found myself wincing. Jasmine needed positive encouragement and we all needed to look forward, not back.

Lou's next statement came out of the blue. 'Right. I won't be your social worker from now on, Jasmine. You will have a new social worker called Stewart.'

'Oh,' Jasmine said, completely unperturbed.

'Nobody mentioned this,' I said to Lou. 'When did it all happen?'

'Very recently. I'm moving to a new department.' It was obvious from the way she spoke she was not going to provide me with any further information.

After giving me Stewart's contact details and telling me he would be in touch before the end of the week, Lou promptly got to her feet. 'Good luck, both of you. I hope it all works out. It's been lovely to know you, Jasmine.'

'Thanks,' Jasmine said. She looked a bit confused and bit her lip. 'Is Stewart a nice man or is he horrible?'

'I've never met him, but I'm sure he's nice,' Lou said. Minutes later, she was gone. I was left with the impression that she had never really bonded with Jasmine in the short time she was her social worker and was perhaps relieved to have her off her caseload. I hoped Jasmine didn't feel slighted; she had been let down by her parents, and Fran, to a lesser extent, and she really did not need to feel let down by another adult who had responsibility for her well-being.

Needless to say, Jasmine's question about whether Stewart was nice or horrible reminded me of when she'd asked the same thing of the head teacher, Mr Weatherstone. She'd also asked me if my dad had been nice or horrible, I suddenly recalled. It's not unusual for a child who's been treated badly by their father to be mistrustful of men, and particularly men in authority. Jasmine seemed fine with Jonathan, thankfully, although I'd noticed she did gravitate towards me more than him. *Bless her heart,* I thought. *No little girl should have to worry about whether men are going to be horrible.*

Jasmine was up very early on Wednesday. She was very excited about going to school and was bouncing around just as she had done when she was going out with her grandparents. Jonathan and I walked to school with both girls and Jasmine never stopped talking.

'Can you go to the toilet when you want? Can you run in the playground? What if I can't do the work? Am I allowed to make a pot?'

'A pot?' I asked. 'What do you mean?'

It turned out Jasmine had done a bit of pottery at her old school. It sounded like this was one of the activities the SEN group did when the class teacher thought they couldn't cope with something on the curriculum. Erica had done some pottery in her art classes and when I told Jasmine this she looked absolutely thrilled.

'I'm going to tell Miss Dowden and Miss Jenson I can make pots,' she said.

I was impressed she remembered both the teachers' names because, to be perfectly honest, Jonathan and I had only remembered one each!

Miss Dowden came out into the playground to meet us and she introduced Jasmine to a few of the children who were already in line. Jasmine started babbling away, asking lots of questions, and when the bell went she filed in with confidence, without looking back at us.

The morning seemed to fly by. Jonathan and I had lots of jobs to do in the shop and the house and, before we knew it, it was time to collect Jasmine after her half day. The two of us walked back to school together and reported to reception.

'Let's hope this is good news,' Jonathan said, rubbing his hands together to warm himself up.

We'd discussed how Jasmine's trial session could have gone either way. Though we were getting to know her quite well by now, the fact remained that she was unpredictable.

Once we'd signed in at reception we had to wait while a boy from Year 6 who was on 'runner' duty at the office went to fetch Jasmine from her classroom. She appeared a few minutes later, accompanied by Miss Jenson. The two of them were beaming and talking animatedly.

'How was it?' I asked, feeling optimistic.

'Great!' Jasmine boomed, giving a little hop, skip and a jump as she approached us. '*So* good. I had a good time! It's better than my last school.'

Miss Jenson giggled and gave us a thumbs-up. 'I think

that says it all,' she smiled. 'Jasmine's been a pleasure to have in the classroom this morning. She's a very welcome addition to the class.'

Jasmine grinned and looked very pleased with herself. I could have hugged Miss Jenson. This kind of positive support was exactly what Jasmine needed.

'That's such good news,' I said.

'So, can I start school tomorrow, like properly?' Jasmine asked.

Miss Jenson said that from the teachers' point of view she was more than welcome to start the next day.

'It's fine with us too,' I said. Jasmine was nodding and bouncing on her toes. 'I'll have a word with the office and check that's OK with the head . . .'

The receptionist we'd met previously had appeared at the front desk and overheard our conversation. 'No need, Mrs Hart. I've spoken to Mr Weatherstone this morning and that's what he was expecting,' she said. 'There's some more paperwork for you here. There are a few forms to fill out, about school dinners, allergies and such like. If you can get those back to us as soon as possible – later today or in the morning – that would be perfect.'

I knew one of the forms would be about whether we'd be paying for school meals, which we would. Children in care never qualify for free school meals and so we have always paid for them. There would also be questions about Jasmine's social worker and so on. I appreciated the way the receptionist handled this. Sometimes people in positions of authority, or power, make unnecessary mention of the fact a child is in care, but she treated us in the same way as I imagined she would any other family.

Overall, I was very impressed by the very swift and efficient way the school had dealt with Jasmine's application. Mr Weatherstone may well have come in for criticism for running a tight ship, but I for one was not complaining. We've known kids to be stuck at home for days, weeks or even months when they should have been in school, and all because of red tape and inefficiency from schools, the local education authority or both. I've been known to write to our local MP and even Downing Street when children have been forced to miss out on their precious education through no fault of their own.

All things considered, I was feeling upbeat and optimistic about this new chapter in Jasmine's life.

Quite touchingly, she refused to take off her uniform that afternoon and watched the clock for when we could return to school to collect Erica. Unfortunately, Erica came out of school looking somewhat crushed and cross, which put an immediate dampener on things. Her teacher called me over.

'Is everything OK?'

'I'm afraid Erica was teased by some of the other children.'

The teacher explained that after seeing her arriving with Jasmine and talking to her in the playground at break time, three boys in Erica's class had asked her if they were sisters. Erica was irritated by this and told them that of course she and Jasmine weren't sisters. 'It looks like she got very annoyed that they would think this and pointed out that they looked very different. It seems this raised more questions, and the boys didn't let it go.'

'So they asked if she was in care?'

'We're not sure who said what, but it appears that way.' The young male teacher blushed slightly as he said this.

'Did they make fun of her for being in care?'

He coughed rather nervously. 'Yes, it appears that way. I'll be speaking to the parents of the boys involved.'

My heart sank. Only that morning I'd been feeling so thankful at how sensitively the receptionist had handled Jasmine's move into the school, and now this had happened. *Poor Erica*, I thought.

A minority of kids don't mind saying they are in care and they aren't bothered who knows that they are fostered, but I knew that Erica was definitely not one of them. She never called me Angela in front of people and never corrected anybody who referred to me as her mum. What had happened with these boys would almost certainly be a setback for her, and I was afraid it could also impact on how she treated Jasmine, especially at school. The only saving grace was that Erica said nothing about what had happened to Jasmine, even when pressed.

'Are you mad about something? Did something happen? Erica, was your teacher mean or nasty? Did you get loads of homework? Do you have to do detention?'

Erica was very patient. 'No, I don't want to talk about it.'

'OK. What did you have for school dinner? What's for tea, Angela?'

Jasmine was off on another of her marathon babbling

sessions, blasting out questions in all directions and not waiting for the answers before going on to the next thing. For once, I was very grateful.

Jasmine phoned her grandparents that evening and they arranged to take her out again, on Saturday. When I spoke to Pearl she told me she had a tear in her eye.

'I've never heard her so enthusiastic about school. I don't know what you're doing, but you're doing something right.'

'Well, it's more to do with the school than me,' I laughed. before adding cautiously, 'And let's not forget she's only done half a day! But so far so good. It's great to see her buzzing the way she is, and she's thrilled she can see you again at the weekend.'

Pearl told me that she and Lenny had decided to try to see more of Jasmine than they had in recent months.

'We worried when she was with Fran that if we kept turning up it might make things difficult. We thought it could be unsettling, and we didn't want to do anything that might get anyone's back up at Social Services. Now everything's going so well with you, we just want to see more of her.'

I told her I understood and I didn't contradict her comment that 'everything was going so well with us'. Pearl didn't know about the various problems we'd had with Jasmine but, for the time being at least, it felt right to keep it that way. I didn't want her to worry. It was early days, as I'd said, and in any case Pearl and Lenny were powerless to change the situation.

'Can you even begin to imagine what it must be like to see your grandchild taken into care, and then seeing them unhappy and not being able to intervene?' I said to Jonathan.

'No, I can't. It must be very, very difficult.'

'Agonising, I'd say. Especially when you are willing to take that grandchild in. It doesn't bear thinking about.'

'No, when you put it like that it really doesn't.'

We agreed that we wanted to help the situation as best we could. We would do our utmost to make sure Jasmine was happy in our care, and we'd help ensure she spent as much time with her grandparents as possible. When the time was right, I thought, I'd have a word with Pearl about possibly appealing against the Social Services decision, if it were appropriate, and ask her whether she had done anything about seeking legal advice from a solicitor.

12

'You don't know how awkward I can be if I want to'

Miss Dowden came dashing out of Jasmine's classroom at home time on Thursday, her first full day in school.

'Can I have a word?'

Jasmine had bounded out of school looking as excited and enthusiastic as she had that morning, when she'd been so looking forward to joining her new class.

Jonathan stayed with Jasmine in the playground while I popped into the classroom to talk to Miss Dowden.

'All good this morning, but we had a bit of an issue this afternoon,' she said, speaking rapidly but with a kind and friendly tone in her voice. 'Has Jasmine made strange noises before?'

'What kind of noises?' I asked. I immediately thought of the animal noises and the 'zoom' sounds she'd made, but I wanted to hear what Miss Dowden had to say before discussing what had happened at home.

'Just strange noises. I don't know how I'd describe them really. Groaning. Growling, but when I say growling, it was like it came from her stomach. It was kind of guttural, does that ring any bells?'

I told Miss Dowden we had heard Jasmine make a variety of strange noises at home, though the 'guttural' description didn't exactly fit with what I'd heard.

'How do you deal with it at home?' she asked.

'I just ask her to stop, remind her she is disturbing other people, that sort of thing. I try not to give her too much attention.'

Miss Dowden nodded. 'I see. I asked her nicely to stop at first and then I had to tell her off, as she was disrupting the class. Then she got worse. Perhaps the attention she got was counterproductive. I'll bear that in mind if it happens again.'

I thanked Miss Dowden, wished her luck and asked her to keep me posted. I liked the way she'd handled our conversation. Some teachers have confronted us, almost as if they are blaming us for how a child has behaved. There was none of that with Miss Dowden. She seemed to be purely focused on tackling Jasmine's behaviour and I was happy to let her do her job, even if she had told Jasmine off. Similarly, I didn't confront Jasmine about what had happened in the classroom. Over time we've learned that it's best to let the teachers deal with anything that happens at school. We generally have enough to cope with at home, and our attention is best focused on what happens when the child is with us.

Jasmine had been given spellings that day, but when I asked if she wanted me to help her learn them before dinner she was very dismissive.

'No, there's no point. I'm thick and I won't remember any of them.'

'What? That's not true at all!'

After several more attempts at encouraging Jasmine to learn the spellings, which were all met with the same response, I hatched a plot.

'I tell you what, I'll give you 15p for every word you can spell correctly in your test tomorrow.'

She thought about this carefully and agreed. Then she sat over her spelling book quietly for a full ten minutes before covering up each word and attempting to write it out correctly.

'I can test you, if you want me to?'

'No.'

I wanted to remind her to say 'no thank you', but that was not a battle to pick at this moment in time.

'OK. Let me know if you change your mind.'

I carried on preparing the dinner.

Jasmine huffed and puffed as she read back over her work. Then I heard her growl, which made me jump. Throwing down her pencil, she declared, 'You don't know how awkward I can be if I want to!'

Just at that moment, Anthony walked in the kitchen. He chuckled. 'I can be awkward as well,' he said, 'and I bet I can be more awkward than you!'

'You can't!'

'I can! One of the customers in the pub called me an awkward git today.'

'Anthony!' I said, throwing him a look.

'Git? Is that a swear word?' Jasmine started laughing.

'Oh sorry. Actually, I think he said awkward bug—' Anthony was teasing me, and he stopped himself from completing the word.

Now it was Mum's turn to join in. She'd half-heard the conversation as she'd walked slowly across the hall and into the kitchen. 'Has somebody been calling you names, Anthony?' She frowned and looked terribly concerned.

This is all we need! I thought. *What was it I was saying to Miss Dowden about not giving too much attention when kids are creating drama?*

'Go on, tell her, Anthony,' Jasmine goaded. 'Tell her what the man called you!' She started giggling and banging her hands on the table in excitement.

'No, I can't,' Anthony said.

'Go on!'

'No, I can't!'

'Please! Say it again, Anthony.'

'No.'

'Why not?'

'Angela will kill me!'

'You're a spoilsport!' Jasmine had a bit of a scowl on her face now and I think Anthony must have picked up on this.

'See!' he replied cheekily, smiling and looking her in the eye. 'I told you I could be more awkward than you!'

He put his fists up and jokingly pretended to spar with her. It was something I'd seen Anthony do with Jonathan, when he was mucking about or pretending to be cross. Playfulness like this is usually a great way of connecting with a child. Our fostering training has taught us the PACE method, which stands for 'playfulness, acceptance, curiosity and empathy'. The playfulness helps defuse a situation; acceptance relates to accepting the child but not their aggression or other poor behaviour; you require curiosity in order to detect a child's needs, and empathy underpins everything because you need to be able to put yourself in the child's shoes in order to relate to them and ultimately help them. Anthony didn't need any training or encouraging to be playful; it was just the way he was built. Unfortunately, on this occasion it wasn't helpful at all because when Jasmine was confronted with Anthony's raised fists she froze and the colour drained from her face.

It was one of those moments when I sensed the atmosphere change instantly. I think it was the same for my mum and Anthony. We all prickled and took a sharp intake of breath, and I felt my stomach turn over.

Then in bounced Erica.

'What's wrong?' she said, stopping in her tracks and appearing worried, as she looked around at us all. Kids who've known trauma often have a knack of reading a room in a split second. They can spot when something's off like nobody else, because they have become accustomed, consciously or subconsciously, to being on red alert for trouble. Sadly, it's an instinctive method of self-protection.

'It's OK, Erica,' I soothed. 'Right. Jasmine, shall we clear away your spellings now and perhaps you two girls could lay the table in the dining room?'

I started picking out cutlery from the drawer and telling

everyone what we were eating that evening, which included lemon meringue pie, one of Jasmine's favourites. Erica still looked a bit spooked but she took the knives and forks from me and asked Jasmine, 'Are you coming?'

'What?'

'Can you help me lay the table?'

'What? Why?'

It was as if she hadn't been present in the room for the previous few minutes.

The doorbell rang.

'I'll go!' Anthony said cheerfully. I think he was glad of an excuse to exit the room.

'Who's that?' Jasmine asked cautiously.

'Don't worry,' I said, 'it's probably just carol singers!'

'Carol singers?' Mum tutted. 'It's far too early for carol singers, surely?'

I resisted the urge to roll my eyes at my mother for this unnecessary challenge.

The colour had returned to Jasmine's cheeks and she got to her feet, I was pleased to see.

'Really, who would call at this time?' Mum groaned. 'You're just about to serve the dinner up.'

I smiled to myself, thinking how strange it was that my own mother, who had lived around the corner for all the years we had fostered, and with whom I was in regular contact, didn't know the half of how my life revolved. I was well used to our doorbell ringing when we weren't expecting visitors. There was one young man we used to foster who would *deliberately* call at dinner time, knowing that we tended to eat at the same time each evening. When you've had dozens of kids living in your home over the years it becomes quite a hub, just like most family homes, except ours has had more kids passing through it than an average family. Having kept in contact with so many of the children who had stayed with us until they left care, and with a good number of them still living in our neighbourhood, sometimes we felt like we lived in Piccadilly Circus. 'Angela!' Anthony called. 'It's for you!'

'Jasmine, sweetheart, can you please help Erica now?' I passed her the salt and pepper to carry to the dining table. She nodded and, thankfully, gave me a little smile as she took them off me.

'Great,' I smiled brightly. 'Thanks for setting the table, girls. That's a big help.'

Anthony was standing in the hallway, looking out of our wide-open front door.

A blast of Baltic-cold air had blown in. I felt myself shudder and pulled my cardigan tighter around my shoulders.

'It's Diane,' Anthony said, turning to look at me.

'Diane!' I exclaimed, instantly brightening.

Anthony looked relieved that I reacted that way and he stepped aside for me.

'Diane! Come in!' I said, introducing her to Anthony, who now gave her a friendly, welcoming smile.

Diane had lived with us for several years during her teens. She was in her twenties now and had been living independently for some time. We'd kept in regular touch and she had looked after the house for us a couple of times when we'd gone away.

'Er, thanks. I hope I'm not disturbing you.'

Diane was generally a very vivacious girl and I could tell she was not herself.

'Not at all, sweetheart. In fact, I'm serving up dinner shortly. Want to join us?'

I'd learned that it never really works if you make a fuss or immediately start to pry when there seems to be a problem. It's far better to offer the hand of friendship, welcome someone in and let them talk to you in their own good time.

'Yes, that would be great, thanks.'

Diane gave me a grateful smile. I noticed she had a holdall with her and I immediately started to think about where we could put her and if she'd be comfortable on the sofa bed in the lounge, as that was the only spare bed we had. I knew she was police-checked, as she had worked at the local play scheme that summer and had babysat for us in the past. At least that was one less thing to worry about.

Jonathan had just finished work and was delighted to see Diane, and Mum said she remembered her well and how lovely it was to see her again. Everyone was gathered in the hallway, and Erica and Jasmine came out of the dining room to see what all the fuss was about.

'Girls, this is Diane. She used to live with us. Diane, this is Erica and this is Jasmine.'

Erica and Jasmine looked very curious and interested in Diane, in the way young girls often do when faced with a 'grown up' young woman. To be fair, Diane had was particularly striking. She had jet black, short bobbed hair and wore thick eyeliner with large Amy Winehouse-style flicks and a diamond stud in her nose.

'I like your hair,' Erica said, 'and your shoes.' I hadn't even noticed the footwear, but Diane was sporting a pair of Dr Martens shoes that were painted with flowers.

Jasmine stared at the nose stud intently but said nothing.

Quietly, I asked Diane if she needed to stay the night.

'If that's OK?' she said, sounding very grateful. She explained that she was moving flats and had got her dates muddled up. She'd handed her keys back on her old flat that afternoon but couldn't move into her new place until the next day.

'The landlord was really nice and let me store my stuff in the bedsit next door as it was empty, but he can't have me staying there. It's uninhabitable, he said. I have nowhere else to go.'

I told her it was absolutely fine, as long as she didn't mind the sofa bed.

'Thanks,' she said, breathing out a sigh of relief. 'That'll sort me right out.'

I felt sorry for Diane. Mixing up dates like this is the sort of thing that can happen to anyone. Most young adults have a family to fall back on in times of need, but those who have been brought up in care sometimes have nobody to turn to. I hated the fact she must have been stressed about this. Given that it was nearly six o'clock, I imagined she'd tried other options before coming to us.

'Remember what Jonathan and I told you when you

moved out? We're always here for you. You should have let us know sooner. You could even have stored your stuff here.'

'I know, and thanks. But I was hoping I'd be able to sort myself out without bothering you this time. You must think I'm useless!'

'No, not at all. And I don't want to hear you say that, ever again,' I chided gently. 'Do you hear me?'

'Yes, Angela,' she smiled. This had been something I'd said to her on many occasions previously, as for years I'd encouraged Diane to build her confidence and self-esteem. She'd stayed with us on a few different occasions since leaving care, but, as I'd said to her, we were always willing to help and didn't ever judge her.

'Anyhow, it's absolutely lovely to see you,' I said brightly. 'Now, let's get some dinner. I've made a hot pot and dumplings. There's plenty to go around.'

Diane visibly relaxed.

Her presence inevitably changed the dynamic around the dinner table. Anthony started off being quieter than usual; I guess it's not unusual for an eighteen-year-old boy to be slightly intimidated in the company of an eye-catching young woman he's never met before. Mum, Jonathan and I were very keen to catch up with Diane's news and there was plenty of it, as she'd changed jobs three times and had two boyfriends since we'd last seen her.

The girls looked quite awestruck when she spoke about doing belly button piercing in the hairdressing and beauty salon she worked at. The boyfriends were both dismissed as 'muppets', which started an amusing conversation between Anthony and Mum, who had only ever heard that word used when describing Miss Piggy and Kermit. Anthony had Mum in stitches, doing an impression of Kermit as he explained how the word is used to describe someone you see as a 'loser' or a bit of an idiot.

Jasmine was very excited to discover that Diane could do French plaits.

'Can you do my hair?' she asked. 'I love French plaits. My mum—' She stopped herself. 'I used to have French plaits sometimes. Can I have French plaits, Angela? I saw another girl at school had them. Can I? Can I, Angela?'

'If Diane's happy to do it, it's fine with me,' I said. 'I think they're very neat and great for school.'

After dinner, Erica sat at the dining table to do her home-work and Diane did Jasmine's hair in the lounge. Mum was very interested to see how Diane did the plaits, and she chatted to the girls while Jonathan and I cleared up and Anthony went off to do a shift in the pub.

'Jasmine very nearly mentioned her mum, did you notice?' I said to Jonathan.

'Yes, I did. Maybe something about Diane's visit reminded her of her?'

'Maybe. Anyway, she seems to be in a good mood.'

I'd taken Mum a cup of coffee and there was a good atmosphere in the lounge. Jasmine's hair was coming on a treat. She was sitting very still, as Diane had asked her to, and was joining in with a lively conversation about Rihanna, who Diane loved.

When we'd finished in the kitchen, Jonathan went up to the lounge and sat in his favourite armchair with his newspaper while I went upstairs to sort out some bedding for Diane. By this time, Jasmine's hair was finished and she was admiring herself in the mirror above the fireplace.

Mum went to the loo and then Diane stood up and said she'd help me with the bedding.

'Are you pleased with your plaits?' Jonathan asked, after Diane left the room.

As he looked up from his paper, he watched in astonishment as Jasmine flung herself on the floor theatrically and let out a shrill cry.

'Jasmine! What are you doing? Are you OK?'

'You don't care! You did it! You pushed me! I hate you! You're the same. You're worse than that, what's his name? That Fran's husband. Get away from me! I hate you, Jonathan.'

Jasmine was writhing around on the hearthrug, as if she'd been hurt or was in pain. Jonathan was seated several yards away from her, had seen exactly what she'd done and knew there was nothing wrong with her. He got to his feet and went to leave the room, instinctively thinking it was best to put as much distance between himself and Jasmine. To his surprise, Erica was standing in the doorway, looking shocked and confused.

'What's she doing?' she asked.

Jasmine heard her. 'Jonathan pushed me over. Jonathan did it. He pushed me down.'

'Erica, come with me. I think it's best we leave Jasmine. She isn't hurt. Let's get Angela.'

Jonathan quickly escorted Erica up the stairs to the top landing, where I was standing with Diane, collecting bedding from the airing cupboard.

I could tell immediately that there was a problem.

'What on earth happened?'

'It's Jasmine. She said I pushed her over when we were alone in the lounge.'

I was about to suggest that Erica go into her bedroom, but she blurted out, 'I saw what happened, I saw everything.'

'You did?' Relief percolated through Jonathan's voice.

'Yes. She just kind of chucked herself on the rug by the fire. It was a bit weird.'

Erica explained that she had stopped in her tracks when she saw what Jasmine did and hovered in the doorway as the theatrics played out.

'Thank you, Erica. I can deal with this now. Thanks for telling us what you saw.'

'Is she, like, OK?'

I told her I was sure Jasmine would be perfectly fine. 'We all do silly things sometimes,' I said.

Jonathan and I returned to the lounge together, to find Jasmine watching TV with Mum as if nothing had happened. We said nothing but kept a close eye on her for the rest of the evening, and I had a gentle word with her before bed.

'Jasmine, please make sure you tell the truth,' I said. 'Jonathan didn't push you, we all know that.'

'Well, he might have!' she blurted. She looked flushed in the face and had a defensive look in her eyes.

'He didn't. I know he didn't. He would never do that. Is there something you're worried about?'

'No.'

'OK, well, we'll leave it at that. You know you can talk to me about anything at all, don't you?'

'Yes,' she said. 'But I don't want to. You wouldn't understand and I could stab myself if I wanted to.'

'Stab yourself? Jasmine, please don't talk like that. You are a lovely girl. We don't want you to come to any harm at all. Let's all try to get along, be kind to one another and to ourselves. What do you think?'

'When am I seeing Granny and Granddad?'

'At the weekend. Saturday.'

'OK, I won't be awkward.'

'That's good. Night night.'

I made a note in my diary in case Jasmine repeated the accusation to her social worker. I was half expecting trouble that night, even though Jasmine hadn't rattled the bunk bed for ages. Thankfully, she went straight to sleep. I'd had a word with Erica, suggesting she didn't mention what she saw in the lounge, and she was more than happy to agree to this. As I've said, Erica was good at withdrawing from potential conflict, and it suited her to say nothing.

'Poor Erica,' I said. 'Jasmine's caused quite a lot of disruption to her life, hasn't she?'

Jonathan nodded. 'When we see Pearl and Lenny again,

I think maybe it's time to ask a few more questions about their dealings with Social Services. Maybe it's worth them appealing sooner rather than later? I think Jasmine would be happier with them, I really do, and it would suit Erica too, I'm sure.'

I had to agree. School would be an issue, as Jasmine would have to move again, but hopefully it would be her last move. It did seem the best way forward, for all concerned.

13

'You're a lovely girl and don't you forget it!'

Once again, we found ourselves very much looking forward to Jasmine's day out with Pearl and Lenny. It couldn't come soon enough, in fact, and on the Saturday morning I was counting down the hours until they arrived at our door.

The day after Jasmine's worrying performance in the lounge, she had had a terrible day at school. Miss Dowden caught my eye when I went to collect the girls at home time, and she gave me a thumbs-down.

'What's happened?' I asked, going over to chat in private while Jasmine and Erica went to collect their coats and Jonathan waited in the playground.

'I'm afraid that after the spelling test this morning Jasmine refused to do any work and was cheeky to Miss Jenson, who became quite upset. Then she made a mess and refused to clear up. When asked to tidy up she pushed past another pupil, called her 'spotty' and stormed out of the classroom. We had to keep her in at afternoon break time, and in the last lesson she started making animal noises again, grunting and so on. I had to remove her from the classroom as she was disrupting the other children and stopping them from learning.'

I could detect a note of disappointment in Miss Dowden's voice, and she also sounded less understanding and friendly than she had done previously. I wasn't sure if it was simply because she was worn out on a Friday afternoon, or was already reaching the end of her tether with Jasmine after her few days in the classroom.

'I'm sorry to hear that. What did she do when she was excluded from the classroom?'

'She was given work to do in the thinking room. We had a support teacher watching her.'

I knew that the 'thinking' room was basically isolation, and my heart sank.

'What can we do to support you?' I asked.

Miss Dowden gave me several worksheets. 'This is the work Jasmine missed in class today. She refused to do any of these tasks, even in the thinking room. If you could try to get her to do these sheets as homework over the weekend it would be a big help. I think it would also be good if she would apologise to Miss Jenson. Perhaps she could write a note?'

I agreed to this, but I must admit I had a few alarm bells ringing in my head. Miss Dowden was a kind and competent teacher and I knew she was only following school policy in the way she had treated Jasmine. However, I couldn't help thinking that preventing Jasmine from running outside in the fresh air at break time, excluding her from the classroom

and placing her in isolation were counterproductive meas-
ures. The school's ways of dealing with a disruptive, damaged
child didn't tie in with the more understanding, nurturing
and engaging techniques we were doing our best to practise
at home.

Inevitably, I wasn't really surprised that Jasmine hadn't
responded well to effectively being given 'time out' rather
than 'time in'. I imagined she would have felt punished
rather than understood and supported, and this would most
likely have made her feel even more disgruntled.

It wasn't appropriate for me to approach the school
about my concerns at such an early stage – after all, she'd
only done two and a half days – but I thought that, potentially, I might have to have a word with Miss Dowden, when
the time felt right. Perhaps I would ask whether Jasmine
could do some art or pottery when she needed to be taken
away from the classroom, rather than being placed in the
thinking room.

Back home, after giving the girls a drink and a snack, I
sat with Jasmine and went through as much of the work
as I felt she could manage. I also encouraged her to design
a 'sorry' card on the computer for Miss Jenson. Kids are
normally shattered by Friday afternoon, although of course
Jasmine hadn't done the full week in school. She seemed
to be alert and had plenty of energy, so I thought it was
wise to strike while the iron was hot and get this making
a card for Miss Jenson out of the way before her day out
with Granny and Granddad. I really wanted Jasmine to
have a great day out and hoped that we could then enjoy

a relaxed day together on the Sunday, before starting a fresh week at school.

'What do I need to make a sorry card for?' Jasmine had asked, a puzzled expression on her face.

Even before we'd arrived back at the house after walking home from school, Jasmine seemed to have genuinely forgotten the events of earlier in the day. Without telling her off, I tactfully reminded her that Miss Jenson had been upset when things hadn't gone well in the classroom, and that Jasmine had missed break and spent time in the thinking room because she was not working or behaving in the way she was expected to.

'Oh, yeah. OK. I'll do a nice card to say sorry to Miss Jenson. I didn't mean it. She's nice.'

Jasmine spent ages designing the card, choosing different fonts, adding colours and pictures and typing out a short message that read, 'Sorry for being bad.' I encouraged her to change the wording to, 'Sorry for not behaving well and making you feel upset.' She agreed to this and seemed to appreciate it when I explained that it was her behaviour that wasn't up to scratch, but that this did not mean she was a bad person. I'd told her this before, but it was as if it were the first time she'd heard it.

'You're a lovely girl and don't you forget it!' I said.

Jasmine smiled at me and then suddenly remembered something.

'I got seven right!' she said.

'Seven what?'

'Spellings! I got seven out of ten. We did the spelling test this morning, so you owe me, er, let's see . . .' She scribbled down a sum on a piece of paper and worked it out with impressive speed. '£1.05!' she announced triumphantly.

It was my turn to smile. 'I told you that you could do it! And how good is your maths, too? You've worked out seven times 15p with no problem at all.'

Jonathan walked in. 'We were hoping we could get away with paying you 30p,' he winked. 'Shame your maths is so good.'

'Well, too bad, it's £1.05!' she said, holding out her hand.

I counted out the money from my purse. When we first started fostering I'd have thought twice about handing over money after a bad report from school that same day. However, I've learned that when consequences are illogical or unrelated to the 'offence', children see them as a punishment, which only creates more negative behaviour. If I'd gone back on my word about paying her 15p per correct spelling, Jasmine would have been confused and affronted and might have lost her temper or caused trouble.

'Well done on working hard on your spellings,' I reiterated as I gave her the money, hopefully leaving her in no doubt that this reward was tied exclusively to the spelling test.

Once Jasmine's card for Miss Jenson was printed out successfully, I popped upstairs to bring my log for Social Services up to date. In amongst my paperwork I saw a handout we'd been given at a training session. It read, 'Beneath every behaviour there is a feeling, and beneath each feeling is a need. When we meet that need, rather than focusing on the behaviour, we begin to deal with the cause not the symptom.'

I sat and looked at this handout for a few minutes, rereading the words as I digested them. Jasmine's poor behaviour was ultimately caused by the terrible events of her upbringing. We, and the school, had to focus on how this made her feel and give her the help she needed as a result of her childhood experiences. Not only was she not a bad person, as I'd told her more than once, but unfortunately she could not help her behaviour. She needed everyone involved in her care and education to understand this, not punish her when she transgressed.

A sadness descended on me, because the more I thought about it, the more I felt Jonathan and I were ill-equipped to deal with Jasmine's needs. There were huge holes in our knowledge about her background and upbringing, and to add to her woes Jasmine was now in a school where discipline ruled and, potentially, her behaviour was being punished without any nod whatsoever to her unique needs.

Diane was still with us – Jonathan and I are well used to 'just one night' turning into more – but we weren't at all bothered by this; in fact, we loved having her to stay. We decided to have a Chinese takeaway as a treat for everyone, which we sometimes did on a Friday night. Anthony would miss out as he had gone to work and was having his meal at the pub, but I knew Mum enjoyed a Chinese every once in a while. She would have sweet and sour chicken, and egg fried rice as usual, I imagined.

'Girls, what would you like?' I gave Jasmine and Erica the menu to look at.

There was a warm atmosphere in the lounge and Mum, Diane and Jonathan were chatting about this and that. Erica stared at the menu unenthusiastically. She had been quieter than usual since Jasmine's accusation against Jonathan, and I'd noticed she'd been spending her free time on her own, listening to music with headphones on or just looking the other way when we sat around the table or walked to school.

'Erica, you like those chicken satay skewers, don't you?' She shrugged. 'Yeah.'

'Let's get some of those then. And how about we get a chicken chow mein to share?'

Jonathan's ears pricked up. He agreed to us ordering chicken chow mein and made a joke about not wanting to share.

'Sounds all right to me,' Diane said. 'This is such a treat! I can't remember the last time I had a Chinese.'

'No!' Jasmine suddenly shouted. 'No, no, no! I'm not!'

Her outburst came completely out of the blue. We all looked at her in surprise as she jumped up from the sofa, sending the menu flying. Then she ran down the stairs to the kitchen shouting, 'Look at the green door! Green door! Green door! Green door, red door, orange door. Orange door! Fire!'

Mum gave me a pitying look, as if to say, 'What did I tell you? She's not right, that girl.'

'Oh dear,' I said, getting to my feet, 'I'll go and see if she's OK.' I quickly added, 'I'd like some mixed vegetables and shall we also have some prawn toast to share? Let's get the order phoned through. They're very busy on a Friday night.'

Erica nodded at the mention of prawn toast, though I don't think she could have cared less what we ate that night. It was clear she'd had a bellyful of Jasmine.

'Shall I go and check on Jasmine?' Diane offered. 'I don't mind.'

'Thanks Diane, that's kind, but I'll go.' Jasmine hadn't seemed upset or angry; just strangely animated. I thought it wouldn't do any harm to let her blow off a bit of steam, rather than chasing after her and giving her immediate attention.

'Jonathan, can you phone the order through? I'll let you pick something for Jasmine.'

'Of course,' he said. 'What am I having, or have you all decided that for me?'

I laughed, though I didn't really feel like it. Jasmine's outburst had soured the mood. I quickly read the order out loud before handing it to Jonathan. 'Happy with that?'

'Perfect.'

'Actually, can I change mine?' Mum piped up. 'I'm not sure I'm in the mood for sweet and sour, it might be a bit spicy for me. Can I have a look at the menu?'

She started fumbling for her reading glasses and realised she had left them in her bedroom.

'Don't worry, Mum, I can read it out, if it's easier.'

Mum decided she would like to order the chicken and sweetcorn soup, but might try some of the other dishes, if that was OK.

'Fine, Mum,' I said. 'We've got lots of choice, we can all share. Right, I'll go and see Jasmine.'

Jonathan started to dial the number of our local takeaway

and Diane, Mum and Erica carried on watching TV. I left the lounge and walked down the stairs.

I fully expected to find Jasmine running up and down the hall or darting in and out of the kitchen, but she wasn't there. I had a quick look in the dining room and utility room and called her name in case she was in the downstairs loo, but she wasn't anywhere on the ground floor of the house. She'd had time to go back upstairs and then carry on up to the bedroom while I'd read the menu to Mum, I realised. I wouldn't necessarily have heard her pass by the lounge, what with all our chatter and the TV on in the background. I'd go up and check, I thought, though I wasn't unduly worried. There was no noise coming from her bedroom, as far as I could tell, and I certainly couldn't hear her shouting any more. Maybe it was good to leave her while she was quiet like this.

I quickly put some plates to warm on a low heat in the oven and was about to start collecting cutlery and soy sauce for the table when I felt a cold draught blow through the kitchen. It was the sort of sharp, icy blast that races in when you open the front door in deepest winter, and I realised ours must have blown open. It was very unusual for this to happen. We were always very particular about safety, and our heavy wooden door was usually locked from the inside. It had been part of our assessment to draw a plan of an escape route from our house, in case of a fire. Children needed to know where the key was to open the door if it was locked, and we always kept keys in the same places, near the front and back doors. I'd explain this to all the children when I went through the house rules at the start of their placement. With so many people coming and going, I supposed it was possible someone simply hadn't shut the door fully, by accident, and had perhaps forgotten we liked to keep it locked. It was windy that night, and it could have blown open if someone had left it ajar by mistake. I closed it tight shut and turned the key in the lock before heading up to the girls' bedroom.

As I climbed the stairs I tried to remember who the last person was to come in. Was it Diane? She had popped round to see a neighbour earlier. Or was Anthony the last one to go through the door, on his way out to work?

I knocked on the girls' bedroom door and got no answer.

'Jasmine, are you OK? I'm going to come in, sweetheart. I just want to check you're OK.'

Still no answer. I pushed the bedroom door open and carried on talking as I did so, not wanting to alarm her or suddenly invade her privacy. 'I just want to check you're OK, sweetheart. Jonathan is ordering lots of different food, I'm sure there'll be something you like . . .'

There was nobody in the bedroom and I suddenly felt my heart tighten. Racing back down the stairs, I poked my head in the lounge and called Jonathan to come out and 'help me with something'. He shot down the stairs after me as I told him the bad news: 'I can't find Jasmine. I think she must have run off, out of the house.'

'Where have you checked?'

'She's not in her room or downstairs. And the front door was ajar.'

He let out a sigh.

Jonathan has always been the best person for the job when it comes to chasing after a runaway child. He's been a good runner all his life and has headed off many a child at the pass, surprising them with his speed and agility. However, this was not your standard scenario, because it was not a chase situation and we were not even certain she had run out of the house. We quickly checked the other bedrooms and the bathrooms, and realised that Jasmine's shoes were missing, and that's when we both had to admit she really must have run off. I calculated she could have been gone for at least five minutes, possibly more.

'I'll go and look for her,' Jonathan said.

She had not taken her coat, I saw, which was very worrying on such a bitterly cold night. Also, we had no idea which direction she'd run in, and it was pitch black outside. Not only that, we had to consider the fact that, just the day before, Jasmine had wrongly accused Jonathan of pushing her over. What if he caught up with her in the dark and she made a malicious allegation, with no witnesses?

'Don't do that. I'll call Social Services and we'll both go after her.'

'Right, yes. Good plan.'

Jonathan began to put on his shoes and a coat. 'I'll get the big torch.'

It was after office hours so I called the duty manager on the out-of-hours number, giving my name and Jasmine's name and age. Before I explained the reason for my call, the social worker on duty interrupted me.

'Angela Hart? That's a happy accident. My name's Stewart. I'm Jasmine's new social worker. I meant to call you this week, but it just got so busy, and my hours have been messed up because I'm duty manager all weekend.' He paused and then finally asked what the reason for my call was.

I explained about Jasmine running off and said we had no experience of her doing this and had no idea if there was any history of her running away.

'Oh,' he said. 'I've been having a look through her notes this week, to familiarise myself with the case. She runs off quite a lot. It's not unusual. How long's she been gone?'

Great, I thought. *We could have done with knowing that.*

'At least five minutes, maybe a little more.'

'Only five minutes?' Stewart sounded surprised that I'd called in so quickly. The rule is that you call Social Services in the first instance to log a 'runner', and if the child doesn't turn up you call the police an hour later if it's dark, or two hours later during daylight hours.

'I'd give it another ten minutes or so, she'll come back I'm sure. I'll log the call.'

He made a comment about the fact it 'wasn't late' as it wasn't yet six thirty, but to my mind that was completely beside the point because it was a dark, winter's night and Jasmine was only eight years old. Before I could reply Stewart started talking about the fact he needed to make an appointment to visit us the following week, but my mind was not on that particular conversation. All I could think about was that Jasmine was a vulnerable little girl and she'd gone out into the night without her coat, and not in a stable state of mind.

'OK, thanks,' I said, not really feeling like thanking him at all. 'Good to make contact. Hopefully I'll speak to you very soon. I'll wait to hear about the appointment next week.'

I ended the call as quickly as I possibly could without being impolite, though I was thinking, *Does Stewart understand the seriousness of this situation?*

I relayed to Jonathan what Stewart had said.

'Are you serious?'

'Totally.'

Before we left the house together, I discreetly explained the situation to Diane. We gave her some cash and asked her to pay for the takeaway if it turned up before we did. If Mum asked, I told Diane to quietly explain what had happened, and we all agreed to simply tell Erica that Jonathan and I had had to go out but would be back as soon as possible. We'd explain more if she asked questions, of course, but hopefully there would be no need and we'd be home before Erica knew it, with Jasmine safe and sound.

'I'm sorry about . . .' Diane started. 'I remember . . .' she looked slightly pained. 'It's made me think . . .'

'Don't worry, Diane. Hopefully see you very soon. But don't wait for us to eat, we'll heat ours up if need be.'

I had a good idea what Diane was thinking. She had done several runners during her time with us in her troublesome teenage years. Perhaps it was only now, seeing the anxiety etched on our faces, that she understood how frightening it is for carers and parents when a child goes missing, even if only for a matter of minutes.

Jonathan and I headed in the direction of the town as we figured that this was the most likely route Jasmine would have taken, as she had not yet been in the opposite direction. It was also better lit. We both had our mobile phones switched on and Diane was going to call us if Jasmine arrived home.

'Jasmine? Are you there?'

We called out constantly, poking the torch into every alleyway and shop doorway.

'Everything OK?' a kind voice asked. A face was illuminated under a lamppost. We recognised the man as one of our customers, though we didn't really know him.

'Fine, thanks,' Jonathan and I chimed hurriedly, in unison. Obviously, we weren't fine, but our instincts – terribly British, I guess – made us react that way. It was probably no bad thing, as telling a virtual stranger that a young girl was out on her own would not necessarily have been a smart move, not at this stage. It was too early to push the alarm bells in public. Jonathan and I were clinging on to optimism, keeping the faith that this would all be over very soon, just as Stewart had intimated on the phone. Telling our customer that we'd lost a child in our care would have only escalated this drama and we didn't want that. We had to believe we would nip it in the bud any moment now, and that Jasmine would appear around the very next corner.

'Let's turn back and check the playing field,' I said to

Jonathan when we reached the end of the road beyond ours and the street lamps started to thin out.

'Good idea. I'd don't think she'd have got this far.'

We hurried through the back roads and entered the playing field behind our house via a dimly lit passageway beyond the play area.

'Is that her?' Jonathan suddenly exclaimed, pointing at the swings. He sounded relieved as he spoke. I squinted and looked at the distant figure leaning between the chains of the slowly swaying swing. The play area was deserted and dusted in fog. Jonathan quickly removed his glasses, wiped them and looked again. We were a few paces closer now, and it had become achingly obvious the 'figure' on the swing was a large doll of some description. When we got up close, we realised it was a Jasmine-sized effigy of Guy Fawkes. The straw and foam-filled puppet was damp and dirty-faced and I reckoned he must have been kicking around the field since Bonfire Night. No doubt some kids had thought it would be funny to tie him to the swing.

Jonathan shone his torch around the field somewhat haphazardly. This was starting to feel more desperate now. I could see the muscle in the side of Jonathan's jaw twitching randomly, as it often does in testing situations like this.

'Let's check our garden,' I suggested.

We'd had kids hide in our garden before today, and it's not uncommon for young children to stay close to home even when they are supposedly 'running away'.

'We probably should have done that first,' Jonathan muttered.

'I'm not sure. It was the front door that was open, why would she go out the front in order to hide in the back garden?'

Jonathan ran across the playing field, towards the back entrance to our garden, calling Jasmine's name. I had a job keeping up with him.

'Jasmine, are you there?' I called. 'Jasmine, can you hear me?' My voice seemed to echo around me then disappear hopelessly into the freezing air.

Jonathan had to reach over our back gate to unlock it. He struggled because his hands were so cold. We were both puffing out white clouds of breath into the night air. I looked up and saw the stars were shining brightly, which gave me a glimmer of hope.

'Jasmine, I know you're here,' I said loudly as I walked through the gate. 'The takeaway will arrive soon. Come on into the house with us. Let's have some food. It's cold out here. Jasmine, can you hear me? I'm not cross, I just want you to be safe and warm. Can you hear me?'

There was no response. The wind had dropped and the garden seemed quieter than I had ever known it. Jonathan and I went back into the house.

'Any luck?' It was Diane.

'No. What time is it now?' I looked at the clock and worked out that Jasmine had been gone for about fifteen minutes. Waiting another forty-five minutes before we called the police seemed far too long, but that was the rule. An hour in the dark. That's what Social Services decreed was a suitable cut-off time for a runaway child, even if that child was only eight years old.

The doorbell rang and Jonathan and I rushed to open it, hearts pounding in anticipation.

'Delivery for Jonathan Hart?'

'Ah, yes. Thank you very much indeed. Let me fetch the money. What do we owe you?'

Diane was already handing Jonathan the cash he'd left her in charge of. He passed her the brown paper takeaway bag, took the money and paid the delivery man.

'Keep the change,' he said politely.

'Thanks, mate. Have a great evening!'

'You too. Bye now!'

The polite smile slid off Jonathan's face as soon as he shut the front door.

'I'm calling Stewart again,' I told him. 'We can't just do nothing. It's ridiculous. We need to call the police. I'm going to tell Stewart I'm phoning the police now. I'm not waiting another forty-five minutes. She's eight, for God's sake.'

Just at that moment we heard a clatter coming from the utility room. I'd checked in there just before we'd gone out because kids have hidden behind the door of the utility room in the past, but Jasmine had been nowhere to be seen.

I gently opened the door, just in time to see her emerging from the large cupboard beside the washing machine. It was one of those awkward-shaped corner cupboards in which things get lost or forgotten. As a result, I hardly used it, save for storing a few spare dishcloths, pegs and rubber gloves. It was virtually empty, but even so, I was surprised Jasmine had managed to squeeze herself in there.

'Jasmine! There you are!'

'Yes, here I am. Red door.' She was staring around the room, her eyes wide and unfocused.

'We've been outside looking for you.'

'Why?'

'We thought you'd gone out.'

'Did you? Why? I went in this door. Orange door. Is it orange?'

The cupboard was the colour of oak. I had no idea what she meant by red door and orange door, or what she'd been trying to say earlier, when she'd talked about the green door and fire.

Jasmine was talking in her baby voice now, but I don't think she was trying to feign ignorance. She seemed to be genuinely confused about why we had gone looking outside for her, and what she had been doing, hiding in the cupboard with the pegs and dishcloths.

'Did you phone the policeman?'

'No, sweetheart, but I was thinking about it. We were very worried.'

Jonathan popped his head around the corner and gave me a thumbs-up. He'd heard everything.

'I'll take the Chinese through to the table and call everybody down, shall I? You hungry, Jasmine?'

'Yes,' she said. 'Erm, don't you want to tell me off? Don't you have to hit me?'

Jonathan gave an exaggerated frown. 'What? Why would I do that?'

'Because you thought I ran away.'

'I'm just glad you are here, safe and sound,' he said. 'I'm glad to know you didn't run away. I didn't like to think of you out there in the freezing cold without a coat. It's very dark and cold. Oh, by the way, did you open the front door for any reason?'

Jasmine's face was a picture.

Though she didn't confirm this, we both had a good idea what had happened. It looked to us like Jasmine had put her shoes on, stuck her nose out the door, thought better of it when she realised how cold and dark it was and had instead decided to hide herself in the warmth of the utility room. She'd probably got in the cupboard when she heard me coming down the stairs and putting the plates in the oven, and thought she had no way out without being spotted.

While Jonathan organised the meal and got everyone around the table, I called Stewart and told him we'd found Jasmine, and that she was fine and we were about to sit down and eat.

'I knew she wouldn't be far away,' he said in a rather superior tone, which I didn't think was appropriate. We'd had a horrible, worrying time and Stewart didn't seem to acknowledge this at all. More importantly, he didn't ask after Jasmine in any way, not even to enquire where we'd found her or why she'd run off in the first place.

We made an appointment for him to visit after school on Tuesday of the following week. He said he'd confirm this when he was at his usual desk on Monday.

'Fine. I'll let Jasmine know. Thanks.'

'Cheerio,' he said. 'I can't tell you how envious I am that you've got a Friday night off and I'm stuck in here. Enjoy your meal!'

I opened my mouth to respond and decided better of it. The best and most empathetic social workers always said the opposite, complimenting us on the fact we were on duty 24/7, unlike them. Their kind words often gave us a boost when we most needed it, but Stewart had left me feeling irritated and wound up. Firstly, he'd treated the disappearance of an eight-year-old girl far too casually, in my opinion, and now he was inferring that our work for the day was done.

We might have been having a takeaway, but I certainly didn't feel like I was off duty. My nerves were frayed and I was extremely worried about Jasmine. Clearly, her mental state wasn't right. She was a traumatised child and it seemed to me she had a great many demons to deal with, possibly more than we'd realised.

'I think we really need to get to the bottom of why she talks about fire and seems to have a thing about it,' I said to Jonathan later on that evening. 'All of this is too worrying.'

We'd had conversations about this before, inevitably, but this was the first time we listed all the incidents and references that bothered us. Jasmine had made several mentions of fire or reacted to fire in an unusual way. Looking back, she'd lost control when I asked if she wanted to see the bonfire on the playing field not long after she first arrived, then she'd rampaged wildly around the lounge when I offered to switch on the fire for my mum when I was up the stepladder hanging the Christmas cards. 'I know who started the fire,' she'd screeched. 'I TOLD HIM WHO STARTED IT! I TOLD HIM! I TOLD HIM!' At the start of her stay, there had been that strange episode in the department store, after we saw Santa's grotto. I hadn't thought about this at the time, but was it the fake fireplace, with its red, yellow and orange cellophane flames that had made her freeze? Did the realistic display trigger some bad memories or associations? This evening's outburst of 'green door, red door, orange door. Orange door! Fire!' only added to our fears.

'It's the first thing I'm going to ask Stewart about when he comes on Tuesday,' I said. 'We have to know if there is something on her records that might explain this behaviour. He already knows more than us. We had no idea she had a history of running off. What else don't we know?'

The rest of the evening passed without further incident, and in fact Jasmine was good company and enjoyed her take-away. At bedtime she asked me for a cuddle, which was unusual, and the next morning she was up early, getting ready for her trip out with her grandparents.

I was very glad Pearl and Lenny were picking her up and, as I've said, on the Saturday morning I was counting the hours until Jasmine went out. She was behaving perfectly well but I felt on alert, fearing that we could have another incident at any moment, and not wanting one. Erica was keeping a very low profile and staying out of Jasmine's way, and I imagined she felt the same as I did. There was something so unpredictable about Jasmine, and you never knew which version of her was going to come to the fore. It was like walking on eggshells.

Happily, just like on the other occasions when she'd gone out with her grandparents, Jasmine left us in a good mood and came back excited, if a little hyper, having clearly had a great day. Pearl and Lenny had taken her to the cinema to see the Disney film *WALL-E* and they'd had a meal in one of the restaurants at the out-of-town retail park.

Unfortunately, there was no opportunity to talk to them in private – they turned up just as we were all seeing Diane off and they had to dash – but it didn't matter. After the running away scare, we felt that talking to Stewart was our priority now. Once we'd put together a few more pieces of Jasmine's puzzling background, we felt we'd be better placed to help her and work out what was best for her future.

14

'I'm going to report you to Social Services!'

Stewart came to the house on the Tuesday after school, as planned. He was young – late twenties, I'd say – and had a confident swagger about him.

'How are you getting on, young lady?' he asked Jasmine.

'Er, OK.'

'I'm taking over where your old social worker Lou left off. I expect Angela and Jonathan here have told you that?'

'Er, yes.'

'Good. So, are you happy here? Do you like Angela and Jonathan? Is there anything you'd like to tell me?'

Jonathan and I swapped glances. While these were questions Stewart needed to ask, his manner was quite brusque and businesslike. We couldn't imagine he'd get much out of Jasmine by firing questions so directly at her like this and, unfortunately, we were right.

'Er, no,' she said. 'I mean, yes, I like Angela.' She paused then added, somewhat reluctantly, 'And Jonathan.' Then she said, 'No.'

'No what?' Stewart asked, sounding a little impatient.

'No, there isn't something to tell you.'

She clamped her lips tight shut.

'Are you sure? You can talk to me in private? We need to have a little chat in private before I go, so you can tell me anything you like then. Do you understand that?'

She looked at the floor.

'Like why you ran away the other night?'

'OK, erm, no, I don't.'

Her eyes were still trained on the lounge carpet.

I didn't think Jasmine was going to open up to Stewart, at least not at this first encounter. Stewart had been so brusque on the phone on Friday night that he didn't even know she hadn't actually run away and had been hiding in the utility room. Clearly, this was not a great question to ask her. Though I'm sure he was trying his best, Stewart wasn't coming across as a particularly warm and empathetic person. He spoke almost as if reading from a script, like he was going through the motions and trying to do so as quickly and efficiently as possible.

'Can I go to my room?' Jasmine asked, still looking down and avoiding eye contact.

We said she could, and we were happy about this, as we had lots we wanted to discuss with Stewart out of her earshot.

These last two days Jasmine had been in trouble again at school, to the point where Mr Weatherstone had got involved. We'd had more issues at home, too.

While Miss Jenson had been very pleased with her 'sorry'

card and had hoped for a fresh start on Monday morning, Jasmine had continued to disrupt the class, make rude and personal remarks to other pupils and, once again, had refused to do the work she was asked.

For example, she would not fill in her 'news' book, although I have to say I had a lot of sympathy with this. Children in care often struggle to write about a weekend spent with foster carers, or seeing relatives they aren't able to live with, while all the other kids are talking about what they did at home with their mum and dad and siblings. It's a problem we've seen before. Making cards for Mother's Day or Father's Day and working on family trees are, understandably, other minefields for kids in care.

In her second period on Monday Jasmine had been excluded from the art class for making a mess with the paints and throwing pencils. She had missed her break as punishment for her poor behaviour, and then at lunchtime she had been found fighting with another child, who she'd apparently had in some kind of headlock in the girls' toilets. This was the point at which she was taken to Mr Weatherstone's office. The head had told her he had a 'zero tolerance' approach to fighting and disruptive behaviour of that nature and said she would be excluded in a week's time if she didn't change her attitude and stop causing trouble for herself and others.

I got a double thumbs-down from Miss Dowden across the playground on Monday afternoon. I felt quite nauseous as I walked towards her, fearing what I was about to hear.

'There's no reasoning with Jasmine,' she told me, looking

exacerbated. 'When I try to engage with her she seems to switch off. She goes kind of wide-eyed and vacant, do you know what I mean?'

'Yes,' I said reluctantly, thinking of the times when Jasmine had frozen and stared into space. 'Can she have more time with Miss Jenson or a teaching assistant? At home I find she's better when she's engaged in an activity or has one-to-one attention. I don't think stopping her from burning off energy at playtime or doing things she enjoys, like art, is helping.'

'I'll see what we can do, but it's a question of resources and priorities.'

Miss Dowden made a comment about Jasmine not being statemented despite having some special needs. I knew an SEN would have strengthened the case for Jasmine to have an assigned teaching assistant, ideally on a one-to-one basis. It seemed obvious that she did need more help than she was receiving from Miss Jenson and the special needs group she joined sometimes.

'Do you think we should have Jasmine statemented, as a matter of urgency?' I asked.

Miss Dowden considered this. 'I was going to monitor her for a little longer before having this conversation, but now you've brought it up, I think she has some psychological problems. I'm not an expert, but I think that rather than having her academic needs assessed – I feel she is a bright girl, in many ways – the priority should be to have her see a psychologist, to find out what's going on up there.' Miss Dowden tapped her head with a pencil. 'I've got no idea, you see, and that's starting to worry me. I'm afraid we might not be able to cope with her.' She made a reference to Mr Weatherstone and his stringent rules on discipline and protecting all pupils from having their learning disrupted by others. 'I'd hate to see her excluded, but it's going to be out of my hands if she carries on like this.'

That evening we had a terrible job getting Jasmine home from school. Thankfully, Erica was in a club and so she missed the miserable and very frustrating walk home that Jonathan and I endured. Jasmine ran into trees, banging her fists on them and threatening to hit her head. She also picked up a stick and said she'd hit herself, and she made loud yelping noises.

'Sweetheart, please stop doing that. You're going to harm yourself.'

People were staring at her and kids were laughing, but she seemed oblivious.

'I want to go on the school trip,' she spat out, eyes darting everywhere.

'What school trip? Tell me about it.'

'If anyone makes me go to school tomorrow, I'll hit them with a stick!'

'Sweetheart, is there a school trip?'

'Not for me! Not for me! They won't let me go!'

I eventually coaxed her into telling me that there was a trip to a local museum coming up, after Christmas. The children had all been given consent forms to take home but one of the teachers had warned Jasmine that she would not be going if she didn't behave herself.

'They said they'll make me stay in. Well they can! I don't want to go to that stinking school anyway.'

She was fizzing with anger and energy, and when we eventually reached the house she refused to come in through the front door as usual. Instead, she ran into the shop and deliberately kicked over a tub of cut flowers. Water splashed into the middle of the shop floor and an elderly couple who were browsing jumped at the commotion.

'Goodness, I wondered what on earth that was!' the gentleman remarked.

'A whirling dervish!' his wife replied, trying to smile at Jasmine. All she got was a growl in reply.

'Sorry,' I said as Jonathan and I tried to steer Jasmine out of the shop and Barbara fetched the mop, giving us a sympathetic smile as she did so.

'I want to go that way!' Jasmine yelled, pointing behind the counter. We didn't normally go into the house through the shop unless we were working.

'Please come this way,' I said, indicating that I wanted to leave via the front door of the shop, the way we'd come in. 'It's locked up at the back.'

'Grrr!'

Jasmine shot out of the shop door and said she was going to run up the street and not come back. I was shivering with cold and was desperate to get inside and put the kettle on.

'I'm running! I'm running! I'm going to do it! Zoooom!'

'I tell you what,' Jonathan said slowly, 'if you're serious about running away, Jasmine, why don't you pack a rucksack?'

Jasmine stopped in her tracks and looked at him suspiciously.

'Take a few supplies, maybe? Want me to help you? I mean, if I was running away, I'd take a flask of coffee, some chocolate biscuits, maybe a map and a torch . . .'

Finally, something had got through to Jasmine. She stared at Jonathan, incredulous.

'What? Are you throwing me out?'

'No, not at all. I just don't want you running off with only your school bookbag. Don't you want some extra clothes? Perhaps a sandwich? Angela, do you think you could make a packed lunch and I could go and find a rucksack?'

Jasmine was furious to have her bluff called like this.

'I'm going to report you to Social Services!' she huffed. 'You're trying to get me lost! I'm going in the house, whether you like it or not.'

We tried not to let her see that we were not just mightily relieved, but really rather amused by this about-turn.

Unfortunately, this small victory was immediately followed by yet more trouble. Once inside the house Jasmine kicked the radiator, threw her shoes down the hall and slung her coat on the floor, refusing to pick it up.

'Why don't you listen to some music or we could play a game?'

'Part of me wants to and part of me doesn't.'

'Come on, let's make a hot drink and find something you'd like to play.'

'No, I want to listen to some music.'

She put the radio on in the kitchen. The Beatles' 'A Hard

Day's Night' was on, appropriately enough, and I made the mistake of saying I loved the song. This prompted Jasmine to attempt to sabotage my enjoyment of it. When it got to the words 'I've been working like a dog', Jasmine started barking as loudly as she could. When I asked her to stop she turned the volume up full blast and began rampaging down the hall and up the stairs.

'I don't mind loud music,' I called after her, trying some of Jonathan's reverse psychology. 'Shall I turn it up louder? I love this one.'

'No thank you!' a voice called. It was Mum. She was standing on the landing outside the lounge. 'Angela,' she said, 'what on earth is going on?'

I turned the radio down.

'I think you need to ask Jasmine, not me.'

Mum looked at Jasmine, who kicked her way up the stairs, banging the wall with the flat of her hand before barging past Mum and into the lounge. It was clearly not worth questioning Jasmine, who now seemed to be in a furious world of her own.

'I think I'm going to go for a lie down,' Mum said, rolling her eyes.

'I don't blame you. I might do the same myself.'

By now I could hear Jasmine's footsteps in the lounge, hammering through the ceiling. I wondered whether to leave her to burn herself out, but it was too risky. She was in such an agitated mood she might hurt herself, I thought.

Jonathan joined me and we went up the stairs together.

When I pushed open the lounge door I saw Jasmine standing on the sofa, holding a table lamp in her hand.

'I can throw this,' she said. 'I could hit my head with it and smash my head in.' She stared at us, smirking and going cross-eyed.

'Jasmine, sweetheart, it would break my heart if you got hurt. I don't want you to hurt yourself. You're a lovely girl. I can see you're very angry and agitated. Why don't you give that to me and sit down?'

'Grrrrrr! Grrrrrr! Grrrrrr!'

She threw the lamp on a cushion, jumped off the sofa and ran up to the light switch, which she started flicking on and off repeatedly.

'I'm going to make a cup of tea,' Jonathan said. 'Who wants one?'

'Me, please,' I said wearily.

I put the table lamp back in its place and sat down in one of the armchairs while Jonathan went to the kitchen. Despite her threats, I didn't think Jasmine was intent on inflicting any harm on herself. It was possible she might accidentally hurt herself with all this rampaging round, but Jonathan and I both had the impression she just wanted to shock us, or get our attention, in order to make us see how angry she was. It was a cry for help, we supposed. The poor girl didn't know how else to express herself. She was full of pent-up aggression because of how she had been treated in the past, or at least that's how it seemed to us.

I picked up a magazine and started doing a wordsearch. Meanwhile, Jasmine continued flicking the light switch and then started running around the coffee table in circles, making grunting noises, animal sounds and dramatic growls.

'Would you like a pear drop?' I offered. 'It sounds like you're hurting your throat.'

'You don't know what it's like to be me! You don't know anything!'

'What do I need to know? Sweetheart, come and sit down with me and talk to me. I'd like to help you.'

'No! No! I know you people! I know you don't care because NOBODY cares! Not even Granny and Granddad because otherwise I'd be living with them and not in this stinking house.'

I took a deep breath. 'Jasmine, that is not true. Your granny and granddad love you very much indeed.'

'Not fair! Not fair!'

She darted out the door and ran up to her bedroom, where she started playing music at top volume. Erica, fortunately, was still out at her club. Normally I'd have left Jasmine to it, as I've done with children in the past who've tried to antagonise us by turning up the volume. 'It's fine by us, we like loud music,' we've said many times, much to the annoyance of children who are trying to protest. However, Mum was attempting to have a nap in her bedroom along the corridor, so I couldn't ignore this. I went up and knocked on the bedroom door.

'Jasmine, I'm going to have to ask you to turn down the music because Mum is trying to have a rest.'

She ignored me so I took a step into the room after telling

her, loudly, what I was going to do. 'You *can* play music up here,' I said to her, as I stood in her bedroom doorway, 'but not at that volume. Mum is trying to have a rest.'

'I don't want to turn it down!' she shouted, bolting past me and out of the room.

I switched off the music and followed her. I didn't make a fuss but instead just kept an eye on her, watching as she raced back down to the lounge, did a circuit around the coffee table and carried on down to the kitchen. All the while she continued her angry rampage, flicking on switches, hurtling herself around the furniture and making a range of odd noises.

Eventually, Jonathan and I sat in the kitchen and had a cup of tea. We took it in turns to check on Jasmine every now and again, making sure she was safe as she dashed between rooms chaotically, but mostly we let her blow herself out.

Eventually, after almost an hour of this carry-on, Jasmine finally calmed down. When she began to flag, I put the TV on for her and didn't attempt to tackle her on her behaviour. There did not seem any point, as she was in such a hostile and unresponsive mood. Intermittently, she was smirking and going cross-eyed. Needless to say, I didn't bother suggesting she did her homework; it was very clear that would have been an abortive task.

It took all our efforts to get Jasmine to eat a meal, have a shower, clean her teeth and get into bed without kicking off again that evening. Erica had studiously ignored her when she got dropped off by a friend after her club, and

Mum told me yet again that she didn't think Jasmine was 'right' or 'normal'.

For Erica's sake, we considered moving Jasmine to the sofa bed that Diane had vacated in the lounge, but then thought better of it. Social Services would not see this as acceptable, as each foster child is meant to have a proper bedroom, even if it's shared, although for one night it might have helped. Also, though we hated to think along these lines, we didn't trust Jasmine to be alone in a room with a fire. As I've said, by now we had genuine concerns that something had happened with a fire, but we didn't know what. We had one of those gas fires designed to look like a real fire, set in the hearth and with a chimney. There was a switch beside it to turn on the gas and it wouldn't have been impossible for her to work out how to light it, if she really wanted to. We hoped we were overthinking things, but we couldn't take the risk.

Today had also been very testing.

'Good morning, Jasmine,' Mum had said brightly at breakfast time.

They were alone in the kitchen together for a few moments, as I'd popped out to the bin. Mum was making good, steady progress with her recovery and was moving about much more easily, every day. She looked better than I'd seen her in ages and was in a very chirpy mood.

'Ugh? What?'

'I said good morning, Jasmine!'

We'd all learned that it was best to treat every day as a

fresh, new start with Jasmine. Normally, that's what she did herself. No matter what had gone on the day before, she invariably carried on as if nothing had happened, or at least as if she couldn't remember what had happened.

'It's not good, not a good morning, Thelma,' Jasmine said. She spoke in a monotone voice that sounded quite spooky, and she stared coldly at Mum.

'Oh, why's that darling?'

Jasmine's reply floored poor Mum.

'You know what, when I lived at home, my house, I mean, my dad put a knife to my throat and threw me in the shed and tried to burn me.'

'Oh dear, I didn't expect you to say anything like that. That's really awful.'

Jasmine locked her eyes on Mum's for a few moments before pouring herself a bowl of cereal. Mum was very shocked but she quietly drank her coffee and left it there. She knew not to probe and to simply report anything like this back to me. When she shared the conversation later, she admitted she had actually been lost for words.

'I had no idea what to say. I felt like I'd been punched. You know that feeling? It knocked the stuffing out of me, hearing Jasmine talk like that.'

'I'm sorry to hear that, Mum. We don't know if what Jasmine said is true, so please try not to worry about it. Her new social worker is coming over later and I will tell him about this. It's a job for the professionals.'

* * *

I'd hoped Jasmine would have a better day in school, but it wasn't to be. Miss Dowden told me she had introduced a 'three strikes and you're out' chart on the wall. I didn't agree with that kind of thing, as it was like a 'naughty chart' in my mind, when what Jasmine needed was praising for her good behaviour. Anyhow, I had no control over this; it was a new system that Mr Weatherstone was introducing across the school, apparently, to improve behaviour. The rule was that if a child had three strikes in one day they had to go and see him.

'Did she have three strikes?'

'I'm afraid she did.'

Jasmine had earned her first strike when she rocked in her chair and gave cheek to Miss Jenson when asked to stop. Strike two came at lunchtime when she hit another child with an empty juice bottle.

'What was strike three?'

'Fighting in the playground. She whipped two other children with a rope and made threats to kill them. She had to be held by a member of staff. I'm sorry, Mrs Hart, but she had to see Mr Weatherstone, and he would like her to cool off at home for a week.'

'You mean she's excluded?'

'Yes, I'm afraid so.'

My face must have fallen and Miss Dowden gave me a pitying look.

'I'd hoped school would help improve her behaviour,' I said. 'I'm sorry.'

'It's not your fault, Mrs Hart. 'Please don't apologise.'

Miss Dowden then seemed to steel herself before telling me she had been thinking about Jasmine's mental health again. She said she now considered it to be a 'priority' to have Jasmine seen by a professional. 'She said something to Miss Jenson today that was disturbing, to say the least.'

I was on pins as I asked, 'What did she say?'

'Miss Jenson asked the children if they had ever done something without thinking of the consequences. One child said she ate some chocolate from her grandmother's handbag and got diarrhoea. Everyone was laughing and then Jasmine had her turn.'

'Go on.'

'She said that she stole a box of matches from her dad's pocket and lit a piece of paper in her bedroom. She said she put the burning paper in her laundry bin and left the room. Then the house caught fire. The other children laughed and said she was making it up but Miss Jenson wasn't sure. Jasmine didn't appear to be attention-seeking when she told this story, that's the impression Miss Jenson had. Jasmine spoke quietly and in a serious way.'

'I see.' My blood ran cold. I told Miss Dowden, truthfully, that Social Services had not told us of any history of Jasmine having started a fire. 'That's very alarming,' I said. 'Thank you for telling me. I'll pass that on to the social workers.'

Now here we were on Tuesday afternoon, with Jasmine's new social worker. An awful lot had happened in the last couple of days, but the first question I wanted to ask Stewart, after Jasmine had gone up to her room, was what he could tell us about any history of a fire in the family home.

I passed on what she'd said in school that day. 'As I've noted in my log, we've already had some concerns about Jasmine having been involved with fire in some way. Now this has happened, our concerns are obviously stronger and we want to know more. Can you tell us anything? Was there a fire in the family home?'

'Yes,' he said, somewhat casually. 'I've seen a note somewhere in her files about a fire. There wasn't much detail, I'm afraid.'

Jonathan and I were on the edge of our seats. 'What can you tell us?'

'It happened about a year before Jasmine was taken into care, I believe. It was unexplained but it did start in her bedroom. She said something to her previous carer about it just before the placement broke down.'

'Fran knew about it?'

'Yes, I've got the most recent notes here.'

Stewart flicked through some paperwork and located the reference he was looking for. 'Fran noted, "Jasmine told my husband that she knew who started the fire and it wasn't her mum or dad."'

'That's it?'

'Yes, that's all it says.'

Jonathan had gone pale. Over the years, the one thing he'd put his foot down about was having a so-called 'fire-starter' in the house. 'I can handle anything else, but not that,' I'd heard him say, not just to me but to other foster carers and several of our trainers and support social workers. The fear that he would not be able to protect me and any children living in the house was what fuelled his viewpoint.

Right now, I knew he'd be thinking about my mum, Anthony and Erica as well as Jasmine and us; *I* certainly was. There was also the shop to think about. It was attached to the house. The potential devastation a house fire could cause was terrifying.

'Stewart, we should have been told about this,' I said. 'I feel like we've been kept in the dark. No wonder her placement with Fran started to break down. It's all making sense now.'

'Hang on a minute,' Stewart said, rather sharply. 'There is no evidence that Jasmine started the fire. Nothing in her file says she started it. It was unexplained. What happened to innocent until proven guilty?' He let out a strange, snorting laugh, which seemed wholly inappropriate.

'I don't think it's funny,' Jonathan said. 'This is a damaged child we're talking about. From what Jasmine has said, potentially it is not safe for her to be in this house with us and the other people who live here.'

'Look,' Stewart said, 'if any of your property or effects got damaged, you could claim on your household insurance. You know that, don't you?'

That was not the point and I was shocked at his attitude.

'Stewart,' I said, 'even before this conversation, as you know, we had grave concerns about Jasmine. The school thinks she needs to be psychologically assessed and so do we. This now needs to happen as a matter of urgency. Is there anything you can do to get her an appointment with an expert as soon as possible?'

'I'll do my best,' he said. 'Any other concerns you'd like to tell me about before I have a chat with Jasmine?'

I ran through the other problems we'd had, which took some time, and ended with the news that Jasmine had been excluded from school that day. I also asked Stewart if he could tell us anything else about Jasmine's background.

'We don't know anything about her mother, for example. We heard through her grandmother that she disappeared, but that's all. Is there anything else you can tell us?'

'Her mother? I'm afraid I don't know. I'll have to go back over the file, but I don't think there's anything else.'

'Where is her father, can I ask?'

'I don't know. There is no contact and so we wouldn't know.'

Stewart spoke very briefly to Jasmine. Afterwards she said, 'I don't know why he asked me about the fire. Last time I talked about that I got into *so* much trouble. Does he want to get me into trouble?'

My attempts to get her to continue this conversation failed. 'What am I going to do when I'm off school?' she asked. 'Can you take me swimming? Can you take me to that museum?'

'Jasmine, I'm not sure, I haven't had time to think about it yet.' I knew that children excluded from school were not supposed to be out around town. We were expected to keep them at home, but in the back of my mind I was already wondering if this was the best way of handling Jasmine. It seemed to me akin to keeping her in at break time then wondering why she got frustrated and needed to let off steam in the classroom.

'How are you feeling?' I asked.

'Cool. Great. Erica is not happy that I'm off school, ha ha ha! L is for loser, L is for loser!' She made an L shape with her thumb and index finger.

'Jasmine, that's not kind, please stop saying that.'

She placed her hands over her ears and ran off shouting, 'Nee-nah! Nee-nah! Nee-nah!'

Our support social worker, Caitlin, phoned up shortly after Stewart left.

I brought her up to speed and, though I didn't criticise Stewart directly, I think she could tell I wasn't exactly enthusing about him. To my surprise it turned out she had known him for years and rated him highly.

'He's a great social worker. I don't think you have anything to worry about, but of course feel free to call me about any problems at all.'

'Well I never,' I said to Jonathan. 'Maybe he was just having an off day.'

'The jury's still out,' he replied. 'Mind you, what was it he said? Innocent until proven guilty!'

We both had a laugh. I think we needed one.

15

'She needs to sort herself out!'

Happily, Stewart did come up trumps on the very important issue of Jasmine's psychological assessment. Even though it wasn't strictly his job, he managed to help us fix up an appointment with a specialist psychologist at impressive speed. It would take place early in the New Year, which was excellent news. Sometimes we'd waited six months or more for appointments like this to come through, so we were happy to settle for that.

We were very grateful, although of course it didn't solve our immediate problems and concerns. We still had to struggle on with Jasmine and her behaviour continued to test us. I was worn out trying to keep her occupied and out of trouble during her exclusion, but we got by without too many dramas. I asked the head teacher for permission to take Jasmine out during the day, explaining that her behaviour improved when she was occupied and had an outlet for her energy. He agreed that we could go out and we decided to take her swimming, which proved to be a lifesaver. She thoroughly enjoyed it and it seemed to improve her mood and help her to sleep more soundly. We went almost every day, and also took her on several long walks. On the following Tuesday, which was the last day she was excluded from school, I found her in the garden, trying to make friends with the neighbour's cat. She was chasing her round because she wanted to pick her up, but Dusty jumped up onto the fence and ran away. It got me thinking that perhaps we should get Jasmine a pet, as she'd asked when we visited George and his animals. I still wasn't prepared to get a rabbit or a guinea pig. I felt we had too much on our plate to take on a commitment like that, but I wondered about getting some goldfish.

Jonathan thought about this and said it wasn't a bad idea, commenting that it would be a good way to teach both girls about caring and looking after a pet.

'Let's get two fish and the girls can name one each,' he said. We both felt it would be good for them to have one each and share the responsibility of feeding them and helping to change the water in the tank.

We got the fish the next day, after Jasmine had returned to school. Jonathan and I bought them at the pet shop on the retail park, along with a tank and a bag full of paraphernalia, including pink-coloured fake coral, an electric blue castle with a bridge and some plastic seaweed.

We had decided to tell the girls that the fish belonged to everyone in the house. They could name one each and it was up to them to feed them and help change the water, but they were everybody's pets. Though we didn't spell it out, this was to stop any problems that might occur if one of the girls moved out and wanted to take a fish with them, which might not be possible.

'Jaws,' Jasmine said. 'I'm calling mine Jaws.'

'That's a great name!' Erica laughed.

Both girls were thrilled to bits with the fish. Jonathan set the tank up in the kitchen and we unveiled it after we all arrived home from school. Thankfully, Jasmine had had a good report that day and was in very good spirits.

'What are you calling yours?'

'Bullseye,' Erica said.

'Why?'

'His eyes are kind of red, see? Much redder than Jaws's eyes. They look like bullseyes, on a dart board.'

'I like that, Erica,' I said. 'It's very clever. And we won't forget which fish is which.'

Pearl phoned that evening to ask if they could take Jasmine out again, perhaps a week on Saturday? 'It's fine by us. She was excluded from school though, just to let you know. She's been out for a week and has returned today.' I reassured her it had been a good day, and the teacher was pleased with how she had behaved.

Pearl sighed. 'I hoped all that would stop now she's settled in with you. Why was she excluded this time?'

'Fighting in the playground, amongst other things.'

'Not again!' Pearl said. She clearly knew more than we did about Jasmine's school record.

'To be honest, Pearl, I haven't been given any details about her previous exclusions. I knew she'd been out of school, of course, but I had no idea she'd been excluded for fighting before.'

'Oh yes. Fighting, giving cheek, not doing work, disrupting the class. That's been the biggest problem. They don't like it when she disrupts the other kids, do they?'

While Pearl was in a talkative mood, and Jasmine was in the other room, I decided to ask a few more questions.

'There's been mention of a fire, at the family home. That's something else I didn't know about. Can you tell me anything about it?'

'A fire? No, I'm sorry. I can't help you there. If there was one, I never heard about it.'

'Also, what about her mother, if you don't mind me asking?'

'What do you want to know?'

'I don't know anything at all about her. You told me she disappeared but Jasmine has never mentioned her.'

'Well, I'm not surprised. We haven't seen hide nor hair of her since she upped and left. Not a dicky bird. That's where the trouble started, if you ask me.'

'I see.'

I left a gap, but Pearl didn't offer any more information and I didn't push for more. It's generally best to wait for relatives to fill in the blanks but seeing as Social Services had given us so little and Pearl seemed open to chat, it hadn't felt wrong to ask a couple of questions. I wanted to ask about Jasmine's scar too, but I felt I'd pushed my luck already and I didn't want to upset Pearl in any way.

Before I called Jasmine to the phone I asked Pearl about her dealings with Social Services, and the decision made about not allowing Jasmine to live with them.

'Have you considered appealing?'

'It's funny you should ask that. We've kept quiet about it as we don't want to get Jasmine's hopes up, or destabilise her placement with you, but the answer is yes. We've decided we're not giving up, not without a fight. I'm very sorry she was excluded from school again, but maybe that shows you she's not as happy or settled as she could be. I don't mean any disrespect to you and Jonathan – we have nothing but admiration for you – but maybe that's something that might go in our favour, you never know.'

I told Pearl I understood, thanked her for being so frank and honest with me and said we would do anything we could to help her appeal. I also gave her the news about Jasmine's upcoming appointment with the psychologist.

I found myself feeling glad I'd mentioned the fire. The last thing I'd want to do would be to keep any other potential carers in the dark. I'd taken some comfort from the fact Pearl had not heard about it. I hoped that must mean it had not been a major incident, as presumably, if it had, news of the blaze would have been all over the neighbourhood.

I called Jasmine to the phone. 'Your granny wants to talk to you. She and your granddad would like to take you out next weekend.'

'Oh!' Jasmine said, looking bemused. She seemed

genuinely surprised by this, which was odd, given that this was not the first time they had taken her out.

She took the phone and I heard her making plans and telling Pearl about the goldfish. 'Next Saturday, not this Saturday, twelve o'clock,' she said twice, as if trying to commit it to her memory. Then she called me over to check this was OK before telling her granny she was looking forward to seeing her.

'That's good news, isn't it?' I said. 'It'll be lovely to see your grandparents again.'

Jasmine suddenly had a very serious look on her face. 'Do I have to go out with them?'

I was puzzled by this. I wondered if she meant did she have to go out, or could they stay in. 'It's fine by me if you want to stay here and see them, but you always enjoy going out.'

She stared at me and didn't reply for a moment.

'Do I have to go out with them?' she repeated.

'No, you can stay in.'

'Do I have to stay in with them?'

I wasn't sure where Jasmine was going with this. 'No, you don't have to stay in, you can go out with them. They'd like to take you out, as usual.'

She scowled and looked angry and disappointed.

'Do you want to go out with your grandparents?'

'What?' she blurted, sounding incredulous. 'Of course I do! Why wouldn't I?'

'Great. That's great.'

'It's twelve o'clock on Saturday, not this Saturday but next Saturday,' she repeated.

'Great. I'll write that down. That's settled then.'

She scowled at me again. Like I say, I had no idea how her mind worked.

'Guess what?' Jasmine said, when she came out of school one afternoon. She hadn't been back in the classroom for long since her exclusion and we'd had some mixed reports. I looked towards Miss Dowden, who thankfully gave me a big smile and an enthusiastic thumbs-up.

'What is it, Jasmine?' I replied.

'I won the road safety competition.'

'Did you? Very well done. What did you do to win?'

Jasmine explained that every child in the school had been asked to design a poster that would be displayed around the perimeter of the school and in the surrounding roads, asking motorists to slow down and park considerately.

'Mine was the best! I'm going to meet the mayor. I'm going to have my picture taken with him and I'm going to be in the newspaper!'

Jonathan and I gave each other a quick glance, acknowledging the fact this latter point would have to be carefully handled. Of course, the reason Jasmine was not allowed to live with her grandparents was because her father knew where they lived, and there were fears he might have contact with her. We were sure Social Services would not want Jasmine to appear in a newspaper, with the name of her new school displayed. Clearly, this would make her very easy to track down, if that's what her father wanted to do.

'Jasmine, that's absolutely brilliant. Well done, sweetheart. That is such good news. Can I see the poster?'

'Really?'

'Yes, of course. I'd love to see it.'

'OK, let's ask Miss Dowden,' she said, looking very pleased that I was so interested.

Miss Dowden was delighted to show us the poster and discreetly told me that they had been trying to give Jasmine a boost by handing her this victory.

'I think it's worked,' I said. 'I'm very pleased.' While Jasmine showed Jonathan some of her other artwork I took the opportunity to mention that, unfortunately, we couldn't let Jasmine appear in the local paper.

'I'm not sure what you mean, Mrs Hart.'

'It's because she's in care—' I started to explain.

Miss Dowden interrupted me and said that she completely understood why a child in care might not be able to appear in a newspaper, but there was no plan for this to happen.

'Oh, that's odd. Jasmine just told us the mayor was coming and she was having her picture taken with him and would appear in the local paper.'

Miss Dowden smiled. 'I think her imagination has got a little bit carried away. We called her up onto the stage in assembly this morning and Mr Weatherstone shook her hand and the whole school applauded. She seemed to love being in the spotlight and has been in a very good mood all day. But no, she's not being pictured for the local paper.' After a pause, Miss Dowden said there was a newspaper clipping on the classroom wall of a child who'd won a different prize and had appeared in the local paper with the mayor. 'Maybe Jasmine put two and two together and came up with five!'

Jasmine was a pleasure to be around that evening. She helped Jonathan clean out the fish tank, which we'd decided to install in the dining room, and she did her homework without being asked. She was also very kind to Erica, who had just found out her grandmother was poorly. Caring for the fish together seemed to have bonded the girls a little more.

'Will she die?' Jasmine asked Erica gently.

'Maybe, but I hope not.'

'That's sad. Do you want to listen to some music? It might make you feel happier.'

Erica shrugged and Jasmine played her one of her favourite CDs in the bedroom.

Jonathan and I dared to hope that Jasmine may have turned a corner. Our hopes were fuelled by the fact that for several consecutive days after winning the road safety competition she didn't miss any playtimes and avoided the thinking room. She also worked hard on her homework and got all her spellings right, which was a first. We rewarded her with £1.50, which we promised she could spend along with her pocket money when we went shopping at the weekend.

Very disappointingly, the day after the spelling test I spotted Miss Dowden giving me a thumbs-down and looking glum.

'What happened?'

'I don't know. It was like the flick of a switch. One minute she was fine, working on making Christmas cards, and the next she flew into a terrible rage. She threw all the art supplies on the floor and started shouting and banging her head against the door. I had to take hold of her, in a safe hold, as I was afraid she was going to hurt herself. I told her she needed to calm down. I could feel her pulse in her wrists, and it was going completely wild. She broke free from me – she's surprisingly strong – and then she tried to run off the school premises. Luckily, one of the PE teachers saw her and managed to stop her.'

I was very sorry to hear this. This was such bad news, after she'd had several positive days.

'Did you say she was working on Christmas cards?'

'Yes, that's right. She was making one for her grand-parents, and it was really good, but she tore it up I'm afraid, along with another one she'd been working on.'

I wondered if this was the trigger. No doubt most of the other children were making cards for their mum and dad or their siblings. Christmas can be a difficult time generally for children in care, and we were in mid-December now. The countdown was well and truly underway, and I imagined this would not be helping Jasmine. Whatever had happened in the family home, she would have memories of Christmases past, and that would be difficult for her to cope with. Not only that, but Pearl and Lenny had had to cancel their planned day out, which she had started to look forward to. Unfortunately, Lenny had fallen off a ladder when putting some decorations up outside their house. He'd sprained his wrist and had one arm in a sling. As he was the only driver they had no way of getting to us. I offered to run Jasmine out to meet them halfway, but Pearl explained that Lenny wasn't really up to it. 'Thanks, but it's knocked him for six and he just needs to take it easy. After all, I don't want him to be crocked at Christmas!'

The walk home from school was extremely difficult after the Christmas card incident that day. Jasmine tugged at Erica's coat, trying to pull her backwards.

'Get off me, Jasmine! What are you doing?'

'Just messing!' she said, with a smirk on her face.

'Well don't! It's so annoying!'

'Do you wish you were dead?'

Erica didn't dignify this with a response. Instead, she put her head down and marched on ahead.

'Jasmine, that is not a nice question,' Jonathan said. 'I don't want to hear you ask that question of anybody again.'

'Why? Are you scared of dying? Is her grandmother going to die? I wish I could tie a piece of string around my neck and die and then I wouldn't have to be HERE with YOU! I wouldn't have to sit on your stinking chairs and eat her stinking food!'

She pointed at me, and several parents and children on the path looked over to see what all the fuss was about.

Jonathan and I didn't respond to this. Sometimes you know when to stay quiet, and this was one of those times. Nothing we said was going to turn Jasmine's mood around, it would only be asking for more trouble.

Mum was in the kitchen when we eventually got home. The walk had taken double the time it normally did because Jasmine kept dragging her feet.

'How was school?' Mum asked brightly.

'It was good until I saw her,' Erica said moodily. 'She needs to sort herself out!'

Jasmine smirked and asked, 'Can I phone my granny?' As she said this she gave Erica a catty look.

'Yes,' I said. 'Let's go up to the lounge.'

Mum gave me an encouraging smile. 'Good idea,' she said. 'I'll make a pot of tea.'

'Great, thank you.' *At least Mum's improving*, I thought to myself.

On the way up to the lounge I had a gentle word with Jasmine.

'Sweetheart, I think you need to be kinder to Erica. Her grandmother is very ill.'

'Oh!' she said, in an overly dramatic way. 'Do you think she might be jealous that I can phone my granny and she can't? Her granny's in hospital, isn't she? I didn't think of that! Do you think that might have wound her up?'

Jasmine seemed to be behaving in a sneaky and mean way. This was a side of her I hadn't seen before, and I didn't like it. I decided to call her bluff.

'Gosh!' I said. 'I didn't think of that either. I'm sure Erica wasn't thinking along those lines. She's a very nice girl. I don't think she would be jealous about you phoning your grandmother. But now you mention it, perhaps it would be best if you don't talk to Erica about her granny, or yours. We don't want to upset her in any way, do we?'

'No,' Jasmine said. 'We don't want to upset Erica.' She fixed her eyes on mine and gave me a lingering smirk. 'We don't want to upset Erica.' I felt goosebumps prickle my arms. We had so many concerns about Jasmine. On top of the worries we had about her history with fire, the numerous references to death she made disturbed us greatly. Jonathan and I were being very vigilant about this. I recorded every reference and we'd had a very serious conversation about whether or not she might be displaying suicidal tendencies, or at least was in danger of harming herself.

I wanted to discuss all of this with Caitlin, but we'd been told that she was ill and had been signed off work. As for Stewart, he was proving difficult to get hold of. I'd left several messages for him to call me back but had heard nothing for a couple of weeks.

'We don't want to upset Erica.' I had a new fear to add to the list. Might Jasmine harm Erica?

Of course she could. That was what the voice in my head was saying, and once I heard it I couldn't stop thinking about it.

Jasmine phoned her granny. 'I've been making you a Christmas card,' she said sweetly. 'Can I come to your house for Christmas?'

Pearl must have asked if she could speak to me because Jasmine came over and whispered in my ear, 'Granny wants me to stay with her and Granddad at Christmas. Can you talk to her?'

'Of course,' I smiled.

'Hello, Pearl. How are you? How's Lenny getting on?'

'Not bad, thanks. Hopefully the sling can come off soon. How are you?'

'Fine, thanks,' I said, though to be honest I was feeling very far from fine at that moment in time.

'Has Jazz spoken to you about Christmas?'

'No, she hasn't, Pearl, but she just told me that you'd like her to stay with you. Is that right?'

'Oh no, I'm afraid not. That's why I wanted to have a word. Jazz has been asking and asking, but we're not going to be here. We're staying with some old family friends. I must have told her half a dozen times but she seems to forget. I'm wondering if she thought things might have changed because of Lenny's arm but that's not going to stop us. We're travelling on the train so he doesn't have to drive. It was all arranged ages ago. Can you explain it to her? I'd hate her to get upset about it, especially after we had to cancel our day out with her.'

'I see, yes, I'll talk to her, no problem. I did wonder, actually . . .' I stopped myself saying any more as Jasmine was listening, but it had occurred to me that Social Services might not have been keen on that arrangement in any case.

'By the way,' Pearl interjected, 'I wouldn't have planned to go away if Social Services weren't being so slow, and so obstructive. I want you to know that. If we had our way, we'd have Jazz living with us by now. You know that, and I've told Jazz that too. Maybe that's not helpful, but I'd hate her to think we're not bothered or not even trying.' I heard

Lenny rib Pearl in the background. 'You're wittering again,' he chided. 'Let Angela get a word in edgeways!'

'Of course, Pearl. I understand. Can you hold the line a moment?'

I asked Jasmine if she would go and see if Mum needed any help making the tea.

'OK,' she said. 'But can I speak to Granny again?'

'Yes, sweetheart. I'll give you a shout in a minute or two.'

'Your mum won't need help with the tea. Erica can help. Where is Jonathan?'

'Please go and see. Besides, I'd like to have a quick word with Pearl in private, if you don't mind.'

Jasmine narrowed her eyes and walked out of the room.

'Sorry, Pearl. I'm back now and Jasmine is out of the room. Don't worry about Christmas, I had assumed she was with us, of course. I'll talk it through with her so there's no confusion. How long are you away?'

'Only five days, we'll be back on the 28th. If it fits in with you, we'll take Jazz out and do something nice as soon as we're back.'

'That sounds good, she'll love that, I'm sure. If you don't mind me asking, is there any news at all about your appeal?'

Pearl sighed. 'Not really. Getting hold of the right people is so long-winded but I've got an appointment booked in with someone high up. I can't remember her name. Lenny might remember.' There was a pause and I heard her asking Lenny, who said he didn't know the woman's name either, but that she was 'in charge of case managers, or something like that.'

'We've been bounced up and up the chain, which I suppose can't be a bad thing. I'll go right to the top if need be. We'd so love to have Jazz living with us and we have no intention of letting her dad have any contact with her. I've told them until I'm blue in the face. Hopefully they will start listening. It's so frustrating. I think common sense needs to be applied here. I mean, there's you with a houseful and Jazz hasn't even got her own bedroom. I'm not being funny, Angela, but it doesn't make sense, does it . . .?'

There were lots of other things I wanted to discuss with Pearl, but now was not the time and, besides, it was not my place. Social Services had to be the ones to fill her in on all the notes I'd made and any results and assessments we received from Jasmine's upcoming psychological appointment.

Before I said any more, Pearl was off again. 'We've been decorating our spare bedroom, ready for when she can come and stay. It's nearly finished and I'd love to show it to her but, as things stand, I'm not allowed to even bring her to the house. Ludicrous, isn't it? I'm actually glad we're away at Christmas. How could I tell her she's not allowed to stay with us, her own grandparents?'

'Do you know where your son is living?' I ventured. 'I mean, is he still in the area?'

'That's a very good question, and do you know what? Not one person in Social Services has bothered to ask me that. I've told them all I know, of course, but it doesn't make a jot of difference.' She sighed before continuing. 'He's disappeared, just like her mother. The rumour is he's gone abroad.

We're trying to find out if there is any truth in that. I'm hoping there is, and that he's not planning to come back.' She added that she wouldn't be surprised if Social Services knew more than she did about her son's whereabouts.

'OK,' I said. 'Jasmine's back. I'll let you explain to her about Christmas again. It's great news that she'll see you when you get back from your travels.'

'Thanks. No problem. I was thinking of maybe getting some pantomime tickets but I won't mention it yet, just in case. Thanks, Angela.'

When Jasmine had finished talking to Pearl, she immediately told me she wasn't bothered that she couldn't go to her granny and granddad's for Christmas.

'It's all fine,' she said. 'It's cool! I want to go to Aunty Ruth's anyway, because she has lots of money and will buy me loads of presents.'

She ran off. I'd never heard of Aunty Ruth and would probably have to ask Pearl about her too, seeing as she seemed to be the only person I was receiving information from right now.

16

'You do it because you get paid'

Jasmine was refusing to shower, which told me she was trying to wrestle some control over her life. I tried every trick in the book to get her in the bathroom, including asking if she wanted to choose her own shower gel and other nice smellies from the local chemist. This is something that's worked in the past, on the suggestion of our foster care trainers, but it didn't sway Jasmine. She turned her nose up and said, 'What would you do that for when you've got loads of smellies in the house already?'

'Anyway,' she added, 'I'll have a shower when I go to Aunty Ruth's.'

'Who's Aunty Ruth?'

'I told you before. I'm going to Aunty Ruth's for Christmas. Durgh!'

'I didn't know you had an Aunty Ruth.'

'Haven't I already told you? Nobody listens to me! She's my rich aunty. She's the one I'm spending Christmas with. She has loads of money and she lets me do what I want and doesn't mind if I have dirty feet.'

'OK, but you still need to have a shower tonight.'

Jasmine rampaged around the house, jumping on furniture and deliberately making her hands dirty by poking her fingers into the soil of a large rubber plant we had in the hall. In the lounge, she picked up her advent calendar and threatened to eat all the remaining chocolates.

'Why would you do that?' Mum asked.

'Because then I'll get more.'

I told her that she would not get more, and it was her choice if she wanted to finish them all off at once.

'OK then, I won't! See how you like that!'

Then she ran up to her bedroom.

Mum gave me yet another meaningful look.

'Angela,' she started.

'I know, Mum, she's hard work.'

'She is. I was wondering, perhaps, if I should think about getting back to my place sooner rather than later. I'm feeling so much better and you have an awful lot on your hands, dear.'

I told Mum that I certainly didn't want her moving out on account of Jasmine. She'd seen the GP this week and had been advised not to get carried away with her recovery, and to continue to take it easy despite the excellent progress she was making.

'We can handle Jasmine,' I assured her. 'Please don't change your plans. We want you to stay for Christmas, we really do. You will stay, won't you?'

Erica rushed into the lounge before Mum could reply.

She looked thoroughly fed up. 'Angela, I think Jasmine needs to see a doctor.'

'What? What's happened?' I was shocked and had visions of Jasmine having injured herself in some way.

'She's talking to herself. Well, when I say talking to herself, she's talking to the teddies and dolls, but it's all weird stuff. It's like she's gone loopy or something. It's not like she's playing with them. It's freaking me out. She needs her head examining.'

Erica said she'd been trying to read in the bedroom when Jasmine had burst in. I told her I'd go up and see what was going on.

'Come in!' Jasmine said brightly when I knocked on the bedroom door.

'Hello, sweetheart, are you OK?'

'No, but what are you going to do about it? You can kill me if you want.'

'Jasmine, please don't say things like that. I like you very much. You're a lovely girl and I want you to be happy, and clean, and well looked after. That is why I ask you to take showers and clean your teeth, and I make sure your clothes are washed and ironed and you have healthy food to eat.'

'You do it because you get paid.' She turned to the teddies. 'She does it because she gets paid. We know, don't we?'

'We have the florists and that pays our bills. We don't foster for the money. We foster children like you and Erica because we want to help. I want to help you. I want to support you. I'm here for you and I would be here for you even if I wasn't fostering you anymore.'

She stared at me and said nothing. 'We used to foster Anthony,' I reminded her, 'but even though he's not in care anymore we are still helping him, because we care about him. There is no need to be rude to me. We all just want to get along, live nicely together and be as happy as we can be.'

I didn't get through to Jasmine. She started talking to her dolls and teddies again, saying odd things and ignoring me. It was as if I wasn't even in the room.

'I went through the red door,' she said. 'Green door, red door.' Then she told a Sindy doll, 'I told them and I shouldn't have. Just look at that. Would you hit me?'

She took the doll, made it punch her in the arm and then turned and smirked at me.

'Sweetheart, I'm going downstairs now. You know where I am if you want me. I'll be up again shortly.'

I felt I had no choice but to leave her to it. When I got downstairs I apologised to Erica for the fact she couldn't relax in her own bedroom. Then, for the next hour or so, I checked on Jasmine regularly. She either studiously ignored me or made pointed remarks, via the teddies, such as, 'Here she is again. Don't tell her anything, I'm warning you!'

That night Jasmine banged on the wall and woke Erica up, which she hadn't done for many weeks.

I didn't sleep well and my nerves were twanging. When I did sleep, I had an awful dream in which I saw Jasmine running away down the street, her fair hair billowing out behind her. I couldn't catch her up, and when she looked back the scar on her head stood out because it looked much bigger than it was in real life, and it was an angry, blood red instead of its typical silvery colour.

'I'm not sure I can take much more of this,' I said to Jonathan in the morning. 'I feel like we're on a tightrope.'

Jasmine had been with us for more than six weeks now, though it felt like longer. Our first placement meeting was overdue as, by rights, this should take place every six weeks, organised by the child's social worker. A placement meeting is a forum to discuss any issues relating to the child, such as their family background, any medical issues, their day-to-day care, schooling and safe-caring strategies. Unfortunately, we hadn't heard from Stewart for a few weeks, and he'd failed to return half a dozen calls.

'It's starting to feel like we're being deliberately ignored,' I commented after yet another one of my calls to Stewart went straight to answerphone.

'Well, it's a busy time of year for everyone,' Jonathan reasoned. 'And it's not as if we haven't seen anything of him at all, just not recently.'

'You're being generous,' I said, 'but I suppose it is the season of goodwill. I just feel uneasy about the fact he seems to have gone incommunicado, that's all, and I don't like to ignore my gut instinct. That's always a dangerous thing to do.'

Finally, we got a brief message to say Stewart would pay us a visit before Christmas. He left this on our answerphone at home, telling me the date and time and that he would 'drop in' to the house.

'At last!' I said. 'If we hadn't seen him this week, we'd have been into the New Year before we knew it, and there's a lot to talk about.'

When I checked my diary I saw it had been almost three weeks since Stewart had last been in contact with us. I also realised I'd fixed up to see a friend on the day of his visit, which I hastily rearranged. My friend was very understanding when I explained how important it was for me to see the social worker.

By chance, Caitlin phoned me on the morning of Stewart's visit, which was unexpected. We'd been told that her period of sick leave had been extended, and she was now signed off on long-term sick leave.

'It's stress,' Caitlin told me. 'I just wanted you to know, in case you thought it was something more serious.'

'Well, that is serious,' I said. 'I'm sorry to hear that.'

I wasn't exactly surprised that stress was the cause of her sick leave. Caitlin worked over and above her allotted hours on a regular basis, taking calls even if she was at home, and rarely failing to pick up her mobile at any time of the day. She never seemed to switch off and I knew she also became emotionally involved with some of the carers and children she was responsible for, which is something of an occupational hazard for social workers.

I gently told her off. 'You shouldn't be ringing me when you're off sick. You need to rest and stop worrying about other people.'

'I know, but I realise you don't have another support

social worker. I just wanted to make sure you are OK, and to wish you a Happy Christmas. How's it going?'

I didn't want to burden Caitlin with any extra worry so I was somewhat economical with the truth. The fact of the matter was, Jonathan and I had reached the point where we were seriously questioning how long we could go on with Jasmine.

She had received a two-day exclusion from school, for having a temper tantrum in the greenhouse and pulling up saplings, and also for fighting. This time she had caused another child to have a nosebleed. When she was at home it was very taxing trying to keep her entertained and out of trouble.

'We're doing OK,' I told Caitlin. 'Jasmine's grandparents have stepped up their efforts to take her in and we're hoping that might come off. We think it will be better for her to be with family, or maybe in a single placement, but of course it's so close to Christmas so nothing will happen now. We'll have to wait until the New Year to find out more.' I told her about the psychological assessment that was booked in, and I also explained that Stewart was due to visit that afternoon.

'Good luck and I hope everything goes well. And how is Erica?'

'She's OK, but I'm sure she'd prefer it if Jasmine wasn't here, to be honest. It's been disruptive for her, having Jasmine in her bedroom and at the same school.' I explained that Erica was going to stay with relatives for a few weeks over Christmas and was really looking forward to it.

'Diane's going to come for dinner on Christmas Day, so that will be nice,' I added.

Caitlin laughed. 'Typical of you to have one out and one in. How many will you have for dinner?'

'Six,' I said. 'Me and Jonathan, Mum, Diane, Anthony and Jasmine.'

'Lovely! It should be fun. It's great to have a full house at Christmas.'

I asked after Caitlin's family and she asked after my mum and Anthony.

'Mum's doing extremely well, thanks. Back to her old self, more or less, but the GP has warned her not to get too carried away. She'll be moving back home before long. Anthony's great. Full of beans. I expect he'll also be ready to move out before too long. He's almost saved enough to get a flat and start his HGV training.'

Caitlin said she was pleased to hear the good news.

'Merry Christmas, Angela. Give my best to Jonathan and hopefully I'll be back at work before we know it.'

'Merry Christmas, Caitlin. I appreciate the call.'

Jonathan was outside cleaning the windows when Stewart arrived.

'What are you doing up there?' Stewart asked, craning his neck to look up at Jonathan, who was perched on a ladder.

'Cleaning the windows.'

'I can see that,' he said disapprovingly, looking at his watch. 'But we've got a meeting.'

Jonathan bristled. No other social worker had ever

expected us to be standing on ceremony, waiting for their arrival. They were often running late and it would not make sense to sit and wait on the dot of the appointment time. Nevertheless, Jonathan dutifully came down from the ladder and showed Stewart into the kitchen. I could tell immediately that the atmosphere between the two of them was a bit tense. Perhaps as a result of this, Jonathan was quicker to cut to the chase than perhaps he normally would have been.

'I have to tell you, Stewart, we're not really very happy with how this placement has been managed.'

I was making a pot of tea and was quite taken aback at Jonathan's frankness.

'Aren't you?' Stewart replied, arching one eyebrow. 'And why is that?'

Jonathan had a list of things to discuss that we had talked about privately. He went through it calmly, while Stewart listened in silence. It included the fact we'd been given so little background information that we'd felt rather coerced into keeping Jasmine on when things had broken down with Fran, even though we didn't have a separate bedroom for her, and that nobody had prepared us for the fact Jasmine had a history of being excluded from school.

'We still feel like we're in the dark about so many things.' He gave the fire at the family home as an example. 'I understand that Jasmine's moving in with us was sudden and unplanned, but it feels like Social Services were very quick to allow her respite stay to turn into a placement, despite being very slow to fill us in on some important details.'

I gave Jonathan an encouraging smile: I felt he'd summed this up well and had made our point politely but firmly.

Stewart asked if we'd discussed this with Caitlin.

'No,' I told him. 'She's off on sick leave, isn't she?'

'Oh yes,' Stewart said vaguely. Either he didn't know about this or had forgotten, I thought. He cleared his throat. 'Look, there is always a choice,' he said starkly. 'Do you want her out?'

'I wouldn't put it like that,' Jonathan said, clearly unimpressed by Stewart's abruptness and turn of phrase. 'We want what's best for her, and we are very unsure whether staying with us is the best long-term solution for Jasmine. It would be good to talk about this, be armed with as much information as possible, and to feel that our opinion is being heard, that's all.'

'That's why I'm here,' Stewart said, somewhat sarcastically. 'That's what placement meetings are for.'

I told him we hadn't realised this was the six-weekly placement meeting; when he booked the appointment he'd made it sound like he would be simply calling in for a catch-up visit.

'I thought it was obvious. I take it Jasmine's in?'

'Yes, she is. The girls broke up from school yesterday.'

'Well there's no problem, is there?'

I poured us all a cup of tea, set out a plate of biscuits and helped myself to a chocolate digestive. I saw Jonathan take a deep breath.

We talked about the psychology appointment – it was going to take place in the first week in January – and thanked Stewart for setting it up. But Stewart looked ill at ease – vexed, even – and began to run one hand through his thinning hair.

'We're very grateful you got that booked up so quickly,' I said. 'We have been questioning whether Jasmine is safe. This is one of the reasons we think she might be better off in a single placement, where she can get more one-to-one care and attention.'

'Is this what Jasmine wants?'

This was an unexpected question and Jonathan and I looked at each other. It's not something we would ever discuss with any child, not knowing if a placement move was a realistic possibility and having no power over what Social Services might decide.

'I think she would be happy living with her grandparents and that would be the best move for her,' I replied. 'I wouldn't want her to go through the disruption of starting another placement that may go wrong, because what would happen then?'

Stewart didn't answer me, and he continued to look annoyed. I would not have been surprised if he'd stood up and walked out of the room; it looked like he would rather have been anywhere but in our kitchen, talking to Jonathan and me.

'What are your thoughts, Stewart?' I asked eventually. 'Is there anything you can tell us, any feedback at all?'

Stewart's reply left us scratching our heads. 'I agree that this does not sound like the best placement for Jasmine but if aunts and uncles were set up locally to take her out, and the correct support was put in place, it could work. Failing that, we could look at placing her in a special unit or children's home, if things don't go in favour of the grandparents.'

'We have not been told about any aunts and uncles. She's spoken of Aunty Ruth recently, but there has been no previous mention of her, not from Social Services, nor from her previous carer or grandparents. Where are these aunts and uncles?'

'I don't know. I'll have to look into that.'

I questioned whether Social Services might have the same concerns about aunts and uncles as they did about Jasmine's grandparents.

'What do you mean?' Stewart looked bemused.

'I mean, Social Services have concerns about Jasmine's father making contact through Pearl and Lenny. Surely if she lived with other family members there might be similar concerns?'

Stewart didn't seem to have an answer to this. 'Let me make a note of that,' he said, scratching his head. 'You make a valid point. May I see Jasmine?'

'I'll fetch her,' Jonathan said. 'She's just in the dining room, on the computer.'

As Jonathan stood up, Stewart asked if Jasmine had made any further allegations against him. He'd obviously read my notes about the time Jasmine threw herself on the floor in the lounge and accused him of pushing her.

'No,' Jonathan said. 'She has not.'

Neither of us could put our finger on why, but Stewart seemed intent on rubbing Jonathan up the wrong way. I stood up and we fetched Jasmine together. She pulled a face when we said Stewart would like a word, but she came off the computer without complaint.

'Here she is,' I said. 'You can both go up to the lounge and we'll stay in the kitchen.'

'Who are you again?' Jasmine suddenly asked, staring at her social worker.

Stewart looked annoyed and a little embarrassed. 'I'm your social worker. Don't you remember we met a few weeks ago?'

'Oh yeah.'

I showed them up to the lounge and, no more than five minutes later, Stewart and Jasmine came back downstairs and into the kitchen.

'All done,' Stewart said. 'I wish you all a very Happy Christmas. Good luck with the appointment.'

With the Christmas break, we knew we wouldn't see Stewart again until after the psychological assessment. 'Thanks again for fixing that up, and please let us know if there's any news from your end.'

'You're very welcome,' Stewart said, putting his shoulders back and finally looking less riled.

I was genuinely very grateful to him for making that appointment, but unfortunately it seemed to me that this was about all he'd done for Jasmine in the time he'd been her social worker. He didn't appear to have been any support to her, or to have made any effort to really get to know her.

Just as he was going out the door he turned back and said to Jasmine, 'What did you say your aunty was called?'

She looked shocked.

'What aunty?'

'Aunty Ruth?' I offered.

'Oh, that was a joke! You fell for it! Ha ha, I don't have an Aunty Ruth, silly!'

'Do you have any aunties or uncles at all you are in touch with?' Jonathan asked.

'No,' she said.

'Leave it with me,' Stewart said, dashing off. He looked like he couldn't get away fast enough.

The next day I decided to call Stewart and ask him if he'd checked Jasmine's records for other relatives. I was quite surprised when he picked up the phone straight away and also had a definitive answer for me.

'Yes,' he said briskly. 'I've dealt with that. There are none, so that was all a red herring.'

'Really? I'm a bit confused. Why did you think there were aunts and uncles who might be able to support Jasmine?'

He told me that he'd been 'misled' by some old notes. It seemed that Jasmine must have invented aunties and uncles in her initial interviews with Social Services, just as she had with 'Aunty Ruth'. I imagined the poor girl had done this because she wanted to live with other family members, rather than being taken into care.

'I see,' I said. 'That's unfortunate.'

I actually felt it was careless of Stewart too, though of course I didn't say this. Clearly, Stewart had only read half the notes, perhaps in haste, and before the placement meeting it seemed he had not got to the part where Jasmine's file spelled out that the 'aunts and uncles' were a figment of her imagination. It was an embarrassing mistake for Stewart to have made and he clearly didn't want to dwell on it.

'Yes, it is unfortunate. I'm very busy, I'll have to go now. Merry Christmas!'

'I'm not sure his mind's on the job,' I said to Jonathan when I put the phone down.

'I'm not sure he's even cut out for the job,' Jonathan replied. It was uncharacteristic of him to be so blunt, but that's how strongly he felt.

We found out the next day, through a phone call from Pearl, that Stewart had recently been in contact with her and Lenny as part of Social Services' assessment of whether or not they could take her on. Stewart had completely failed to mention this at the meeting with us, even when we had specifically mentioned Jasmine's grandparents. Nothing seemed joined up; in fact, it was all quite a muddle. With Pearl and Lenny's appeal, Jasmine's life was already caught up in red tape. The last thing she needed was a social worker who seemed so distracted, I thought.

'What she really needs is a social worker who's going to roll his sleeves up and fight for her,' I said.

'Yes,' Jonathan agreed. 'Instead of fighting me!'

17

'You'll never be able to foster kids again!'

Erica went off to stay with her relatives and, in the last couple of days running up to Christmas, Jasmine was a delight to be with. She helped me wrap presents, deliver cards, make mince pies and create a decoration that was to be the centre-piece for our table.

'Will Father Christmas come down the chimney?' she asked, wide-eyed.

'I expect so,' I said. 'That's what he normally does. We'll leave him one of our mince pies and a carrot for Rudolph.'

'Can we? What about drinks? Shall we give him a drink? How about a whisker?'

I smiled to myself and thought what a joy it was to hear Jasmine sounding like any other excited eight-year-old.

'A whisky, do you mean?'

She giggled at her mistake. 'Whisker, ha ha! Father Christmas would laugh his head off if he heard me say that!'

* * *

Jasmine was first up on Christmas Day and she came hammering on our door.

'He's been! He's been! Come and see what I've got!'

'Have you opened your stocking?'

'Yes! I got a CD player! He must have got my letter I wrote in school! I got colouring pens and a chocolate selection box and a dance mat and a new pair of slippers and that *WALL-E* cuddly toy I wanted . . .'

Her eyes were shining and she was bouncing on her toes, like she usually did when she was excited.

I'd asked Jasmine the night before if she could come and get us when she woke up, so we could watch her open her stocking. She must have forgotten, which was understandable, though I would have loved to see her little face light up. This moment made up for it. I loved to see her like this, full of energy and life and with a big grin on her face.

Diane was a treasure while I prepared the dinner, playing games with Jasmine and painting her nails in lots of different sparkly colours. We were eating early – at one o'clock – because one of Jonathan's brothers and his wife, plus two of our nephews and their families, were coming over in the afternoon. It had been years since we'd seen this set of relatives on Christmas Day, and we were really looking forward to it.

Our meal was delicious and I loved having Mum, Diane and Anthony around the table with us. Anthony was on great form, reading all the terrible jokes out of the crackers in silly voices, pretending he'd singed his eyebrows on the flames when we lit the Christmas pudding and teasing my mum about being drunk when she had probably only sipped an inch of wine with her meal.

'Isn't it lovely?' I said, looking at everyone gathered together.

'It is,' Jonathan said. 'What a great day, and I can't wait to see my brother and all his lot. What a treat.'

'Who is coming?' Jasmine asked, for the umpteenth time. 'Who are they, again?'

'One of my brothers and his wife, plus their two sons – our nephews – and their children,' Jonathan told her. 'My nephews have five children between them.' He ran through the names of everyone, showed Jasmine a photograph and pointed out how old the children were. They ranged in age from four to fourteen and included an eight-year-old girl, Bethany. Naturally, we hope she and Jasmine might hit it off, as they were so close in age.

By the time our visitors arrived, Jasmine was completely absorbed in playing with her new dance mat. It was one of those sensor pad mats that you rigged up to the television, and you had to follow the steps on the screen and try to keep in time with the music. Diane had played with Jasmine for a while and Anthony had had a go too, though he was hilariously uncoordinated. Jasmine was taking a solo challenge, watched by Diane, when we introduced her to our relatives.

'Hello Jasmine, can Bethany play with you?' her mum, Caroline, asked.

'What?' Jasmine said, snapping her head round. She looked annoyed to have been interrupted, and she missed her step.

'Jasmine, I think it would be kind if you let Bethany play with you, after you've finished your turn,' Diane said.

'You've made me go wrong now! Grrr!'

'Never mind. Look, you can press reset and have another go.'

Jasmine did as Diane suggested and begrudgingly said Bethany could have a go next, after she'd finished the round she was on. We'd set the mat up on a small TV we kept as a spare. It was in the dining room, and we pushed the table against the wall to make room.

'Can you watch them?' I asked Diane, as I wanted to fetch drinks for the visitors.

'Sure,' she grinned. 'I'm hoping I'll get another turn. I think Father Christmas has come up trumps.'

Caroline and I left the dining room and went into the kitchen and started to fix the drinks. Jonathan came in and I told him Jasmine had been a bit grumpy.

'I'll go and pop my head round the door,' he said. 'Make sure she's settled down.'

'Thanks,' Caroline said. 'You know what little girls can be like!'

Jonathan crossed the hall to the dining room and moments later I heard a commotion. Jasmine was shouting, 'Ow, ow, ow!'

'What's happened?' I said, dashing to the dining room.

'He pushed me!' Jasmine said. She was writhing around on the dance mat, clutching her arm and still saying 'Ow, ow, ow'. 'I'm going to tell that social worker what he did!' she spat. 'Ow! You'll never be able to foster kids again! Never! Ow!'

Caroline was right behind me. I turned and saw her face: she looked mortified on Jonathan's behalf.

'I was nowhere near,' he said. The colour had drained from his face, and he looked at me in alarm. He was standing at the back of the dining room, by the door.

'Bethany, love, did you see what happened?' Caroline asked her daughter.

Wide-eyed, Bethany stepped forward. 'Mummy, Uncle Jonathan didn't push her.' She took another step forward, distancing herself from Jasmine, who was still on the floor and groaning as if in pain. Whispering, Bethany added, 'As soon as that big girl – what's her name? – went to the toilet, she did that. Like, she threw herself down.'

Jasmine heard what Bethany said and got to her feet. 'It's true!' she said, less vehemently than before. 'He pushed me! He did.'

'You come with me,' Caroline said to her daughter. 'We'll leave you to it I think, Angela.'

I nodded, thinking to myself that this sounded very similar to the previous time she had accused Jonathan. Caroline led Bethany up to the lounge, giving Jonathan and me a sympathetic look as she left. Jasmine stayed lying on the floor but turned her back to us. I think she knew she hadn't got away with this one, even before Diane returned and gave us her take on it. She said that she had seen Jonathan enter the dining room just before she went to the toilet. 'I heard Jasmine shouting out well before he had a chance to cross the room and be anywhere near the girls. The timing was all wrong.'

Diane widened her eyes and mouthed to me that she had something else to say.

I stepped into the doorway, where I could still see Jasmine and also talk to Diane without being overheard.

'I don't know what's up with her,' Diane hissed. 'She did something else odd.'

'Go on.'

'Bethany asked Jasmine where her mum was and Jasmine went as still as a statue and started talking weirdly, like a machine or something. She told Bethany, "I never had a mum." I think it spooked Bethany a bit as Jasmine said it without showing any emotion. It was kind of weird. I don't know anything about Jasmine's mum, but what she said just didn't sound right.'

I thanked Diane and said I'd have a word with Jasmine. Jonathan watched discreetly from the doorway as I went up to Jasmine and asked her if she would get up off the floor.

'What's the point?' she seethed. 'I'm not worth it. I shouldn't have any presents. You can send them all back!'

She tugged feebly at the dance mat, in a half-hearted attempt to pull the wires out of the TV.

'Jasmine, of course you deserve Christmas presents. Now please get up.'

She didn't move. I tried to steer the conversation back to what mattered. 'Why are you on the floor, sweetheart?'

'Because he pushed me.'

Her accusatory tone had vanished and she said this in a small, uncertain voice. I knew she didn't believe her own lie.

'Sweetheart, that is not what happened, is it? Tell me what really happened.'

'Who cares? Nobody cares about me. Why don't you just go back to all your visitors?'

She sat up now and pushed her hair back off her face. 'Nobody else has a scar on their head, do they? See this?' She prodded her scar. 'This is mine. You don't have one. You don't know what it's like to be me. You and your mum . . .' She bit her lip.

'Can I give you a cuddle?'

'No. No thanks.'

'Are you sure?'

'Sorry, Angela.'

It was unusual for her to say sorry and I acknowledged this and gave her a grateful smile.

'It's OK, Jasmine. Do you want to tell me anything about your scar? Or anything else? You can, you know.'

I had hunched down so I was on the same level, as it's never a good idea to tower over a child who is probably already feeling small, or perhaps insignificant.

Jasmine shook her head and said she was OK now.

'If you change your mind about the cuddle, let me know. I'm always happy to have a hug.'

She forced the faintest smile.

I had a good idea what was going on here. It was understandable that Jasmine had been unsettled by all our visitors. She'd started the day feeling at the centre of attention, opening her presents from Father Christmas and telling Jonathan and me all about them. She'd been comfortable around the dinner table with the people she knew and, crucially, she was not the odd one out. Diane and Anthony were former foster children of ours and she knew they were also away from their own relatives on Christmas Day. Seeing all these other visitors, our extended family, must have magnified any fears Jasmine had of being seen to be an outsider, or someone who was not as loved and cherished as others. Bethany was with her parents and grandparents and surrounded by cousins and aunts and uncles. It must have been hard for Jasmine not to feel envious, I thought.

It would be a few years before I gained a greater insight into what had happened that day. We went to a training session and learned that kids in care can feel 'invisible' if they are not getting the amount of attention they are used to from their carers. Christmas is a well-known flashpoint, because visitors take away a great deal of your attention. Jonathan and I had been extremely busy, looking after everybody else, while all Jasmine probably wanted was for us to be there for her, cheering her on as she played on her dance mat. Having another eight-year-old girl as part of the team of distractors – a girl she no doubt perceived to be in a luckier position than her – was most likely what lit the blue touchpaper and made Jasmine want to lash out. Jonathan was the focus of her anger, just as he had been before. Sadly, I don't think we needed a training course to work out why that was, given how her father had treated her.

We put a call in to out-of-hours to cover ourselves in case Jasmine stood by her allegation but thankfully, not long after all our visitors had gone, she admitted that Jonathan hadn't pushed her.

'I thought he had,' she started.

'Thought he had?'

'I thought Jonathan pushed me but I got it wrong. Er, yeah. I didn't mean to.'

'OK, thanks for telling me. I'm glad we've got that straightened out.'

She looked relieved that I left it there.

Jasmine joined in some party games and went to bed tired but happy. She was asleep within minutes, I think. Meanwhile, Jonathan and I ended the day feeling exhausted and thankful. The incident had certainly put a dampener on things, but we didn't let it spoil Christmas. On the whole, it had been a brilliant day.

'I wonder what Christmas was like for her at home?' I said when we got into bed.

There was still a large black hole where I wished I saw memories and history for Jasmine. I found it quite disconcerting, knowing so little about her past. We imagined that the previous Christmas could not have been good – from what we'd heard, we reckoned her mother must have gone by then, leaving her alone with her father.

'I hope she had some good ones,' Jonathan said wistfully. 'She certainly knew all about Santa and leaving food for the reindeers. That's all reassuring. She expected a stocking, didn't she? All that has happened before. The turkey, the trimmings. The crackers. All of that. She's had Christmases, Angela.'

I smiled at Jonathan. He could tell I was feeling emotional. I think Christmas sets your emotions off at the best of times. Mum had talked nostalgically about Dad and my brother, who had been taken too soon, many years earlier. Jonathan and his brother had raised a glass to their late parents. I knew poor Anthony and Diane would be feeling the pain of the families they had become estranged from since going into care.

As my head hit the pillow I felt sleep rush over me. It had been a long day and I was absolutely shattered.

'Night, love,' I said. 'Thanks for everything . . .'

There was a polite knock on our bedroom door. I jolted my head up off the pillow.

'Who is it?'

My initial thought was that Mum had got up and needed help.

There was no reply, just another knock.

'I'll go,' I said, switching on my bedside light.

'No, I will.'

Jonathan and I both got out of bed, put on our dressing gowns and answered the knock.

'Oh my god! Jasmine, what on earth . . .'

She had her dressing gown cord looped around her neck and was holding each end out to the side of her. Her face was pale and expressionless, and in the reflected light she had black rings under her eyes.

18

'It's a secret. Shh. Don't tell.'

By New Year we were in crisis. The dressing gown cord incident had knocked us for six and it seemed to plunge Jasmine into a darker, more troubled phase.

'Jasmine, come on now, take that cord off,' I'd cajoled calmly on Christmas night, trying hard not to show my distress and alarm.

She stared back at me, unblinking. The cord was not pulled tight and it was clear that she could not have done any harm to herself simply by holding out each end. The cord was longer than her outstretched arms, and she was statue-still, making no attempt at pulling the cord taut and tightening the loop around her neck. Even so, it was extremely disturbing to see her like this. Her message seemed very clear. She was telling us she wanted to do harm to herself, even if she wasn't actually going to do it.

'Jasmine, why don't we go and get a drink?'

Still no response. I remembered the day she'd got into

trouble at school for behaving badly when the class made Christmas cards.

'I wish I could tie a piece of string around my neck and die and then I wouldn't have to be HERE with YOU!' That's what she'd yelled at Jonathan on the way home that day.

Jonathan said he remembered that too, perhaps at the same time. He took a step back and let me continue to try to engage with Jasmine.

'How about I take you back up to your room? It's late and we've got lovely things planned for tomorrow.'

She continued to stare.

Eventually, when all my efforts fell on deaf ears, Jonathan tried humour. 'How about tying that in a bow, it would look better?' he said, over my shoulder.

That might seem like a flippant way to deal with a situation like this, but sometimes a crass joke makes all the difference. Thankfully, it worked.

'Why would I do that?' Jasmine replied, jolting her head up to look at Jonathan. She was still staring eerily, but at least she had said something.

'Why not?' Jonathan said with a shrug.

'You're weird,' she told him.

She'd dropped her arms to her sides now and the dressing gown cord was hanging loosely down the front of her pyjamas. Jonathan stepped back into our bedroom, sensing that his job was done and thinking he was better off out of the way completely now. I gave him a discreet nod to let him know I would take this from here.

'Come on,' I said brightly, 'I don't know about you, but

I'm really tired. What a long day we've had. What was your favourite part?'

To my relief she turned and started to walk slowly along our landing. She looked like she was sleep-walking, or at least trying to make it look like she was sleep-walking, but I didn't react to this. Instead I chivvied her up the stairs to her bedroom, chatting about the silly cracker jokes and the dance mat.

'I liked having everyone around the table. Wasn't it lovely? What did you enjoy?'

'Not being with my dad,' she said.

'Not being with your dad?'

'Mmm. He hit me. You don't know. When I told them it was me who started it, he got worser and worser and she . . .'

My heart felt like it had stopped. Her babyish use of the word 'worser' grated painfully. She was such a little girl, and she had clearly been horribly abused and traumatised.

'There was a fire engine and smoke coming through the window and my mum.'

She stopped.

'Your mum?'

'She was magicked away. The smoke and the fire came and then she went invisible, away. She's invisible. Out of the green door.'

'Magicked away?'

'It's a secret. Shh. Don't tell.' Jasmine put her fingers to her lips and widened her eyes. I got no further with her that evening. I watched over her until she fell asleep, which thankfully did not take long.

* * *

267

When Jasmine saw her grandparents a few days later, at last she was in a better, brighter mood. I told Pearl what had happened on Christmas night. She couldn't shed any light on Jasmine's worrying actions or comments; there was nothing she could pass on that was new or enlightening.

'She only perked up when she started to get ready to see you,' I said. 'We've done lots of lovely things over the last few days – ice-skating, walks in the park, playing with new games – but Jasmine has been in a bad mood the whole time. I thought she'd be better as Erica is still away and she's had a lot of attention, but no. It's like there's been a black cloud following her around. We're used to her being difficult some of the time, but not all of the time. It's been testing.'

Pearl sympathised. I told her we were managing, but this was stretching the truth. Privately, Jonathan and I were admitting defeat to one another. We were dreading what would happen when Erica came back, if Jasmine was behaving like this when she had our undivided attention. We'd had a terrible temper tantrum at the ice rink, she'd tried to run away in the park and she'd thrown counters from a new board game out of an upstairs window. When Mum tried to stop her she was very rude and started growling and knocking furniture over.

I didn't go into all this detail with Pearl, but I did tell her we were hoping very much that Social Services would make their final decision soon.

'She's always better behaved with you and seems in a happier frame of mind, which is hardly surprising. You're her grandparents, and you love her. She knows that. It's only natural she wants to be with you.'

The truth was, Jonathan and I were at breaking point, and if it hadn't still been the Christmas holidays I'd have been on the phone to Stewart, telling him we felt Jasmine's placement had become unsustainable and was in danger of breaking down.

Erica came home and was glowing with excitement when she told us about the wonderful time she'd had. We had a couple of days when not very much happened and we had no trouble, but the day before the girls were due to return to school Jasmine sank into one of the foulest moods we'd seen, which seemed to poison the atmosphere for everyone. Erica's smiley face fell and she withdrew to her bedroom, looking cowed.

'If anyone makes me go to school tomorrow I'll throw them down the stairs.'

Mum heard Jasmine say this, and she took me to one side. The plan had been for Mum to move back to her own place at the weekend, after her next hospital appointment, but she told me she would like to leave in the next day or two, if that were possible.

'I'm perfectly fit now,' she said tactfully. 'I'm ready to get back into my old routine just as soon as we can get the house ready for me.'

'I understand, Mum. I'm sorry things aren't calmer here. I'll make a start tomorrow and we'll have you home as quickly as we can.'

'It's not your fault. You know I don't like to interfere, but I really do think Jasmine needs some sort of professional help. I'm not suggesting you and Jonathan aren't more than capable, but—'

'We're on the case, Mum. You don't need to worry.'

When I told Jonathan what Mum had said, he had a wry smile on his face. It was her use of the term 'professional help' that prompted this. Foster carers aren't always considered to be 'professionals', even after decades of specialist training. Nevertheless, Social Services leave damaged, traumatised children in our care, often against our better judgement and with less support than we would like. It was nobody's fault. As I've said before, the system is reactive, and a lack of funding means it has to be this way. We accepted that we would probably have to go to the wire with Jasmine, because Social Services had other priorities, including children with no home at all. That's just the way it was, and still is today.

We managed to get Jasmine to school, but it was a terrible struggle. She refused to shower, eat breakfast, clean her teeth, put on her uniform. Everything was a drama. At one point she even barricaded herself in the dining room.

'I'll take Erica,' Jonathan called through the door. 'And Angela will wait and bring you to school when you are ready, Jasmine.'

'What? Why would you do that? What's the point?'

'The point is, you are not ready and you are going to make Erica late.'

I supported Jonathan. 'That's a good idea. You and I will

have to go in via reception and explain why you are late. It's not a problem for me, but the school will not be happy with you.'

Jasmine computed this, no doubt realising that she would be in a hole, as it would be obvious the lateness was her fault and nobody else's.

'That's stupid!' she blurted, bursting out of the dining room. 'What a waste of time. Durgh! I'm getting ready. See if you can stop me!'

Despite this apparent show of willingness, Jasmine started complaining relentlessly on the walk to school, cranking herself up into quite a frenzy.

'I don't want to be in school all day. Can I come out at lunchtime? I don't want to go! I hate school! Why are you forcing me to go? I just don't get it.'

She kept up her grumbling all the way there and had got herself into such a twist that she was shouting very loudly when we reached the path close to the school.

'I hate school! I'll do it! I'll hit someone, I will. Give me a stick!'

Erica was pink with embarrassment and asked if she could walk through the gate with one of her close friends and her mother, who we could see up ahead. I knew them well and said that was fine. I watched Erica run up and greet her friend, and the two of them skipped past the teacher who was on playground duty, making sure no children slipped back out of the gate once they'd been dropped off. Erica's friend's mum turned and gave me a warm smile, which was very welcome.

Poor Erica, I thought. *It's not fair on her, starting her day with all this stress and strife.*

'Jasmine,' I said, when we were alone. 'Please do your best in school today. You're a lovely girl and you are a clever girl. Please work hard and play nicely.'

'If I do, will you let me off?'

'Let you off what?'

She smirked and didn't reply.

I spent most of the day helping Mum prepare for her move home. Her house needed airing and dusting, there was post to deal with and I wanted to get her fridge freezer cleaned out and switched back on, as we'd emptied it when she'd come to stay with us.

It was raining and I was tired by the time I got back to the school at home time. I definitely could have done without receiving a very pronounced thumbs-down from Miss Dowden across the playground.

'Where do I start?' she said wearily. She listed several issues, including throwing equipment, giving cheek to Miss Jenson and refusing to keep quiet and do her work. 'It's such a shame. She seems to be on a path of self-destruction. Is there anything I should know about?'

I said that Christmas in general may have had a negative impact on Jasmine, because of the reasons I've mentioned earlier. Miss Dowden frowned. She seemed upset at this idea. Rain was drumming on my umbrella and she invited me to step inside the classroom.

'It's often a very difficult period for children in care,' I explained, shuddering as I carried my brolly awkwardly through the narrow doorway and accidentally splattered rain in my face. 'Hopefully she'll start to settle, now she's back at school.'

Miss Dowden nodded. 'I hope so too. Good luck tomorrow, by the way. It's her appointment, isn't it?'

'Yes, it is, so we'll be collecting her early.'

'I know. Good luck. Hopefully the assessment will help us all. Fingers crossed.'

Jasmine seemed to be very agitated when we walked home from school that day. 'What is Erica doing? What are we having for dinner? Can I watch TV? How long do I get on the computer?'

She was firing questions out at nobody in particular; her eyes were darting everywhere and she wasn't waiting for answers. Also, Erica was right beside her when she asked what she was doing.

'Why don't you ask Erica what she has got planned this evening?'

Erica ignored her and pulled away to jump over a puddle on the pavement. The girls had not fallen out as such; I'd say they were reluctantly managing to tolerate each other. It had been this way since Erica had come back from her Christmas stay with relatives. Jasmine had asked her nothing about it – I guess she might have been jealous that Erica had family to stay with over the festive period – and Erica had seemed quite happy to keep out of her way and have minimum contact.

The girls had each been making Mum a card to give her when she moved out and I tried to steer the conversation this way. They'd put a great deal of effort into them and I knew Mum would love them. Erica's was extremely neat and she'd spent ages colouring in a border and sticking little sequins on the flowers she'd drawn, while Jasmine's was covered in stickers and busy patterns.

'Mum's going to be so thrilled when she sees her cards. And won't it be great for you to have a room each when she moves out? Jasmine, you can put up some of your new posters on the wall if you like?'

Jasmine frowned and looked at me suspiciously. 'I want to live with Granny and Granddad. Why can't I? It's not fair. I'm ringing them. I'm telling them. Granny said she wants me to move in with her.'

I couldn't control what Pearl or Lenny said to Jasmine on their trips out and I would not have dreamed of interfering, but I didn't think it was helpful for Pearl to keep telling Jasmine she wanted her to live with them. What if it didn't work out?

Before I could answer Jasmine, Erica chimed up. 'I'll miss your mum. Will we ever see her again?'

This gave me a pang, because it reminded me how young Erica was, and of the damage that is done when kids are taken away from members of their family. It's not uncommon for them to think any adult in their life might disappear without trace. Erica knew very well my mum lived close by. She had visited the house before Mum stayed with us and she also knew Mum babysat for us and visited often, and that I had a close relationship with her. Yet still Erica asked the question, 'Will we ever see her again?' I found that very sobering, and sad.

'Of course we'll see her,' I said brightly. 'She'll still be coming around for plenty of visits to our house, and for meals. And we can visit her in her house, like we did before.'

'Really? Oh that's cool!'

'Yes. And as a matter of fact, Mum is going to babysit for us next week.'

Jasmine looked at me accusingly. 'Where are you going? I don't want a babysitter!'

'Don't worry, Jasmine. We have a fostering meeting next week. It's a support session, that's all. Mum said she'll sit with you and Erica, as I think Anthony will be working that evening. She has always babysat for us, for many years. All the years we've been fostering.'

'Absolute joke!' Jasmine said, tossing her hair over her shoulder and pouting like an insolent teenager. 'I'm telling Social Services!'

I let that one go. It was impossible to try to tackle Jasmine's every gripe or criticism head on. I hoped that Anthony's shifts might change, so both he and Mum could babysit together, but I kept this to myself. Leaving Mum alone with the girls was not ideal, I thought, even though she was willing to give it a go.

When we got home Erica said she was going to do her homework in the dining room. Jasmine didn't have any homework and I let her go straight to the lounge to watch TV.

'You can have half an hour, Jasmine, and then I'll help you sort your things out, ready to move into Mum's old room. OK?'

Jasmine smirked as she ran up the stairs to the lounge.

Moments later I heard Erica scream. I dashed to the dining room to see what the matter was and found her holding the card she'd been making for Mum. There was a big blob of dried black paint daubed across the front of it.

'What's happened?'

'It's her! It's Jasmine! She's ruined it on purpose.'

I could see that the art materials had not been put away as neatly as they usually were and there was a small tube of black paint with the lid off. I suggested it could have been an accident as the cards had been stored alongside the paints but Erica was having none of it. She was ranting and raving, accusing Jasmine over and over again.

'It wasn't like this when I left it!'

Tears sprang from her eyes.

'Don't cry, sweetheart. Don't worry, you've got time to make a new one. I can help you, if you like.'

Jasmine appeared at the door. She was smirking and I remembered what she'd said to me that morning, which at the time did not make sense. 'If I do, will you let me off?' she'd said when I asked her to work hard and play nicely in school.

Had Jasmine deliberately spoilt Erica's card? Was this all tied up with the jealousy I suspected she felt about Erica going to stay with relatives at Christmas?

I suspected this was the case but of course I didn't know

for sure. All I knew was that I suddenly felt exhausted by the drama and I was starting to fear that Miss Dowden's words might sadly be very accurate: 'She seems to be on a path of self-destruction.'

If that was true, what did the future hold and how could we help Jasmine get on the right path? I hoped and prayed that the psychology appointment might give us some answers.

19

'Well I hope you behave yourself'

I woke the next morning with a sore throat and telltale aches in my bones, something that always signalled I was coming down with a nasty cold, if not flu.

'Are you sure you'll be OK coming to the psychology appointment?' Jonathan asked.

'Yes. There's no way you're going on your own with her, and we're not missing it.'

'That's not what I asked. Are you well enough?'

'Yes, love. I'll dose myself up today, take it easy and I'll be fine.'

I actually felt dreadful. The card incident had been very upsetting. It took Erica a long time to calm down and then she started crying and screaming all over again when Jasmine came down for dinner.

'She did it! I know she did it!'

Jasmine was adamant she had absolutely nothing to do with it. 'How would I? How could I? When would I?' She smirked and denied all knowledge.

'Anyway, it's only a stupid card! You can easily make another one. What's for dinner? When are we eating?'

Jasmine seemed to be behaving in a deliberately insensitive way, designed to cause offence and trouble. I spent the evening doing my best to keep the girls apart, but they had to sleep in the same room because it had been decided that Mum was staying with us for another two nights, as we'd discovered an issue with her central heating.

'Erica, come and find me immediately if you need anything,' I said at bedtime.

'Don't worry,' she said. 'I'll be OK.'

She turned her head to the wall as I said goodnight. Clearly, her tactic was to ignore Jasmine. I left it there. It's never a good idea to talk about any bad stuff immediately before lights out. It can stop kids sleeping and, in any case, there was not much more to say. I'd comforted Erica and promised I would do my best to get to the bottom of what had happened. Meanwhile Jasmine had tried to carry on as if nothing had happened and there was no point in badgering her about it; hopefully she might tell the truth in her own time, as she had done before. Also, as Jonathan reminded me, we had to remain open-minded and consider that, somehow, it had not been Jasmine's doing.

We had a horrible journey to the psychology appointment. It was icy on the roads and Jasmine was being as awkward as she could possibly be.

'Can you fasten your seat belt?'

'Why?'

'Because we're about to drive off.'

'But why? You're not going to crash are you?'

'Jasmine, just do it please. You know you need to fasten your seat belt.'

She smirked at me, fumbled with the belt, then said she couldn't manage it, even though she'd done it countless times before with no problem.

'I'll do it,' I said, lifting myself out of the passenger seat.

As soon as I was out of the car, pulling my coat around me and sniffling because my nose was running in the cold air, she swiftly fastened her seat belt. I blew my nose crossly and got back into my seat, a shiver running down my spine.

'Shall we have the radio on?' I said, trying to sound as cheerful as possible.

'No. I don't want the radio. Haven't you got any CDs?'

'I've got Rihanna.'

'Nah!'

'Katy Perry?'

'No thanks!'

'Taylor Swift?'

'Who?'

Jasmine liked Rihanna and Katy Perry and knew full well who Taylor Swift was – it was because of Jasmine that these CDs had found their way into the car from Erica's collection – but I let this go.

'Here we go. What about Leona Lewis?'

Jasmine had loved it when Leona Lewis did a guest appearance on *X Factor*. We'd watched it together and she'd told me she was her favourite winner of all time.

'Leona Lewis?' She thought about this for a moment. 'No, is that all you've got?'

I gave up, realising she was going to reject every suggestion I made.

'Yes, I'm afraid so. I'm putting the radio on.'

She complained when the travel news came on, then an advert. I switched the radio off after five minutes. My head was banging and I couldn't take any more of Jasmine's awkwardness. I closed my eyes and waited for my painkillers to kick in. Jonathan tapped my leg. 'Have a rest. I know the way.'

'Thanks,' I muttered wearily.

I'd recently read an article about resentment in one of my fostering magazines. It explained how resentment is an extremely powerful emotion. Children in care are often 'riddled with resentment', an expert was quoted as saying. 'Their resentment is most likely to be deep-rooted and linked to their earlier childhood, but that will not stop them making you the focus of their resentment, as you are the physical representation of the result of the unfolding consequences of their past. As the person towards whom the resentment is focused, you will most likely not be able to do right for doing wrong.'

I thought about this as I sat quietly, trying to shut out the noise of the windscreen wipers gnawing at the ice-covered windscreen and Jasmine's repeated complaints to Jonathan that she had nothing to do.

Jasmine clearly resented her situation, and who could blame her? She had been very unlucky in her life. Both parents had let her down. She was traumatised and angry. She'd been in care for many months and only now was she being seen by an expert, someone who could assess her needs and frailties and hopefully help her cope better in school, and in all situations in her life. It wasn't fair. Poor Jasmine had been let down far too much. I didn't want to let her down, and I felt guilty every time I talked about wanting her to move out and live with her grandparents. Would she feel rejected by us? What if Pearl and Lenny couldn't cope? Then what?

When we arrived at the address of the CAMHS office and consulting rooms, which were on the referral letter, a receptionist told us that the appointment with the psychologist was to last just under an hour. Once consent forms had been signed and a basic medical questionnaire had been filled out – we did the best we could with that, not knowing her full history – a member of staff was called and Jasmine was taken through to a side room.

'We'll be waiting for you when you come out,' I reassured her.

She seemed quiet but was compliant, which was as good as we could hope for.

The assessment was to take place in a room that had a two-way mirror along one side; this was the only thing we'd been told about in advance. We'd seen this type of set-up at police station interview rooms, when children had to give evidence or witness statements, or had a disclosure to make that might prompt a criminal investigation. The idea is to create an environment in which the child feels comfortable enough to talk freely, without feeling they are being watched or recorded, when actually they are, for legal or perhaps safeguarding reasons. In this case, I imagined the room was being used primarily to help Jasmine feel at ease, to allow the psychologist to talk to her one-to-one, without the need for his assistant or anyone else to sit in.

While the assessment took place, Jonathan and I sat on plastic chairs in a draughty waiting room along the corridor, reading out-of-date magazines and listening to traffic on the flyover that arched above the sprawling, rundown building.

The psychologist himself brought Jasmine back to us. He was called Dr Sharma, and, as his name suggested, he was quite charming.

'I'm recommending Jasmine see a colleague of mine,' he smiled. 'I'll file my report as quickly as possible and I will be asking for the appointment to be arranged at the earliest convenience.'

Jasmine looked remarkably relaxed and at ease, so I imagined the two-way mirror system had served its purpose. Dr Sharma's sparky-looking young assistant also smiled at us all, and I saw her give Jasmine an encouraging little wink.

'Very nice to meet you,' Dr Sharma said, shaking Jasmine by the hand. 'You were a very good patient.' The assistant gave Jasmine a friendly little fist pump, which made her giggle.

We thanked them both and left the office feeling surprisingly optimistic. We had no information about what had happened during the appointment, or what Jasmine may or may not have disclosed, but the atmosphere was certainly charged with positivity when she emerged, and Jasmine was in an infinitely better mood than she had been in on the journey there.

'So, how was it?'

'OK. He's funny, that doctor!'

'He seemed very nice.'

'Yeah.' She looked out of the car window, a peaceful look on her face.

'Anyone hungry?' Jonathan asked, when he spotted a Burger King sign. We'd already discussed giving Jasmine a treat on the way home, but he made it sound like a spontaneous decision.

'Yes!' Jasmine cheered. 'Can I have a burger? Can I have fries? Am I allowed Coke?'

She was bouncing in her seat, full of beans. I was transported back to our very first meeting with her. Whatever her issues, Jasmine was, by nature, a lively, talkative and excitable little girl. She had been through the mill and was struggling to come out the other side, and perhaps all she needed was to be supported through this transition. That's what I found myself thinking about. Surely she'd be able to leave her demons in the past, given the right medical care and support? There was nothing I hoped for or wanted to believe more in that moment.

'You can have whatever you fancy, Jasmine,' I said. I generally steer kids away from fizzy drinks and junk food, but I make an exception when we eat out. 'I'm really hungry. I think I'm going to go for a chicken burger, fries and coffee.'

Jonathan playfully rolled his eyes.

'Yes, I know what you're thinking,' I said. 'The New Year diet is still happening, but not just yet. It's too early to start now.'

'And why is that?' he asked.

'We've still got Christmas cake, half a tin of Quality Street and a packet of After Eights, that's why! The rule is, the diet starts when all the Christmas goodies are gone.'

'Oh yes, I remember that from last year,' he said, chortling as he spoke. 'Wasn't it nearly Easter?'

'Very funny,' I said, giving him a sarcastic smile.

I think we both felt mightily relieved that this appointment had happened and at least *something* was being done to address Jasmine's situation. As is often the case, neither of us realised how much pressure we were feeling until a little bit of it was released. We were both slightly giddy that we'd got to this point and Jasmine was in a good frame of mind.

Jasmine's school situation was also looking up. Miss Dowden had decided to put her on a 'behaviour schedule' which we were assured was designed to encourage good behaviour rather than punish bad behaviour.

'I'm very pleased they're trying something new,' I said to Jonathan. 'Things weren't working before with that "three strikes" business. Maybe this will make all the difference.'

'How does this behaviour schedule work?'

'It's basically earning points for good behaviour. It's all about positive support and encouragement.'

Miss Dowden had explained to me that the basic idea

was that Jasmine would have certain targets she needed to achieve, such as 'Stop talking when asked' or 'Tidy up at the end of the session'. If she hit her targets she would get points that added up to earn her some 'carpet time', which was basically time in the activity zone of the classroom, where you could choose to play a game, draw or do a puzzle.

'It sounds just like a star chart,' Jonathan said, looking a little dubious.

We'd long since given up on star charts as we'd found they could be counterproductive, setting kids up to fail and feel disappointed.

'I thought that, but Miss Dowden said there's more to it. You don't have to do anything brilliant to get points and you can gain carpet time quickly – it's not a long-winded schedule. It's about rewarding her for things she should be doing anyway, just a way of keeping her on track.'

Jonathan still looked unconvinced and I had to admit that it did sound a bit like a star chart, now I came to explain it.

'Do you think it's going to work?'

'I don't know. It sounded positive when Miss Dowden explained it, that's all. I'm glad they're trying something new and not giving up on her. That's good news. It has to be.'

Happily, Jasmine had a couple of great weeks at school. I can't describe the rush I felt when I saw Miss Dowden at the door, giving me the thumbs-up at home time, day after day.

'She's done everything she's been asked to do. She was

very kind to another girl who had trouble with the pottery they were working on. Top marks!'

'That's so good to hear.'

One afternoon, I had good news to give Miss Dowden. We'd got Jasmine's second appointment through.

'We should have a clearer picture soon, and hopefully that will improve things further still,' I told the teacher.

'Excellent! Let's hope we've turned a corner. She's had another good day in school and earned house points and extra carpet time for Friday afternoon.'

Things at home were not bad. Jasmine was dragging her heels in the morning quite a lot, she was rude to Jonathan one day when he asked her to carry a bag in from the car and she'd lost her temper and shouted at me when I wouldn't let her have extra time on the computer one afternoon. We got by without too much drama and upset, however, and life felt calmer and more manageable than it had done since Jasmine's arrival.

With Mum back in her own place now, there was less friction between Jasmine and Erica. They didn't have much to do with each other, and the damaged card incident had, thankfully, slipped into the past very quickly, as things often do with young children. We never got to the bottom of what happened. When Jonathan and I looked back we were quite certain that Jasmine had been the last person in the dining room that day, plus that odd exchange about 'will you let me off?' would have taken place shortly after she put the paint on the card, if that's what had happened. We'll never know for sure if she did the damage, but those were the facts.

Stewart paid a visit one afternoon after school, his first since before Christmas. Erica was at a club and Jasmine was home alone with us, which she usually seemed to enjoy. We'd tried to encourage Jasmine to join various clubs, as we do with all the children, but she said she'd prefer to go swimming with us, or just listen to music or play games at home. We didn't push it; one-to-one attention nearly always brought out the best in her.

Jasmine was in a great mood, as she had been told she'd earned enough points on her chart to enable her to go on the long-awaited museum trip that had been mentioned the previous term. She had been so upset when she was told she couldn't go, and now she was very excited.

'We're going on a bus,' she was telling me, just before Stewart arrived. 'We need a packed lunch and a drink and some spending money for the shop. Can I take extra money? Can I buy what I want? I love gift shops. Will they sell sweets and, what's that thing with the words inside?'

'Crossword?' Jonathan said, coming in on the end of the conversation.

'No!' Jasmine roared with laughter. 'It's a stick. It's a stick of rock!'

Stewart looked around sniffily when I showed him into the kitchen.

'Hello,' he said curtly to Jonathan. There was no love lost between them but Jonathan gamely shook the social worker's hand and said, 'Happy New Year, if it's not too late to say that!'

'I think it probably is,' Stewart said in a patronising tone.

I offered Stewart a seat at the kitchen table. I'd made flapjacks that day and laid out a plate, alongside a pot of tea.

'How are you?' he asked Jasmine, as I collected cups and milk.

'Good,' she said. 'I'm going to a museum.'

'That's good,' he said frostily. 'Well I hope you behave yourself.'

He pulled out some notes, sighing heavily as he did so.

'I hear there has been all kinds of trouble. Christmas Day did not go very well, did it? In fact, it went so badly that Angela had to call out-of-hours to report your behaviour.' He gave her a disapproving look.

I was shocked Stewart had brought this incident up, and in this way, so many weeks later. Even to me, it felt like it had happened an age ago.

'You accused Jonathan of pushing you over,' Stewart went on, 'but that wasn't true, was it?'

I felt myself bristle and I could tell Jonathan's hackles were up too. In the beginning, I had told Jasmine that it was my duty to report incidents to Social Services, as I do with all children. However, I never reminded her of the fact I wrote notes in my log that I routinely passed on to the social workers, or that I called the duty officer with problems out of hours. I'd hoped that she gave it very little thought, if any. My notes and messages were designed to help inform the social workers, so they could help us manage her placement in the best way possible. I certainly would never have expected her social worker to rub her nose in what I'd said, but that's what it felt like.

Jasmine suddenly lunged for the teapot, an angry look on her face.

'Don't!' I called, but it was too late. She gave it a sharp shove and it smashed to the floor, boiling tea splattering up the side of the kitchen unit. Now the cups were clattering to the floor too, and the plate of flapjacks.

'I hate you! I hate you! I hate you all! You just spy on me like weirdos! I'll report all of you! I know how to get you!'

Jasmine fled and Stewart tutted and complained that there was tea splashed on his trouser leg. Minutes later he was gone, muttering that he supposed the meeting would have to end there. We had not discussed any of the positive things that had happened since the start of the year, at school and with Jasmine's next appointment coming through so quickly. We also wanted an update on Pearl and Lenny's appeal, but Stewart was already heading to the door.

'I'll call you,' he said. 'I need to go and clean myself up before my next appointment.'

We didn't delay him; Jasmine was shouting, 'I hate you all! I'll kill myself!' and stomping angrily up the stairs. Our priority was to make sure she was safe.

20

'Does it hurt?'

Jasmine screamed and shouted and raged around the house for hours after Stewart left. One minute she was flapping her arms and charging down the landing, howling, growling and snarling as she had done before. The next she was bursting into the living room saying, 'I'm going to break my head! I'm going to smash into the mirror and break my head!'

Anthony came home and saw her in full flight. I'd noticed that she normally kept herself in check in front of him, as she looked up to him and thought he was funny and kind. This time, however, she didn't seem to care what Anthony thought and carried on grunting and charging around the house.

'Hey, Jasmine, shall we go and play with the football or the rugby ball?'

'No! What will you do? Tell Angela? Do you have a spy camera? Will you snitch on me too?'

'What? I just thought we could have a game. How about Guess Who?'

'Guess what?' she yelled. 'I don't want to play a stupid game in this stinking house. I hate everyone!'

Anthony shrugged and looked at Jonathan and me.

'Was I ever that bad?'

'You had your moments!' we replied in stereo.

He laughed. 'How come you two are so calm about Jasmine?'

It was true that Jonathan and I were not flustered. There is no point in trying to reason with a child who is being so unreasonable; all you can do is keep an eye on them, tell them you are there for them when they have calmed down and make sure they are safe. Jasmine had lost control and had to blow herself out, that was the unfortunate truth. It was not her fault. We were privately seething with Stewart, but that was something we had to deal with separately.

'Calm? Well, we've fostered dozens of kids over the years,' I said. 'They *all* have their moments. If we react to every single one, that's a lot of moments, and we wouldn't have the energy to be anything other than calm!'

Anthony laughed again. 'Fair play. By the way, I've got a flat lined up. Rent offer accepted, I'll be out of your hair next month.'

We were delighted for him, though of course we'd be sorry to see him move out. His new flat was only a few miles away but, even so, we'd miss him.

'Well done!' we both said.

'Thanks. You've really done me a favour.' He paused and added, 'One day I'm sure Jasmine will look back and see that too.'

It seemed only five minutes ago when we were wringing our hands over Anthony, who got into all kinds of scrapes and frequently caused chaos in our house during his teens. His wise words were a comfort now, and it gave me so much hope for Jasmine to see how well Anthony had turned out. His problems had been very different to Jasmine's, but either way he had been a troubled, challenging boy. I felt a swell of pride as I looked at him.

The next morning, Jasmine wouldn't shower when I asked her to and called me a 'bitch' when I asked her to eat her breakfast and clean her teeth. 'Bitch,' she repeated when I asked her to put on her shoes. I'd never heard her use that word before, and she certainly had never insulted me to my face like this. I think she was trying to get me to react, but I stayed calm and simply told her I did not like that language and asked her not to use it. Poor Erica stayed as quiet as a mouse and looked like she wished the ground would swallow her up.

I realised Jasmine looked exhausted, which I guess was no wonder, as I'd heard her pacing around in the night. Inevitably, we'd not slept very well, and Jonathan and I were both feeling frazzled and defeated before the day had even got going. We'd planned to get some jobs done in the morning and were meeting an old friend for lunch. Normally I really looked forward to seeing this friend and we hadn't got together for ages, but I found myself trying to muster up enthusiasm. I was shattered and felt distracted by Jasmine's situation.

It felt like a miracle that we'd got the girls to school on

time. Jonathan let out a long, slow breath as we walked away from the gates.

'Thank God we've got some time to ourselves,' he said. 'What a terrible start to the day.'

My head was aching. I'd been suffering from lots of headaches lately, which wasn't normal for me.

'This is awful,' I said. 'She's not happy. We're not happy. Erica does nothing but try to avoid her. Even Anthony's got it in the neck from Jasmine now.'

'Stewart really messed up,' Jonathan said baldly.

I hadn't been expecting that. Normally, whenever I start feeling sorry for myself or complaining, Jonathan steps in and stops me spiralling downwards. We'd been together for so many years I often anticipated what he was going to say next, and usually I was right. I'd expected a, 'Never mind, I'm sure things will get better', or 'Let's make the most of today, it'll do us good to see an old friend.'

But instead he'd said, 'Stewart really messed up.' That was a surprise, even though I shared Jonathan's opinion, one hundred per cent. Jasmine had been on an upward curve before he turned up and started raking up Christmas. There was no getting away from that. Stewart had upset the apple cart with his careless way of bringing up difficult issues we'd already dealt with and moved on from.

'I honestly can't work out if he's just inexperienced and still learning the ropes, or if he's being difficult deliberately,' Jonathan said. 'I mean, do you think he brought up Jasmine's story about me pushing her on Christmas Day to have another swipe at *me*? And if so, why?'

It was disheartening to hear Jonathan talk like this. He didn't deserve to be in this position, questioning whether a social worker was on his side. Social workers were meant to support us, not make waves. Jonathan was not normally one to criticise, or to feel in any way sorry for himself. I couldn't blame him, though. Stewart had left us with our noses out of joint, Jasmine included.

The phone rang just before eleven o'clock. Jonathan was folding washing from the tumble dryer and I was upstairs, about to dry my hair, ready to go out for lunch. Jonathan answered the call in the hall, and something in his tone made me stop what I was doing and walk onto the landing outside my bedroom.

I listened, a sinking feeling filling my heart.

'I'm very sorry to hear that. Yes, of course.' He paused, thanked the school secretary and said, 'We'll be back down as soon as we can.'

'What's happened?' I gasped.

'Jasmine apparently went "berserk" in the classroom. Something to do with the child next to her having more paints.'

'And?'

'She pulled the girl's hair, kicked her and ran around the classroom, growling and throwing things off the desks. The teaching assistant had to restrain her. They want us to bring her home, straight away. The behaviour she displayed has breached the school's behaviour policy and they are following their guidelines and excluding her with immediate effect.'

We collected Jasmine by car, me with my wet hair scrunched under a bobble hat so I didn't catch my death of cold. She was to be excluded for a week and we would receive a phone call from the office to fix up an 'urgent' meeting with Mr Weatherstone.

Jasmine was very tight-lipped on the school premises, but once we got in the car she started ranting about how unfair the teachers were being.

'They said I can't go on the trip. They said I can't go swimming.'

I asked her to tell me what had happened, with the paints and so on.

'Nothing! All that stuff with the paints was after.'

'After what?'

'After the assembly thing.'

'What assembly thing?'

She refused to tell us what this was, but she grumbled that she had lost some of the reward points she had earned on her behaviour schedule and this meant she was to lose the museum visit and her right to go swimming with the rest of the class. It sounded like this was what triggered her subsequent rampage with the paints and her attack on her classmate, but the facts were very unclear.

I'll have to get to the bottom of this, I thought. I was confused about what had gone on with the behaviour schedule. My understanding was that it was to encourage good behaviour, not be used as a stick instead of a carrot, as it seemed to have been. Taking off points seemed unfair when she had already earned them.

When we got home there was a letter on the doormat with some details about Jasmine's appointment with the specialist. It was now just a few days away.

'At least we won't have to ask for time off school,' I said drily.

'Every cloud,' Jonathan said, trying to smile.

Jasmine went to her bedroom and played some music, quietly, thank goodness. Meanwhile, Jonathan and I cancelled our lunch date and had a powwow at the kitchen table. I swallowed two painkillers and defrosted some sausage rolls from the freezer for lunch.

We pledged to make it our mission to do whatever we could to keep Jasmine as calm and collected as possible until her appointment took place. We rejigged a couple of other commitments we had in the diary during school hours over the next few days and asked Barbara to do extra hours in the shop. We also arranged for a good friend, who was also a foster carer, to help us out with Erica's lifts to school and all her clubs and activities.

We wanted to avoid having a battle every time we tried to leave the house with Jasmine, for everyone's sake. If one of us could have taken Erica while the other stayed with Jasmine we'd have done that, but it was not an option. I was concerned that Jasmine might make another allegation against Jonathan if he were alone with her, and he said he was worried for my safety if I was left in sole charge. That may sound an extreme reaction, but unfortunately this was the reality of our situation.

We called Stewart, but there was no answer. A replacement

for our support social worker, Caitlin, had been promised but had still not materialised. Once again, it felt like Pearl was the only person I could really talk to about Jasmine. I phoned her and told her about the exclusion and brought her up to speed about Jasmine's upcoming appointment.

'What a pity,' Pearl soothed. 'Still, at least she can cool down in the comfort of your home. Maybe the break from school will do her good.'

Pearl was remarkably laid-back about her granddaughter's school record, I thought. I'm not complaining; at that moment in time it was helpful to me to be able to talk to someone who knew Jasmine well and took everything in her stride. The last thing I needed was any more drama.

'Any news from your end?' I asked.

'Not a dicky bird. Can we come over at the weekend, take her out? I've got to take one of the cats to the vet in the morning but we could be with you for about one o'clock?'

'Yes, that's fine by me.'

Pearl asked if she could talk to Jasmine.

'I don't want to talk to Granny,' Jasmine said. 'I'm not in the mood. I don't want to talk about school and all that.'

'You don't have to. Your granny would just like a word. And she's going to take you out, with Granddad, at the weekend.'

'Yeah, sure!'

'It's true.'

I held out the phone but Jasmine folded her arms crossly. 'If you make me I'll hurt myself, you know.'

'Jasmine, I'm not going to force you to do anything. I do

not want you to hurt yourself. I care for you a great deal. Your granny and granddad care for you a great deal too. Granny just wants to talk to you.'

'Whatever.'

She took the phone and had a brief chat, which ended with her smiling and telling Pearl, 'See you soon! I can't wait.'

After a tense few days, during which Jasmine lost her temper time and time again over things as trivial as the fact Erica had one extra meatball in her spaghetti at dinnertime, we took her to the appointment with the specialist.

She was seething when she got in the car, having claimed her trainers didn't fit her any longer and we'd failed to do our job properly because we hadn't bought her new ones. I didn't rise to this: claiming clothes and shoes don't fit is akin to refusing to get in the shower or clean teeth. It's another example of what kids who are trying to take control of their muddled life do. The best tactic is to somehow try to give them a choice, so they feel they have some power over the situation.

'Wear flip-flops then,' I said calmly. 'Or your school shoes. It's up to you.'

'What? Are you mad?'

'No, if your trainers don't fit, you will have to wear something that does fit you. You can choose. Which is it to be?'

'I'm not wearing school shoes! Or flip-flops! I'm wearing my trainers. You can't stop me!'

* * *

We didn't know exactly what this appointment would entail. We had been told in advance that she was having an EEG and had been asked to make sure she had clean hair so it worked well, but we'd never come across the test before and didn't really know what to expect. We'd looked it up on the Internet but didn't find a great deal of information. It wasn't until we arrived at the clinic, almost two hours' drive from home, that the three of us had it fully explained to us.

The animated young doctor said, 'Do you know what an EEG is?'

He looked at all three of us, question marks dancing in his eyes. He sounded like he was addressing three young children, but we didn't mind. The important thing, of course, was that Jasmine was made to feel as comfortable as possible, and that was clearly the doctor's aim.

'Not really,' Jonathan and I said.

Jasmine, wide-eyed, shook her head and said no meekly.

'That's not a problem. Let me tell you all about it.'

The doctor looked like he'd performed this routine many times before. He delivered a short, slick presentation, drawing a diagram on the white board behind him as he did so.

'An EEG is a test used to see what's happening in the brain,' he said. 'It tracks and records brain wave patterns. Clever, don't you think?'

He looked at Jasmine and widened his eyes, which were already magnified by his thick, black-rimmed glasses. She stared at him, apparently transfixed. On the board the doctor wrote out the full name of the EEG, spelling it out loud as he did so. 'Electro – en-ce-pha-lo-gram. There! Electroencephalogram. But we don't need to worry about saying that. We can just call it an EEG.'

He then drew a circle for a head and added an arrow pointing to the top of the circle, which he labelled 'scalp'. Next he added lots of smaller circles onto the scalp, which were attached to thin wires leading to a machine.

'No matter what you are doing, even sleeping, your brain gives off electric waves. These discs (he pointed to the little circles) are put on your scalp. That's why we asked you to have clean hair, so they can stick on properly. You do have clean hair, don't you?'

Jasmine nodded and smiled.

'Phew!' the doctor said theatrically.

Jasmine giggled and he went on to explain that the discs talk to the machine via the little wires – or electrodes – coming off them.

'When the test is done we'll end up with lots of wavy lines on the computer screen, which will tell us what your brainwaves are doing. Amazing, isn't it?'

Jasmine blinked. 'Does it hurt?'

'Not at all. But you do have to do one thing, and that is stay still. Can you do that for me?'

She nodded with confidence.

Jonathan and I were told the procedure would take about an hour and that we were welcome to sit in, which we said we'd like to do.

We were all taken to another room where Jasmine was asked to lie still on a bed. Jonathan and I tried to blend into the background as much as possible, so as not to create any distraction. We read some leaflets while the doctor and a nurse got to work.

What little information I had found on the Internet about EEGs had left me slightly confused, as the articles I read focused on how they are used to identify the risk of seizures and epilepsy. There had never been any mention of Jasmine having a seizure, or any question she had epilepsy, so I didn't really understand how this test was going to help her.

The leaflet I read now explained more. 'EEGs can also identify causes of sleep disorders and changes in behaviour and they are sometimes used to evaluate brain activity after a severe head injury.'

I nudged Jonathan and pointed to this sentence. He raised his eyebrows. We both stayed very quiet. We felt it was important to be present for Jasmine, to show support and be on hand in case she needed us, but we were anxious not to do anything to disturb the test.

My mind started to work overtime. Had Jasmine had a head injury in the past? *Of course she had, she had the scar.* Did that cause her bad temper and her difficult and strange moods? Did she actually have some form of brain damage?

'What pretty hair you have,' I heard the nurse say. 'I'm just going to smooth it down a bit so I can get all these discs in the right place. Such a pretty colour. Mine was exactly that colour when I was your age . . .'

Jasmine seemed relaxed and calm. I smiled – the nurse also looked like she had done this many times before.

'You're doing very well indeed.' The doctor was talking

now. 'I think you might well be the best patient I've had in all week!' There was a pause and he asked, 'How did you get your scar, Jasmine?'

She didn't reply.

'I know a little boy who'd love one like that.' She still gave no answer. 'My nephew, that's who I'm talking about. Always saying he wants one. I think Harry Potter has a lot to answer for!'

I was listening intently. I wasn't sure if the doctor was simply making conversation, trying to distract Jasmine so she stayed calm, or whether he was doing what A & E and passport control staff do, casually asking pertinent questions of a child, in order to check what adults, or files, have already told them.

Jasmine slowly replied. 'I don't really like Harry Potter. I like, erm, *SpongeBob* and *WALL-E* and that TV show with the big art things . . . *Art Attack*. I don't like that film about cars. What's it called?'

'*Cars*?' the doctor said.

'*Cars*. Yes. No, I didn't like that one but *Kung Fu Panda* is really funny!'

Jasmine did everything she was asked and stayed remarkably still. She was commended by the doctor for being a model patient and the test was completed well within the hour.

'Very well done,' the doctor enthused. 'You were absolutely brilliant! Hopefully we'll have some results for you very soon.'

'Is there anything we need to know now?' I ventured, when Jasmine was back on her feet.

'No,' he smiled. 'But like I say, the results should not take long.'

If he'd recognised anything on the screen, this doctor was not going to say so now. *And quite right too*, I thought.

Jasmine was quiet and thoughtful on the way home. We put on a classical music CD, on low volume, to help keep the atmosphere calm. It seemed to work.

We received a letter from the clinic within just a few days. It had already been agreed with Social Services that I would open this and immediately share the contents with them.

When I opened the envelope I saw what looked like a printout from an old-fashioned word-processing machine, one of those with a perforated edge pitted with ring-binder holes that looked like it should have been torn off, but nobody had bothered. There was no covering letter and I had to scan through lots of incomprehensible words and numbers that presumably explained the graph that appeared halfway down the page. To the untrained eye, nothing made any sense. I kept scanning the text, looking for something in plain English, before finally resting on three words at the bottom of the page: 'impaired frontal lobe'. Next to the words were the doctor's name and date of the EEG.

'Impaired frontal lobe.' I said it out loud.

Though it's more than a decade on, I can still remember staring at those three words and hearing them bounce back at me off the kitchen walls. I'm sure I felt the floor beneath me shift a little. This poor little girl had a problem with her brain after all. *Poor Jasmine.*

I knew something about frontal lobes, as it happened. I'd learned about them at training sessions, when we were being taught about behavioural problems in teenagers. I knew that the frontal lobe of the brain plays a key role in 'higher mental functions', like planning and motivating yourself, regulating your mood and behaviour and how you cope with social interactions. I had an idea that a damaged or impaired frontal lobe could be caused by disease or by head trauma. I just hadn't considered that Jasmine might have an impaired frontal lobe. To me, it was something I associated primarily with teenagers, and she hadn't had a disease or a head trauma, had she?

Head trauma.

An image of Jasmine's scar began to burn in my mind's eye. I went to my bedroom, took out my laptop and searched the Internet, hoping there was some other cause, other than disease or head trauma. Other than whatever had caused Jasmine to have that scar on her forehead.

'What causes impaired frontal lobe?' I typed.

Head trauma. There it was again. Disease, it said, giving examples of different diseases. Tumours and neurosurgery also made the list.

Head trauma. What on earth happened to her? Did her father's physical abuse cause this?

It seemed the most likely explanation, but of course I had no proof, no facts. I phoned Stewart and left an urgent message for him to call me.

21

'I just don't get him'

Jasmine had returned to school by the time we saw Stewart again. Mr Weatherstone had given her what amounted to a final warning, telling her that if she transgressed again she would be removed permanently from the school. Social Services had been informed about this, and everyone involved in her care and education had been made aware of her diagnosis. We were informed that Social Services would look into what might be done for Jasmine in the future, in terms of her medical condition, and to my relief, the process of having her statemented was happening, at last. The school had held fire on this while Jasmine was being tested, but now they were in favour of it. I hoped having an SEN would help Jasmine a great deal. She'd receive further help in the classroom and may even qualify for a one-to-one special needs assistant, which I hoped would make all the difference.

Having said all this, it was clear to me that despite Jasmine's diagnosis, and having the SEN in the pipeline, no allowances would be made when it came to matters of discipline. Mr Weatherstone was very consistent when it came to the school rules. If a child could not conform to school behaviour policy, the appropriate steps would be taken, it was as simple as that. Procedure would be strictly followed. Unfortunately, in Jasmine's case, her history meant she was in the last chance saloon.

I crossed my fingers and hoped she would manage to stay out of trouble while we got her statemented. I didn't expect miracles when the paperwork was through, but I hoped that when she finally had her SEN and the support she needed was in place, her behaviour would be less likely to spiral out of control.

Stewart arrived promptly for the meeting at our house, looking like a man who meant business.

'So what's been going on, young lady?' he asked, furrowing his brow and confronting Jasmine the moment he stepped in our front door. 'I hear you had another exclusion and you're running out of road.'

She shrugged and looked at him, deadpan.

'Stewart, can we have a word please, in private?'

He nodded and followed Jonathan and me into the kitchen.

'You go up to the lounge, sweetheart, OK?'

Jasmine obliged – I don't think she needed any encouragement to scoot away from Stewart.

He sat confidently on a kitchen chair, smartly booted and suited, and with his neatly bearded chin thrust forward. I had to walk the other way around the table to get to a chair, as Stewart was taking up an excessive amount of floor space. I don't think I knew the word then, but today I'd describe his posture as 'manspreading'.

'I hope you don't mind me saying this,' I began, 'but I don't think it's going to be helpful to tackle Jasmine about the exclusion.'

I said this as tactfully as I could, adding that this was just my opinion, having got to know Jasmine and her reactions quite well by now. I didn't bring up how she had reacted when he confronted her so undiplomatically about Christmas, but it was uppermost in my mind and I certainly didn't want her to snap and go on the rampage again.

'She's back in school now,' I went on, 'so the exclusion is behind her and she seems to be in quite a good place. If she feels that she's being told off all over again I think it will set her off, and that is not really what we want, is it?'

Stewart clicked his tongue and raised his eyebrows sceptically. He didn't seem convinced, and I don't think he appreciated me speaking out like this.

'I don't think it's going to do any harm to let her know that I'm aware of her behaviour and am not happy about it, or impressed,' he said sharply. 'In fact, it might make her pull her socks up and prevent her from being permanently removed from school.'

It was as if Stewart felt compelled to pull rank and show Jasmine who was boss, which didn't seem appropriate, or helpful. He may have believed that his disapproval would somehow make a positive difference to Jasmine's behaviour.

I hoped he did believe this, and that it wasn't just all about him – but I'm afraid I feared it was, and that a reprimand by him would have exactly the opposite effect to what we hoped for. I felt this quite strongly.

'I don't really agree.'

I didn't find it easy to speak up like this and I felt my throat dry out as my words hit the air. Normally I'd never challenge a social worker. My job is to report to Social Services, feed information to social workers and ask for help and support if needed, but I wanted to do what I felt was best for Jasmine, just as Jonathan did.

'She has this diagnosis now,' I went on. 'She has an impaired frontal lobe. She cannot help her behaviour. I think the focus needs to be on this. We need to treat her with kindness and understanding, as much as we can give her.'

Jonathan nodded and put his hand on mine. Given the tetchy relationship he had with Stewart we had decided it was best if I was the spokesperson this time, but Jonathan wanted to show that we stood as one.

'I hear what you're saying,' Stewart said curtly. It felt like he was paying us lip service. 'I'll take that on board.' He got to his feet. 'I'll go up and have a word in private with her now, if that's OK with you?'

'Of course,' I said, wishing this was something I had the power to prevent.

When he returned to the kitchen quite soon afterwards, Stewart immediately started to talk about Pearl and Lenny's application to take in Jasmine. I imagined Jasmine might have asked him about it. The appeal was in its very final stages, apparently, and we hoped to hear the results before too long.

'Jasmine still wants to live with her grandparents, but I'm not convinced they would be able to cope with her,' Stewart said.

My heart sank. Whoever was assessing Pearl and Lenny's application and making the final decision would have no doubt asked Stewart for his opinion.

'Why is that?'

'Isn't it obvious? Now we know she has this brain condition it's a game changer.'

'But why?' To my mind nothing had really changed, except for the fact it was helpful to know what was going on in Jasmine's brain.

'Why?' Stewart gave an exaggerated, spluttering laugh. 'Can't you see why? They are elderly and now we know she has a condition with a name she's more of a handful than we thought she was.'

'I'm not sure I agree, Stewart. Knowing about the impaired frontal lobe is very useful. It means we now have a much greater understanding of Jasmine's needs, and that will make it easier for her grandparents to look after her, not harder.'

Stewart sucked his teeth and considered this. 'I'm not sure I agree with that logic.'

'OK, maybe we could look at it another way?' I said. 'Now we know she has this condition, it's a challenge for whoever is looking after her. She needs people who love her unconditionally. Family. Grandparents. Pearl and Lenny love her to pieces and if she is "more of a handful than we thought" then who better to care for her than a devoted granny and granddad? They will be prepared to go the extra mile for her. They don't have other kids to look after. They're retired and they are ready, willing and able to take Jasmine in. What's more, she could return to her old neighbourhood, perhaps pick up old friendships. Maybe she could even return to her old school.'

'Well,' Stewart said, getting to his feet, 'the decision will rest on the risk assessment in any case.'

'Risk assessment?'

'Whether her parents making contact via the grandparents is a risk.'

'Parents? We thought Social Services were only concerned about her father making contact through Pearl and Lenny?'

'Sorry, yes. The worry is her dad will get in touch with his parents. They are Pearl and Lenny, aren't they?'

'Yes,' Jonathan and I confirmed, somewhat wearily. 'Pearl and Lenny are Jasmine's paternal grandparents. Of course, that is why there has been such an issue.'

I didn't need to even look at Jonathan to know he'd be feeling as frustrated as I was at Stewart's handling of this situation. It was baffling to us that he needed us to confirm something that was at the core of Jasmine's life. Stewart simply didn't seem to be on the ball, and that was extremely concerning. Jasmine's future was uncertain and her social worker needed to be fully invested in helping her make the right move.

'Her mother has no relatives in this area, no sisters or brothers, no aunts or uncles,' he said. This statement came from nowhere. I'm afraid it seemed like Stewart just threw this into the conversation to show us he had a handle on something, at least.

His phone rang and he snatched it from his pocket.

'Damn!' he said, looking at the incoming number. 'I have to take this. I'll be in touch.'

He walked out of the kitchen and out of our house, mouthing 'bye' as he did so.

'Why did he bother giving his opinion about Pearl and Lenny's capabilities if it's all down to the risk assessment?' I said to Jonathan. 'And how could he make a mistake about her mum, talking about "parents" when it's all about her dad?'

'I have no idea,' Jonathan said, shaking his head. 'I just don't get him.'

It would have been helpful for us to discuss the situation with a support social worker, but even after all these weeks we were still without a replacement for Caitlin. Apparently, there had been a delay because Caitlin had said she was coming back sooner than she'd thought, then suffered a setback and had to change her plans. The uncertainty meant Social Services had stalled their efforts to find us a new social worker. I think we were at the back of the queue again.

Jonathan and I talked about the fact Caitlin had praised Stewart and told us he would do a good job of being Jasmine's social worker. We valued her opinion and wondered what we were missing, as our dealings with him were becoming increasingly frustrating.

* * *

I'm happy to say that Jasmine began to have some of her best days ever at school, getting a thumbs-up from both Mrs Dowden and Miss Jenson at home time.

'Maybe the latest exclusion has done some good after all,' Jonathan commented. 'She seems to be trying very hard.'

'I know, bless her. I just hope she keeps it up and we can get the statement through as quickly as possible. I'm sure that's going to make a massive difference.'

Miss Dowden beamed when she gave me two pieces of good news one afternoon. Jasmine had been given a certificate for 'being kind to others' after helping some younger children with an art project and had also scored a winning run in a game of indoor cricket, which had brought huge cheers from her team.

'I wish you could have seen her face!' Miss Dowden said. 'I've never seen anyone looking so thrilled!'

Things were going well at home too. Jasmine and Erica had been sharing the computer without any problems, and one evening they had even helped each other with their spellings, sitting at the table and testing one another.

'Remember when you put the phone charger in your mouth?' Erica said out of the blue, laughing.

'Ha ha, what a silly thing to do!' Jasmine also laughed. 'Maybe that's why my brain went a bit different.'

I heard the exchange as I wiped the table mats. *Bless her*, I thought. When the moment had been right, we'd told Jasmine that the doctor who did the EEG test had given us the results. 'Your brain sometimes works a little bit differently to other people's,' was how we put it.

It was good to hear that she had interpreted this as her brain going 'a bit different' and didn't mind mentioning it to Erica.

'It was silly!' Erica laughed. 'But you're not boring though.'

Jasmine beamed and I could have kissed Erica, I really could have. It was a kind thing for her to have said.

I think the fact the girls had their own bedrooms had helped their relationship no end. They still had their moments when Jasmine kicked off about something and Erica retreated, but at least they each had their own space now. None of us had to worry about whether Jasmine would wake Erica up in the night, which was a bonus.

The downside of Mum moving out was that Social Services had duly noted that Jasmine now had her own bedroom. We wondered if this might weaken our argument that Jasmine would be better off living with her grandparents. We hoped not. As much as we loved Jasmine – and we *had* become extremely fond of her, despite all the problems – we were more convinced than ever that she would be better off with her granny and granddad. Family bonds are so precious, and the more we got to know Pearl and Lenny, the more we believed that Jasmine would be happier growing up in their house than in foster care. It wasn't just that she would be the only child in the home and would therefore receive more attention. We felt she might lose some of the resentment she felt about her past. Being in foster care was a permanent reminder of her dysfunctional upbringing. If she lived with her granny and granddad, wouldn't she feel less badly treated? It seemed to stand to reason. Not only that, Erica and any other children we had living with us when Anthony moved out would not have to deal with Jasmine's challenging behaviour. That was a big consideration, because we were passed to take in up to three children at any one time and we wanted the best for every child, not just Jasmine.

22

'He told me I will go in a children's home'

'Mrs Hart, I'm afraid there's been an incident, with Jasmine.'

'Oh dear. I see. What's happened? She was in a good mood this morning and I thought things were going so well.'

Jasmine had been back at school for a week by now. The school secretary explained that Jasmine had been involved in an altercation with another child that morning. As a result, she'd been kept in at break and lunchtime. I rolled my eyes as I listened to this, knowing that Jasmine would have been building up steam like a pressure cooker if she hadn't been allowed to run outside in the fresh air.

'Unfortunately, at the end of the lunch break she ran outside and went to find the child she'd had the argument with in the morning. She picked up a large stone and threw it at the other child. Mr Weatherstone is extremely unhappy.'

'Is the child OK?'

'I'm not sure. She's still with the nurse.'

We were asked to collect Jasmine immediately and the secretary told us that the head was requesting a meeting with Jonathan and me, as well as Jasmine's social worker and her teachers as soon as could be arranged. Jasmine was excluded from school but would be required to attend the meeting. Of course, after her previous exclusion we'd been warned she would be permanently excluded if it happened again, and Mr Weatherstone was not one to bend the rules. Our best hope, I thought, would be that the head teacher might allow Jasmine to stay at the school until a new place was found for her.

'Do you think her medical diagnosis might sway Mr Weatherstone?' I said to Jonathan.

He shook his head. 'I think this meeting will be his way of getting Social Services on his side, to set the wheels in motion to find Jasmine an alternative school as soon as possible.'

It took a few days to fix up the meeting, not least because Stewart was incommunicado for a day. We drove to school and Jasmine was very quiet on the way. I wanted to tell her not to worry and that it would all work out in the end, but I didn't want to give her false hope. I may have been her foster carer, but I was not in charge of this meeting, or Jasmine's fate. I felt nervous about what the head would say, and I was also anxious about Stewart, because of the confusing things he said sometimes, and the way he handled us and Jasmine. We still had no support social worker, but a manager from Social Services was attending the meeting, we were told.

'OK, sweetheart?' I said, turning around in my seat to check Jasmine had buckled herself in.

'Do I have to wear a seat belt?'

'Yes, sweetheart. We need you to be safe.'

'What if I don't want to be safe? What if I want to die?'

'Jasmine, sweetheart, please don't talk like that. I know it's not easy going into school in the circumstances . . .'

She leaned forward, poking her head between our seats. 'He told me I will go in a children's home.'

'Who told you that?'

'Him. That man.'

'What man?'

Surely not Mr Weatherstone? I thought, because the head teacher was looming large in my thoughts.

'Jasmine, who said you will go in a children's home?'

'Durrrhhh! Him, that Stewart. He said that if I misbehaved again he would do it.'

'He said that, did he?'

'Yes. He said, "Fourteen days before I move you to a children's home." He said it in your house. He said it in a bad way.'

I thought back to Stewart's last visit, which was roughly two weeks ago. He'd spoken to Jasmine privately, as he always did. He'd certainly had the opportunity to say this, and Jasmine seemed very clear about it.

'Jasmine,' I said cautiously. 'This is the first I have heard about any of this. The meeting today is about your schooling.' With more confidence I added, 'The head teacher called this meeting because of the incident with the large stone in the playground. Nobody is putting you in a children's home.'

She narrowed her eyes. 'I don't believe you.'

I repeated my reassurances and Jonathan backed me up, but Jasmine seemed to have zoned out. She sat back in her seat, pulled her belt across her and clicked it into place absent-mindedly. Her expression was blank; it was as if her mind had left the car and only her body remained.

If Jasmine's allegation was true, I wondered if this was why she'd had such a good week at school following Stewart's visit. Had she been trying her best, so she didn't get put in a children's home? The thought made me shudder and I told myself I had no idea what was true and what wasn't.

I walked Jasmine into the school with a heavy heart. Jonathan was attempting to engage her in conversation about her road safety poster, the plants in the school garden, the weather – anything.

'How about if we go for a big long walk this afternoon? There's a lovely circuit we haven't taken you on yet. It's windy, so perhaps we could take a kite?'

Jasmine ignored him and walked on. It felt more like we were taking a teenager to a court appearance than an eight-year-old girl to a meeting at her primary school.

While Jasmine was asked to wait outside, Jonathan and I were ushered into the head teacher's spacious office, where we were met by Miss Dowden, Miss Jenson, a support teacher and a special needs teacher. Stewart was standing at the back of the room, talking conspiratorially to a woman we recognised immediately. It was Mrs Hutton, the rather stony-faced Social Services manager we'd met at Jasmine's original core meeting, when Lou had had to take Jasmine out of the room as she was growling and kicking the table. I recalled how Jasmine had seemed very ill at ease in Mrs Hutton's company, and how I'd wondered if the manager had perhaps been involved in Jasmine's removal from the family home under the original EPO, which we imagined would have been traumatic.

'Good morning, good morning!' It was Mr Weatherstone, who appeared to be in an uncharacteristically upbeat and jovial mood. 'Thank you all for coming. Do please come and take a seat.'

We had barely had a chance to say hello to the other people gathered. As we took our seats around a large, oval table, we all nodded and said good morning to one another.

Mr Weatherstone cleared his throat. 'I won't beat about the bush,' he said. 'It's my recommendation that Jasmine attend Grove Mount, where her needs will be better met.'

Grove Mount was a PRU (pupil referral unit), catering for kids not able to attend mainstream school. Behavioural problems, mental or physical health issues, being victims of bullying or having special educational needs are the main reasons a child may be referred to a PRU. I knew that children who had been permanently excluded made up a high percentage of the cohort at Grove Mount, and I also knew that this particular unit had a higher than average success rate in returning kids to mainstream school, which was something, at least.

Mr Weatherstone presented a summary of Jasmine's unimpressive track record at his school, giving reasons and dates for all her exclusions. If I wasn't mistaken, he delivered this in an almost triumphant way, as if submitting the crucial, irrefutable pieces of evidence at a trial. *That explains his mood*, I thought. *He can't wait to move her. He knows he has a strong case.*

In turn, each of the teaching staff and both Stewart and Mrs Hutton were asked for their opinion. Each of them said, in so many words, that they felt the PRU was the best place for Jasmine, at least in the short term.

'Do you agree, Mr and Mrs Hart, that it is better for Jasmine to be educated at Grove Mount than to have the disrupted education she is having here, given her frequent exclusions?'

'I would have liked to have seen how she got on once her statement came through. I think her behaviour will improve once she gets the help she needs – help that is tailored to her SEN.' I added that we were waiting to hear from Social Services about additional help they may offer in terms of her medical diagnosis.

'Yes, yes,' said Mr Weatherstone rather impatiently. 'But the fact is, we have a duty to *all* our pupils. We simply cannot afford to wait any longer. Jasmine is missing out on her education and she is disrupting the education of others. This has gone on for long enough. It is also stressful for my teaching staff.'

Mrs Hutton wondered whether Jasmine might respond to a final ultimatum: show us you can behave or you will go to Grove Mount. My heart sank. I wanted to say, 'Look how she's reacted since Stewart told her she'll end up in a children's home,' but I held my tongue, of course. I had no idea if that was true or an invention of Jasmine's. 'I'm not sure an ultimatum is the right tactic,' the young special needs teacher ventured. She flushed bright red as she spoke. I felt very grateful to her for speaking out like this, as she was voicing the concerns Jonathan and I had. 'You see, Jasmine is not *deliberately* misbehaving. She has special needs.'

I gave the teacher a smile and an encouraging nod. Mr Weatherstone also nodded, but he wasn't smiling.

'That, I'm afraid, is the whole point. Jasmine has needs that Grove Mount is far better equipped to deal with than we are. Shall we hear from Jasmine herself? Thank you for your time, Mr and Mrs Hart.'

We were politely dismissed, but dismissed we were, having barely had the chance to contribute.

'We'll wait in reception for you,' I said to Jasmine as she entered the head teacher's office.

We walked along the short corridor leading back to the reception area. Once there, the door automatically locked behind us, and we would need a code from a member of staff or the receptionist to re-enter. We both felt very uneasy as we sat down. Jasmine had looked calm, but not in a good way. She seemed disengaged. I wanted to scoop her into my arms and tell her everything would be all right, but I couldn't.

'This is a fait accompli, isn't it?' I said to Jonathan.

'Seems that way. Mr Weatherstone has made up his mind. This was not about *if* she should be referred, but why and when.'

Jonathan started to wonder out loud if it might not be a bad move. 'Looking on the positive side, at least she'll be spending every day in school and she won't be excluded. At least they have better resources for special needs. And she doesn't have to stay there forever. It does have good results . . .'

'That's true. In any case, if she is allowed to move in with Pearl and Lenny, that will change things again. Perhaps if she does do a stint at Grove Mount, she could then have the option of starting afresh at a new school in her grandparents' neighbourhood. With a statement, and without her reputation following her around, maybe that would work out?'

'Jasmine! Come back here! Jasmine!'

Jonathan and I both heard the teacher shouting and looked up in alarm, our eyes falling on the door we'd just come through. It sounded like the cries were coming from the corridor beyond the head teacher's office, which had classrooms leading off it.

'Grrr! Grrr! I'm going to murder you! Don't touch me! Grrr! Come near me and I'll kill you! I'll hit you! Grrr!'

Jasmine's voice was muffled to our ears, but there was no mistaking how she sounded. There was a manic hiss in her voice; she had lost control. We could hear several voices now, and the sound of something crashing to the floor. We stood and peered through the glass panel of the door. We could see Jasmine charging in the opposite direction to us, pulling posters off the walls, slinging books off shelves, kicking chairs and punching art displays as she did so. Stewart was pursuing her, followed by Miss Dowden and Miss Jenson. Outside the head teacher's office, a shelving unit had been overturned and there were books strewn across the floor. Teachers were opening classroom doors on either side of the corridor, and a small child carrying a register was staring in disbelief.

'Oh my God, she's gone berserk,' I said. Instinctively, I tried the door even though I knew I could not get through. Jonathan pressed the bell on reception.

'Grrr! Woof! Woof! Woof! Grrr! Get back! Grrr! I'll kill someone!' Jasmine's voice was echoing down the corridor. The animal sounds were getting louder, even though Jasmine was travelling away from us. It sounded quite haunting.

A receptionist appeared and we both went up to the desk. 'We're here with Jasmine . . . she just went into the head's office and . . .'

'Yes, I know who you are,' she said kindly. 'Please take a seat.'

'Can we go back through?' I nodded towards the corridor.

'Let me see if Mr Weatherstone is available. Take a seat. I'll be right back.'

The receptionist disappeared through a door at the back of the reception area, which led first to the main office and then to Mr Weatherstone's office beyond that. Before the receptionist reappeared, Mrs Hutton came through the door. She looked ashen.

'What's happened?' I asked. 'Is Jasmine OK? I'd like to go to her.'

'I hoped I could argue successfully to keep her in this school for a while longer at least, but I'm afraid Jasmine has destroyed any last chance of that.'

'But how? What exactly went on in there? She seemed calm only minutes ago.'

Mrs Hutton shook her head. 'You'd better talk to Stewart. He meant well. He couldn't have predicted how Jasmine would react. Good luck, both of you.'

Mrs Hutton hurried away.

'Mr Weatherstone will see you now,' the receptionist said, giving us an incongruous smile.

We were shown into the head's office.

'Jasmine is safe. I understand you heard the commotion. Miss Jenson managed to restrain her, using the safe holding technique we teach at safeguarding. I'm sure you're familiar with this?'

'Yes,' I said. 'We are also trained in safe holding.'

Mr Weatherstone sighed. Somehow, he managed to make us feel as if he were disapproving of us as well as of Jasmine.

'I cannot have Jasmine in my school any longer. She is permanently excluded and I am referring her to Grove Mount. That's my final decision.'

'What happened?' Jonathan said.

Mr Weatherstone coughed. 'Jasmine did not respond well to her social worker. When he tried to engage her in conversation, she lost her temper. I think she is a young lady who needs a far greater level of special needs care than we can provide here.'

'What was the topic of conversation?'

'I believe the social worker asked Jasmine what she was going to do to improve her behaviour, which was a reasonable question. We do try to encourage all of our children to take personal responsibility for their actions.'

Mr Weatherstone rose. 'I'm sorry it's ended like this. I wish you the very best of luck.'

'Thank you,' I said, getting to my feet. There was nothing more to say, or, at least, it was clear Mr Weatherstone had decided there was nothing more he wanted to hear.

'We'd like to see Jasmine now,' Jonathan said. 'Thank you.'

I felt defeated. It is so much easier to deal with poor behaviour if you keep telling yourself 'she can't help it', but Mr Weatherstone did not seem to want to grasp the fact that Jasmine *could not* take responsibility for all her actions. She had an impaired frontal lobe. The most likely explanation for this was that she'd suffered a blow to the head and brain injury as a result of the physical abuse she'd suffered in the family home. Even if that were not the case, there were so many pieces of her puzzle left unexplained. Jasmine needed to be treated with love and understanding, not beaten with a rule book and punished every time she misbehaved. We waited in reception until Jasmine was escorted out to us, by Miss Dowden. Jasmine looked as white as a ghost, save for the scar on her head, which stood out like a bolt of fiery lightning under the harsh lights. She stared straight ahead, with no expression on her face.

'Let's go home,' I said, offering her my hand, which she ignored.

Miss Dowden nodded at Jonathan and me. She looked shocked and sympathetic and hesitant, somehow.

There was something about the teacher's demeanour that made me picture her face several times in the car on the way home. It wasn't until later that evening that I said to Jonathan, 'I think Miss Dowden wanted to tell me something.'

The very next morning I had a call from Stewart. 'Good news,' he said, 'she can live with her grandparents.' He sounded very subdued, considering he was delivering such great news.

'What? That's amazing! Do they know? Can I tell her?'

'I've just told Pearl. You can tell Jasmine, if you like. We've also got her a place lined up at a PRU in their town. It's one of the best.'

'That's wonderful! When can she move?'

'As soon as you like. As soon as we can make arrangements.'

'Stewart, I can't thank you enough! That's absolutely brilliant. Are you sure I can tell her? It's all confirmed? Or do you want to see her? Should you be the one to tell her? This has all happened so fast.'

There was a pause. 'No, I, er, don't need to see her. Obviously, I'll do a handover and all that, but she'll get a new social worker.'

'OK. Also, I'd like to know exactly what happened yesterday at school, after Jonathan and I left the room?'

'I think you got the picture. I'll be writing up the notes. She just went mad when asked about how she was going to behave better. Just lost it, just like that. She will definitely be better off in a PRU.' He couldn't get off the phone quick enough.

After telling Jonathan the good news we called Jasmine into the lounge and sat her down.

'I've just had a phone call from Stewart,' I said brightly. Before I could say another word, Jasmine growled dramatically, sprang up and started charging around the room. She swiped three heavy glass ornaments off the windowsill and shouted, 'I hate him! No! No! I want him to die! Grrr! Grrr! Grr!'

'Jasmine, it's good news I've got for you. Please stop. Come and sit down.'

Jonathan was scooping up the ornaments, all of which had landed on the carpet and were undamaged.

'No harm done here,' he said.

Jasmine ignored him, and me. She started flapping her arms, as if she were trying to fly. Then she bolted out of the door and ran up to her bedroom.

While Jasmine was still upstairs the phone rang. I decided to answer it, as I thought it might be Pearl, ringing to share the good news.

'Mrs Hart? It's Miss Dowden.'

I thanked her for calling. I was going to speak to her when I had the chance, but she'd beaten me to it.

'I'm glad you phoned. In all the commotion, we left rather abruptly yesterday and I still don't really understand what happened.'

'Yes, I thought that might be the case,' the teacher said. 'I wanted to fill you in. I have been asked to write up notes, you see, and I've just done them.'

'Notes?'

I knew it wasn't standard practice for a teacher to write up notes like this. All of a sudden, I had the same feeling in my gut that I usually get when a child is about to disclose something.

'Jasmine lost control after her social worker said something that provoked her,' Miss Dowden said.

'I see. What was it?'

Miss Dowden cleared her throat. 'I heard the social worker telling Jasmine that he would tell her father if she didn't behave. When Jasmine got angry and started to shout, unfortunately he told her that her father was outside the school.' I felt my stomach drop, probably just a fraction of the way Jasmine's had when she heard this. Miss Dowden said she believed Stewart had said this to get Jasmine to behave, but of course it set her off.

'That was when she really lost the plot, I'm afraid. Before she ran down the corridor she kicked over a chair in the head's office and threw herself on the floor, growling. When she was on the floor she was so agitated she started biting the rug, as if she was trying to chew lumps out of it. None of us could get near, as she was lashing out and seemed completely out of control. I think the whole idea that her father might be outside the school premises terrified her, that was quite obvious. Of course, he wasn't there at all. The social worker had used Jasmine's father as a threat, with good intentions, I'm sure. But he lied to her, I'm sorry to say. I'm sure he didn't realise the effect this would have on her.'

I had listened so intently I was almost holding my breath.

'Thank you,' I said. 'Thank you. I'm very glad you told me this.'

'You're welcome. I don't want to interfere and please don't quote me on this, but maybe it would be better if Jasmine had a different social worker? I think you do a marvellous job, by the way, and I hope you don't mind me being so forthright.'

I thanked Miss Dowden very much for her candour and care. I could tell she was nervous about speaking to me so frankly. She had a good heart and, ultimately, she'd put Jasmine first. I admired Miss Dowden and would not dream of breaching her confidence.

I chose not to share with Miss Dowden the news about Jasmine's move to her grandparents' at this point. She did not have long to chat, and I wanted to talk to Jasmine before anybody else. I could pop in and see Miss Dowden when I collected Erica from school another day.

The moment I put the phone down it rang for the third time that morning.

'Angela, it's Pearl. Have you heard?'

'I have, I have! It's wonderful news. I was about to tell Jasmine but maybe you can now?'

'I'd love to. I've been waiting a long time for this moment.'

Jonathan started calling up the stairs, telling Jasmine her granny was on the phone and she had fantastic news.

She appeared on the landing.

'Nothing good happens to me.'

'Want a bet?'

'No.'

'Jasmine, come and talk to your granny. She's got something really good to tell you.'

Reluctantly, Jasmine plodded down the stairs and into the lounge.

'This better not be another trick,' she said, narrowing her eyes at me as she took hold of the receiver.

'No trick. Just good news.'

'Granny?'

Jasmine stood statue-still as she took in the news.

'Are you joking?'

I could hear Pearl's happy voice trilling down the phone.

'Oh God, this is totally awesome. It's true? It's real? Granny! I can't believe it. This is the best day of my whole entire life.'

When she hung up she came and gave me a hug.

'I'll miss you,' she said, 'but I'm glad I'm going.'

I'd settle for that.

23

'I hope she stays happy'

'Angela, do you think she will come back?'

Jasmine was looking out of her bedroom window, her bags packed all around her. It was moving day. Everything seemed to have happened incredibly fast, and Pearl and Lenny were on their way to collect her.

'Who, sweetheart?'

'My mummy.'

I felt goosebumps prickle my arms as I gently told her, truthfully, that I didn't know. I still knew next to nothing about her mother, save for the fact that she had 'disappeared' a year before Jasmine first went into care. As I've said before, I worried about what life was like for Jasmine when she was living alone with her dad for all that time. She had only talked about her mother to me once, when she told me about the fire. *She's invisible now. She was magicked away. The smoke and the fire came and then she went invisible, away. Out of the green door.*

Jasmine continued looking out of her window. 'She *could*

come back,' she said wistfully. 'You can't be invisible forever. She *could* . . . Does she know where Granny lives?'

'Well, I'm not sure,' I said. I didn't know what else to say, and I didn't want to give Jasmine any false hope. I was naturally assuming she would want her mother to come back. Kids are incredibly forgiving when it comes to their parents, and despite the fact Jasmine's mother had left her, I was not surprised she was pining for her. Sadly, children who have been subjected to the most terrible forms of abuse at the hands of their parents very often continue to crave a reunion.

I'd never heard Jasmine say 'mummy' before. I thought she must be missing her, or that the move was a painful reminder of the fact her mother had left her to be brought up by others.

'Did you say you aren't sure?' Jasmine said, this time using her robotic voice.

'Yes. Jasmine. I'm afraid I don't know anything about your mum, really.'

With this, Jasmine turned to face me. I couldn't read her expression. She looked zoned out and deep in thought. She dropped to the floor until she was sitting with her back pressed up against the radiator and her legs stretched out in front of her. There was a Sindy doll lying next to her and she picked it up and spoke to it. I stayed very still and watched and listened.

'It was after that *stupid* fire. Dad was really, really angry. He was like an angry monster with fire coming out of his mouth and smoke and everything.'

She stared at the doll. 'See this?' She pointed to the scar on her forehead.

All of a sudden Jasmine jumped to her feet and climbed up onto the chair next to her desk. Then she clambered up onto the desktop and held the doll high above her head. 'You stupid bitch!' she shouted, hurling the doll across the room as she did so. 'You stupid bitch!'

'Let me help you down,' I said, but Jasmine was three paces ahead of me, clambering off the desk, retrieving the doll and racing out through the bedroom door.

'That'll teach you! Stupid! That'll teach you!' she chanted, as she darted to the top of the stairs.

'That'll teach you, STUPID!' she shouted again, louder this time. With this, she hurled the doll down the stairs with all her might. It hit the living room door down below us before dropping to the floor. Anthony had been in the lounge, watching TV, and he came to see what all the fuss was about. The doll had landed on its back, wide blue eyes staring at the ceiling and blonde hair tumbling across the carpet.

'Hello Sindy, what's up with you?' Anthony said, trying to sound light-hearted and giving a grin I could tell was forced. He looked up at Jasmine. 'You leaving her here for me? Is that your goodbye present? Can I take her to my new flat?'

After a momentary pause, Jasmine allowed herself a little giggle. 'No, silly! I want her back.' She said this in her baby voice.

'Well you can't. You'll have to come and get her if you do.'

'Careful on the stairs,' I shouted, as Jasmine was about

to tear after Anthony. She paused a moment, and gave me a strange, almost serene smile, before chasing off down the stairs. I felt grateful to Anthony for changing her mood like this, and in the heat of the moment I doesn't immediately register the significance of Jasmine's unusual smile.

I listened as Anthony and Jasmine chased around the ground floor of the house. They were laughing and clearly having fun. I sat down on a stair and thought about what had happened in Jasmine's bedroom.

It's not uncommon for kids to act out events they find difficult to put into words. Police officers and other professionals sometimes use dolls specifically for this purpose. I couldn't be sure, of course, but I had to consider that Jasmine was trying to tell me she had been thrown down the stairs by her violent dad. Another thought occurred to me. Had he thrown her mother down the stairs, and that was why she had walked out? Was she the person he called a 'stupid bitch'? A third scenario crossed my mind. Had Jasmine's mother witnessed the attack and fled, instead of helping her daughter?

My mind was whirring. Inevitably, I wondered if being violently thrown down the stairs might have been what caused Jasmine to cut her forehead, ending up with that scar and suffering the impairment to her frontal lobe. Head injury was the likely cause of her condition. I closed my eyes and saw her, in my mind's eye, pointing to the scar on her forehead and saying, 'See this?'

I could feel my heart thumping in my chest as I tried to process everything that had gone on, and then I thought about the smile Jasmine had given me when I told her to be careful on the stairs. That's when I realised Jasmine was probably feeling grateful that I'd told her to be careful. That's why she smiled at me serenely, I thought. It was a heart-rending realisation. No child should have to feel grateful for the fact the person looking after them doesn't want them to hurt themselves on the stairs, or isn't going to throw them down the staircase.

Anthony and Jasmine played chase until they were worn out. It was a pleasure to see them that way. It meant that when Pearl and Lenny arrived to pick their granddaughter up, you would never have imagined we'd had the disturbing drama with the Sindy doll. Jasmine was in a sunny, excitable mood and raring to go.

'Can we play chase in your house, Granddad? Can we?'

'We can do, Jazz, but I think you'll be at an advantage because I'm not as fast as you or Anthony!'

I caught a glance at Anthony. Even though he was moving out himself any day soon, I noticed he seemed very upset about Jasmine's departure. He was probably going to miss her, I thought. They'd got along really well, considering there were so many years between them and they didn't have a great deal in common. In fact, they had become better friends than she and Erica, who had said a rather emotionless goodbye to Jasmine that morning before promptly asking if she could use Jasmine's empty room to practise her dancing! Mum had sent a goodbye card and baked a cake, as she often did when children were moving out, and she had said goodbye to Jasmine the night before, when we'd had a little tea party.

'I'll keep in touch,' Pearl said, 'and when we move we'll let you know our new address. Thank you so much for everything.'

Pearl and Lenny had decided to relocate, near the sea where Lenny grew up, and their house was already on the market. Though they didn't go into any detail, we imagined this was to get away from the past and reduce the risk of Jasmine's father turning up at their door. As we'd discussed, Jasmine would go to the small and well-respected PRU near their home for the time being, and the hope was that she would start Year 5 in a primary in their new seaside town.

Jasmine hugged me tightly before she left. 'Thank you,' she said. 'You're a kind lady.'

'And you're a lovely girl. I hope everything goes really well for you, and I hope it's not long before you all move to the seaside.'

Jonathan high-fived her. 'It's been good to get to know you,' he said. 'I wish you all the very best.' Jasmine gave him a thin smile. Their relationship had not been great, but they'd managed to muddle through and end things on an amicable note. The truth was, Jonathan was relieved to have reached the end of the placement without another allegation against him, and without any fires in the house. He'd had real fears about both issues, and he admitted to me later that he'd lain awake at night worrying about them.

Anthony gave Jasmine a bear hug, which she clearly loved. 'I'll tell you one thing,' he said, 'it's good to talk. Don't keep things bottled up, it's not good for you.' He said this in a jolly but forceful way and then presented her with one of his rugby balls. 'I thought you might like this, as a keepsake.'

She beamed and clutched the ball to her chest, and when she was driven away in the back of Lenny and Pearl's car, I saw she was still clinging on to it. I had a lump in my throat and felt sorry to see her go, in spite of the fact I was sure this was the right move for her.

I turned to Anthony, who looked extremely sad. I'd never heard him dishing out advice as he had done to Jasmine and I was surprised at the emotional impact her leaving seemed to have on him. I asked him if he was OK.

'Yeah, I'm fine. It was just that stuff about her mum. I never knew, you see.'

'Never knew what?' I stopped in my tracks, sensing this was not going to be good.

'You know, about her saying she was going on holiday and all that. What a terrible thing to do. I think that was really harsh on Jasmine.'

'I'm not sure I know the story about her mum going on holiday,' I said.

'Really? Oh, I assumed that was why Jasmine was in care, because of what her mum did.'

Of course, it was our understanding that Jasmine had been taken into care because her father, who was left in sole charge of her after her mum walked out, was physically abusive. I wasn't going to share this detail with Anthony, as I wasn't sure what Jasmine had told him about her dad, or anything else for that matter. I chose my words carefully.

'No. Like I say, I don't know this story about her mum and the holiday. Perhaps I should?'

Anthony nodded. 'OK, it might be important, I don't know.' He took a breath and looked at me very seriously. 'Jasmine told me that when her mum left, she said she was just going away on holiday. She packed a bag and said she was going on the train. Jasmine thought she would be gone for a week or two, that's all.'

He bit his lip and looked visibly moved.

'But she wasn't just going on holiday. She was leaving. Jasmine was left wondering and kind of, like, just waiting and waiting. Then, well, I think she eventually worked it out for herself, that her mum wasn't coming back, I mean, because she never did.'

Anthony shook his head while I felt an icy rush of blood around my heart. I was trying to tell myself this might not be true and Jasmine could have made this story up, but that notion didn't help curb the shock I was feeling. I asked Anthony if there was anything else he should tell me.

'No, that was it. Her mum threw her down the stairs – unbelievable! – and then she just vanished.'

'Her mum threw her down the stairs?'

'That's what Jasmine told me . . . you didn't know that either? What an absolutely evil woman.'

I told Anthony that I hadn't heard that story either and gently cautioned him that it may not be true.

'Yeah, but will you tell Social Services, just in case?'

'Yes, but don't worry, nothing will come back to you. And remember, Jasmine is eight and little girls do sometimes invent stories, so please don't worry yourself too much.'

'But the scar on her head . . . she said that was how she got it, because she hit the corner of a radiator at the bottom of the stairs after her mum threw her in a temper.'

I wanted to say that the scar on her head could have simply been the trigger for Jasmine's story, the visible mark that sparked an overactive imagination. But I didn't because, sadly, that didn't seem to ring true. I hated to admit it to myself, but Jasmine's story sounded very plausible. Perhaps it was little wonder she'd smiled at me in that odd way when I cautioned her to be careful on the stairs.

I gave Anthony the chance to relate anything else that we ought to know about and thanked him for being a friend to Jasmine. As I did so, I remembered what she'd said to me after she told me her mum was 'magicked away'. 'It's a secret. Shh. Don't tell.' That's what's she'd said. I could see her now, pressing her fingers to her lips and widening her blue eyes. Little did I know she'd had a much sadder secret to tell, or at least that's how it seemed.

'Like I say, please don't worry about Jasmine,' I said to Anthony. 'She's with her grandparents now. They love her to bits and she's got a new school lined up and a whole new life ahead of her. But I'll pass on what you have told me to Social Services.'

He asked me if she would have to see a person called Mrs Hutton again.

'Mrs Hutton?' An image of the stony-faced Social Services manager flashed into my mind. 'No, I don't expect so. Why?'

'I've remembered something else. Jasmine said she looks like her mum and it scares her, so I'm glad about that.'

'I see.' I sighed. 'Well, please don't worry about that. Like I say, Jasmine is happy now.'

Her reaction to this woman finally made sense. I'd thought Mrs Hutton might have somehow been present when Jasmine was removed from the family home, but this was the reason she was frightened of the manager. I'd have a quiet word with Social Services about this, as I didn't want their paths to cross again, if it were at all possible.

'I hope she stays happy,' Anthony said wistfully, which I felt was a lovely way to end our conversation. Jasmine *had* been happy when she left our house with Pearl and Lenny. I kept that thought at the front of my mind in the coming days, weeks and months, whenever I thought about her.

Jasmine had left our home in a better position than she'd been in when she arrived, and that is the very least we hope to achieve for every child we care for. In Jasmine's case, in the few short months she'd lived with us, we'd managed to have her medically assessed and had started the process of having her statemented, which Pearl and Lenny were going to see through. She'd connected with Anthony and my mum, and though she didn't exactly hit it off with Erica we'd all made some good memories together. Despite the accusations she made against Jonathan, she did have enjoyable moments with both of us.

341

We received a thank you card a week or so after Jasmine moved out.

'To Angela and Jonathan,' she had printed out in her neatest handwriting. 'Thank you for having me. I had a nice time, love from Jazz xx'

Bless her, I thought. *It sounds like she just popped over for tea.* I wondered if this is how she preferred to view it – more as a social visit than a legally enforced stay in care. You could hardly blame her, if that was how it was.

Pearl had written a longer note, telling us that all was well and that Jasmine had started at the PRU, which she called the 'special school'.

She loves the cats, Stan and Ollie, and we've promised we'll get a dog when we move to the coast. We're teaching her to play darts (it's good for her maths) and we've hired a cottage for half term so we can have a good look at properties down there again. The estate agent doesn't think we'll have any trouble selling our house. We can't thank you enough for all you have done for our Jazz. We're so thrilled everything has worked out so well (we're shattered too though!). All OK with Social Services. I'll keep you posted. Take care of yourselves, Pearl x

Caitlin phoned a few days after we received the thank you card. We knew she was finally coming back to work after her extended sick leave and had been wondering when we'd hear from her.

'How are you, Angela?' she said. 'I've been catching up and I hear there's been a lot going on since we last spoke.'

We knew that Pearl and Lenny were applying to obtain a Special Guardianship Order (SGO) for Jasmine, which would give them parental responsibility over her. We'd been told this would be a formality after the appeal had gone through, and I hoped it would be approved by the courts as soon as possible.

I'd written my last notes on Jasmine the day after she left, which included the comments she'd made about her mum to Anthony. It broke my heart to write the words:

Jasmine told a family friend (a former foster child of ours) that her mother threw her down the stairs and then left. Jasmine said her mother claimed she was going on holiday by train, took one bag but never came back. She said she cut her head on the radiator at the bottom of the stairs, as a result of being thrown down the stairs by her mother. This cut resulted in the scar Jasmine has on her forehead, she said.

I wondered what her father had known. Was he aware Jasmine's mum was leaving for good and, if not, how did he react when the truth dawned? I wondered how much of his anger was stoked by his wife's disappearance, and also how Jasmine had apparently kept this secret for so long.

Stewart had dealt with my notes and had told us a new social worker had already been assigned for Jasmine in her grandparents' town. Not for the first time, he'd sounded in a hurry to end our conversation, despite the fact our paths might not cross again. We'd heard on the grapevine that the school had put in a complaint to Social Services about his behaviour on what turned out to be Jasmine's last day. I assumed he was embarrassed and was probably glad he didn't have to deal with us any longer.

'We're fine,' I told Caitlin, my mind flicking back over all the events of the past months. 'It's good to have you back, and I think it all worked out for the best for Jasmine.'

'Yes, I'm sorry about Stewart. I hadn't realised all that was going on.'

'Well, things don't always run smoothly,' I said, imagining she was talking about the tensions we'd had between us, as well as Stewart's awful mistake at the school.

'Yes, he's had a very tough time, what with all his problems at home,' Caitlin said. 'It's very sad for him.'

I realised we had crossed wires and, once again, I found myself breathing in sharply. 'I'm sorry, Caitlin, I think I'd better stop you there. I don't know anything about Stewart's private life.'

'Oh, I'm sorry,' she said, sounding embarrassed. 'I assumed you knew.' She explained that Stewart had made no secret of the fact he was going through a very acrimonious divorce. 'It's taken a lot out of him, and it's hardly surprising that he's the one signed off sick now.'

'Oh. I didn't know anything about that.'

'Really? Well, things move fast when you reach crisis point, don't they? Talking of which, you have plenty of room for another placement now, don't you? I was wondering, would you and Jonathan consider taking in a fourteen-year-old boy? It's just for respite, his guardian has to have an operation . . .'

Of course, we said yes.

'It just goes to show,' I said, when Jonathan and I reflected on Stewart, 'you never know what is going on in another person's life.'

'Exactly. But it's a pity for Jasmine that he didn't confide in us or go off sick before. If he'd spoken up and taken leave sooner, that terrible drama at the school might never have happened. He was clearly under far too much stress.'

I thought about this.

'You know what? Sometimes things happen for a reason. Don't get me wrong, it was a dreadful thing to do and I hope Stewart has learned a big lesson from it and never makes the same mistake again. But it finally got things moving for Jasmine, didn't it? How many times have we been stuck in a bad situation for way too long? At least it triggered the change she needed.'

We would never know for sure, but we both suspected, quite strongly, that the incident in school prompted Stewart to change his view about Jasmine returning to her grand-parents. He'd originally seemed reluctant to back Pearl and Lenny. We now wondered if this was simply because he had enough on his plate with his own problems and heavy caseload. Maybe it was easier for him to just leave her with us for as long as possible, instead of having to deal with moving her.

Or perhaps he felt he owed it to Jasmine to pull out the stops and help make her wishes come true, after the way he'd provoked her at the school.

Whatever the reasoning, things had happened extremely quickly after Jasmine's meltdown at the school that day. It wasn't for us to say, and we would never have speculated with anyone but each other, but we suspected that Stewart had then wanted her off his books as soon as possible. He no doubt wanted the complaint to be quickly buried, as he had enough to deal with already. No wonder he was signed off with stress, we thought.

'At least we can say all's well that ends well,' Jonathan said. 'Jasmine is happier than she has been in a long while, I think. Pearl and Lenny are delighted, and we can take in more children who hopefully won't rock the boat for Erica so much.'

'I'll drink to that,' I said, chinking my coffee cup against Jonathan's. 'I want Jasmine to blossom. She deserves to stay happy, and I think she's in the very best place she could be.'

Epilogue

Pearl was true to her word and kept in touch. Jasmine 'knuckled down' at the special school, as her grandmother called it, and she managed to finish the academic year without any major dramas. The three of them moved to the coast at the end of August, in time for Jasmine to take up a place in a new mainstream school. At last her SEN had come through, which meant she got all the extra help she needed in the classroom. As far as I know Social Services didn't offer any further help in terms of Jasmine's frontal lobe impairment. Pearl said the social workers she dealt with didn't seem to know what to suggest beyond ensuring she was statemented. They were told she could go on the waiting list for CAMHS if they felt Jasmine needed to see a psychologist, but I'm not sure they ever made that decision.

Jasmine was at a village primary with an excellent reputation for pastoral care, and she settled in well and made a lovely friend. They got a dog, who terrorised the cats – 'but everybody loves him, and especially Jasmine'. The goldfish had been quickly forgotten, which is what we'd hoped. The next children who stayed with us were delighted to look after them.

Pearl always mentioned the fact she and Lenny were 'run

ragged' though she never complained and always sounded upbeat on the phone, and in the occasional postcard when they went on a trip or holiday. Jonathan and I admired them. We knew Jasmine must still have been challenging, given the diagnosis she had, but her grandparents didn't ever dwell on the negative. 'She's the light of our lives,' Pearl said proudly one time. 'Having Jasmine living with us has given me and Lenny a new lease of life, it truly has.'

As time went on, Pearl's phone calls dwindled, which I suppose was inevitable. However, she continued to send the odd postcard and she never failed to send a Christmas card every year. This meant we got annual bulletins, and I kept each one.

For her ninth birthday, Jasmine had a swimming party and her whole class was invited. At ten, she started to play netball and was extremely good at it. I have a photo of her, in pigtails, squashed in the middle of the team photo, with a C for centre on her bib and a proud grin on her face. She won another art competition, in celebration of her school's fiftieth anniversary. Jasmine loved the beach, was good at maths and had her bedroom painted lilac, with a rainbow on the wall above her headboard. 'We both got a few more grey hairs getting that job done!' Pearl wrote.

Jasmine's secondary school career didn't start well, unfortunately. Moving from her small village school to a large comprehensive, an hour away on the bus, clearly threw her off-kilter. Jasmine was suspended and excluded so many times that she was moved to a PRU once more.

When Jasmine was twelve Pearl told us that she had been

placed in a special boarding school, for children with challenging needs. She would stay there from Monday to Friday each week and spend weekends and holidays at home.

'We hope it won't be forever, but for the time being we think it's for the best, for all of us.'

It sounded like they had debated long and hard about allowing her to go to the boarding school, but in the end they'd felt they had no choice.

The following year, Jonathan and I were planning a reunion party for former foster children, which we do from time to time. I wrote and told Pearl and Lenny we were hosting a barbecue in the garden during the school summer holidays and said we would love them to come and bring Jasmine. To our surprise, they accepted. Pearl said she and Lenny were going to use it as an excuse to go and visit some old friends they had in the area, 'while we've still got the energy!'

Jonathan and I were delighted. Generally, we only manage to stay in touch with those youngsters who have lived with us until leaving care. Diane, for instance, is still in contact. She housesits for us from time to time and is doing well for herself, and we continue to see Anthony regularly. He achieved his ambition of becoming an HGV driver and is now engaged to a very sweet girl who works as a carer. On the other hand, Erica only stayed with us for a few months after Jasmine left, when she went to live with a relative in another part of the country. She settled very well and we were very happy for her, and optimistic about her future. We lost touch with her after she moved, as is nearly always the case with young children. It was all thanks to Pearl that we'd kept up with Jasmine's news for so many years. I'd told her many times it was very kind of her to still think of us and keep up the contact, to which she typically replied, 'Why wouldn't we?'

It was quite a moment when I saw Jasmine again. She was a young teenager now, and I hadn't seen a photo of her since she was in primary school, but I'd have recognised her anywhere. Her fair hair still tumbled past her shoulders and her blue eyes were as alert as they had been on that first day, when we met in McDonald's.

'Here she is,' Pearl said, smiling proudly at Jasmine as she presented her granddaughter to me. 'Not changed much, has she?'

'Jasmine! I can't tell you how lovely it is to see you. But you *have* changed! You look so grown up!'

Jasmine gave me a smile and giggled in a slightly self-conscious way. 'You're exactly the same!' she told me.

'Well, I'm not getting any younger, so I'll take that as a compliment!'

Jasmine laughed. She looked kind and eager to please, and there was a calmness about her that she hadn't had before, I thought. I remembered the smirking, erratic and sometimes very angry little girl she once was, and thought how much she had changed.

Anthony had been the first to arrive as he was helping light the barbecue. He and Jonathan immediately walked towards us, smiling and saying hello. Jasmine was polite but seemed quite shy as they made small talk. She clearly didn't recognise Anthony at first and was very taken aback when she realised who he was.

'I hope you've still got that rugby ball?' he teased, after reminding her of his parting gift to her.

'Oh God! I'd forgotten about that, but I remember now. I thought I wouldn't remember anything.' She laughed and said she was more into netball nowadays.

It was all slightly awkward, if I'm honest, but what reunion isn't, in the first few minutes at least, and especially when a young teenager is involved? I was very proud of Jasmine for agreeing to come, and for making such an effort, as she was.

More people arrived and, as usual at these sorts of gatherings, I didn't have half as much time as I wanted to chat to everyone. However, I did find out a few things about Jasmine that day that warmed my heart. She played for a successful netball team and Pearl told me that art therapy was helping to curb her 'short fuse'. Her stay at the boarding school had ended, thank goodness. 'She's starting back in mainstream school next term,' Pearl told me conspiratorially, when we had a moment to ourselves. 'I've been dying to tell you. It's the best news we've had in ages.'

'Is your mum here?' Jasmine asked, as I offered her some cake at the end of the afternoon. I wondered if she was remembering my mum baking a cake for her farewell tea party, all those years before.

'Sadly, no. I lost my mum last year.'

I'd given Pearl and Lenny this news in my last Christmas card, but I didn't expect Jasmine to know, or remember.

'Oh,' she gasped, looking mortified. 'Sorry.'

'Don't be. I was very lucky to have her for so long.'

I regretted telling her the moment the words left my mouth, but Jasmine didn't react in the way I feared she might. Brightly, and without missing a beat, she told me she remembered playing lots of games with my mum.

'She was kind. I liked her.'

'I'm glad you have some happy memories of your time here,' I said. 'And I'm so thrilled you came to see us. Your grandparents are wonderful people. In all these years I've never met a granny quite like yours. She's taken so much trouble to keep in touch with us. She must have a heart of gold.'

'Yeah, she has,' Jasmine grinned. 'Er, she says the same about you. Thanks for, you know, helping me out when I was little.' She blushed slightly and looked at the floor when she said this. I wondered if Pearl had told Jasmine she must thank us for fostering her.

'There's no need to thank me. I'm very glad you came to live with us, Jasmine.'

'Me too,' she said, flicking her eyes across the lawn, to where Anthony was busy pouring drinks. 'It all worked out pretty well, really!'

She pushed her hair away from her forehead as she said this, revealing her scar. I'm sure this was a subconscious move. I looked at the silvery line and it triggered a chain of thought. Until Jasmine confided in Anthony at the end of her placement, we believed her dad was the only parent who had abused her. But then she had told Anthony how her mum had thrown her down the stairs, which had caused so much damage, in so many ways. I'd questioned the truth of this, wondering if Jasmine's story had been the result of a troubled little girl's fervent imagination. Not anymore. Standing before her, in the garden she once played in, I felt those doubts leave me. I knew from Pearl that neither of Jasmine's parents had ever resurfaced and that she had no desire to find them. Her story had to be true, I realised. I thought it was the saddest story I had ever heard.

We have not seen Jasmine since the barbecue, but Pearl continues to write every Christmas. Jasmine managed to stay in mainstream school until she left at sixteen, and then she took up an art foundation course at a local college. Inspired by her own art therapist, who helped Jasmine stay on track after leaving the boarding school, she recently started working in a community centre, helping with art therapy sessions. She still plays netball, for another winning team, and is hoping to move into her own flat with a friend. Pearl and Lenny are in their seventies now and, according to Pearl, 'Jazz is the one looking after us!'

There have been moments over the years when Jonathan and I questioned our instincts and wondered whether it was truly the right thing for us to push for Jasmine to live with her grandparents. Not any longer. Jasmine is thriving, despite the challenges she faces. It's a great privilege to have helped her, in a small way, on her road to happiness. We don't know if we will see her again, but at least we have the memories of the reunion to cherish. Pearl and Lenny have given us a very rare gift, and we can't thank them enough.

The Girl in the Dark

The true story of a runaway child with a secret.
A devastating discovery that changes everything.

There was no sign of her at nine. We had a grandfather clock in the lounge that chimed loudly, making me catch my breath. I usually felt soothed by its steady, predictable rhythm, but tonight it was a countdown timer, an emergency alarm. Each tick-tock taunted me, plucking at my nerves. I was becoming more anxious and irritated as each second passed. It was like waiting for an accident to happen . . .

Melissa is a sweet-natured girl with a disturbing habit of running away. After she's picked up by the police with nowhere else to go, she is locked in a secure unit for young offenders. Social Services beg specialist foster carer Angela Hart to take her in, but can she keep the testing twelve-year-old safe? And will she ever learn what, or who, drove Melissa to run and hide, sometimes in the dead of night?

Available now in paperback and ebook.

The Girl Who Wanted to Belong

The true story of a devastated little girl
and the foster carer who healed her broken heart.

'I'll be very, very good,' she told me. 'I won't make Wendy cross with me.'

'I'm pleased to hear you're going to be well behaved, sweetheart. By the way, have you remembered she prefers you not to call her Wendy?'

'Yes. I need to call her Mum. I don't like calling her Mum, but I will. Mum, Mum, Mum.'

Lucy is eight years old and ends up in foster care after being abandoned by her mum and kicked out by her dad's new partner, Wendy. Two aunties and then her elderly grandmother take her in, but it seems nobody can cope with Lucy's disruptive behaviour. Social Services hope a stay with experienced foster carer Angela will help Lucy settle down. Lucy is desperate for a fresh start back home, but will she ever be able to live in harmony with her stepmother and her stepsister – a girl who was once her best friend at school?

Available now in paperback and ebook.

The Girl With Two Lives

A shocking childhood. A foster carer who understood.
A young girl's life forever changed.

As I stepped back into the kitchen, Danielle looked very proud as she held her notepad up for me to see.

'Finished!' she declared cheerfully. I was surprised to see that the surname Danielle had printed wasn't the one I'd seen on her paperwork from Social Services, and so I asked her casually if she used two different names, which often happens when children come from broken homes.

'Yes,' she said. 'But this is the surname I'm going to use from now on, because it's the name of my forever family.'

Danielle has been excluded from school and her former foster family can no longer cope. She arrives as an emergency placement at the home of foster carer Angela Hart, who soon suspects that there is more to the young girl's disruptive behaviour than meets the eye. Can Angela's specialist training unlock the horrors of Danielle's past and help her start a brave new life?

Available now in paperback and ebook.

The Girl and the Ghosts

The true story of a haunted little girl and the
foster carer who rescued her from the past.

'So, is it a girl or a boy, and how old?'
Jonathan asked as soon as we were alone
in the shop.

My husband knew from the animated
look on my face, and the way I was itching
to talk to him, that our social worker had
been asking us to look after another child.

I filled Jonathan in as quickly as I
could and he gave a thin, sad smile.

'Bruises?' he said. 'And a moody temperament? Poor little
girl. Of course we can manage a few days.'

I gave Jonathan a kiss on the cheek. 'I knew you'd say that.
It's exactly what I thought.'

We were well aware that the few days could run into weeks
or even longer, but we didn't need to discuss this. We'd looked
after dozens of children who had arrived like Maria, emotion-
ally or physically damaged, or both. We'd do whatever it took
to make her feel loved and cared for while she was in our home.

Seven-year-old Maria holds lots of secrets. Why won't she
tell how she got the bruises on her body? Why does she run
and hide? And why does she so want to please her sinister
stepfather?

It takes years for devoted foster carer Angela Hart to
uncover the truth as she helps Maria leave the ghosts of her
past behind.

Available now in paperback and ebook.

The Girl Who Just Wanted to be Loved

A damaged little girl and a foster carer
who wouldn't give up.

The first time we ever saw Keeley was in a Pizza Hut. She was having lunch with her social worker.

'Unfortunately Keeley's current placement is breaking down,' our support social worker, Sandy, had explained. 'We'd like to move her as soon as possible.'

We'd looked after more than thirty youngsters over the years, yet I never failed to feel a surge of excitement at the prospect of caring for another one.

Sandy began by explaining that Keeley was eight years old and had stayed with four sets of carers and been in full-time care with two different families.

'Why have the placements not worked out?' I asked.

'All the foster carers tell similar stories. Keeley's bad behaviour got worse instead of better as time went on. That's why we're keen for you to take her on, Angela. I'm sure you'll do a brilliant job.'

Eight-year-old Keeley looks like the sweetest little girl you could wish to meet, but demons from the past make her behaviour far from angelic. She takes foster carer Angela on a rocky and very demanding emotional ride as she fights daily battles against her deep-rooted psychological problems. Can the love and specialist care Angela and husband Jonathan provide help Keeley triumph against the odds?

Available now in paperback and ebook.

Terrified

The heartbreaking true story of a girl
nobody loved and the woman who saved her.

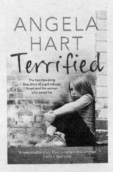

Vicky stared through the windscreen, her eyeballs glazed like marbles. She was sitting completely rigid in her seat, frozen with fear.

I took a deep breath and then asked Vicky as gently as possible, if she was all right.

'I'm here, right beside you, Vicky. Can you hear me? I'm here and I can help you.'

She still didn't respond in any way at all. Her normally rosy cheeks had turned ivory white and the expression of terror on her face was like nothing I'd seen before: I had never seen a child look so scared in all my life.

'Take a deep breath, love. That's what I've just done. Just breathe and try to calm yourself down. You're with me, Angela, and you're safe.'

Vicky seemed all self-assurance and swagger when she came to live with Angela and Jonathan as a temporary foster placement. As Vicky's mask of bravado began to slip, she was overtaken with episodes of complete terror. Will the trust and love Angela and her husband Jonathan provide enable Vicky to finally overcome her shocking past?

Available now in paperback and ebook.